Inside Man
Life as an Irish prison officer

Philip Bray with Anthony Galvin

Gill & Macmillan

Gill & Macmillan Ltd
Hume Avenue
Park West
Dublin 12
with associated companies throughout the world
www.gillmacmillan.ie

© Philip Bray 2008
978 07171 4481 5

Print origination by O'K Graphic Design, Dublin
Printed and bound by ScandBook AB, Sweden

The paper used in this book comes from the wood pulp of
managed forests. For every tree felled, at least one tree is
planted, thereby renewing natural resources.

A CIP catalogue record for this book is available from the British
Library.

5 4 3 2 1

To Janet, Steven and Jillian.
To all who find themselves behind
high, grey walls, the good guys
and the bad guys…

Contents

Acknowledgments

Everyone has a book in them. That was the message that Ryan Tubridy sent over the airways on his RTÉ Radio One show as he announced a competition for a true-life story. The prize was a book contract with the prestigious publishing company, Gill & Macmillan. Against fantastic competitors, I was amazed to come out on top, so here is one man's story. Oh, if you think you recognise yourself in this, it's not you. Every character is composed of many different people mixed into one. Everyone will have a different view and memory of the same events and that's OK – what is written here happens to be mine.

I worked with some fantastic men and women and was proud to wear the uniform. And I met a lot of prisoners who made me think, *There but for the grace of God, go I.*

Fab

July 2008

Chapter 1
'I've Lost the Pulse...'

I was just a year in prison when I came across my first suicide, and it was traumatic. Every prison suicide attracts great media attention, but the truth is that it doesn't happen that often. And nothing can prepare you for it.

That night, I was working outside. It was boring work, patrolling areas where you didn't see anyone for hours on end. The quietness and monotony can get in on you and you welcome any distraction. I was almost relieved when I heard shouting. It was around 1 a.m. and I still had several hours to put in.

I ran around the side of the prison until I was under the wall of D Class, and I could see two prisoners yelling through the window.

'Let us out, for fuck's sake! Hurry, Officer!' They were screaming, their panic unmistakable.

I ran straight to the safe room and told the Assistant Chief Officer we had an emergency in D Class. I grabbed the keys and ran to D as fast as I could.

The officer in charge of D was down the landing, trying to peer into a four-man cell.

'What's going on, Eddie?' I yelled.

'I don't know, I can't see through the spyhole.'

The two prisoners who had called to me outside were up against the door, banging and shouting, and we couldn't see past them into the cell. We ordered them to stand back, but we might as well have been shouting at the sea. They kept pounding on the door, demanding to be let out. They were begging, pleading, screaming.

The first thought that crosses your mind in a situation like that is that it could be an escape attempt. The two prisoners were English and had been working as scaffolders at the Alcan plant in Askeaton. They were fit and strong and I didn't fancy tackling them in the narrow, dark landing.

I went around to the side of the cell, where there was another, larger peephole. Looking in, I could see the two panicked men beating on the cell door. The three beds were empty. There was an ominous shape hanging from the light fitting in the centre of the cell.

'Open the door, Eddie!' I screamed.

The two Englishmen tumbled out, completely terrified. We opened another three-man cell and bundled the cowering men in on top of three sleepy inmates who hadn't a clue what was happening.

I was the first to enter the first cell. The prisoner was dangling from the light in the centre, eerily still. I could see that he had made a noose from strips of sheets and had used that to hang himself. I immediately grabbed him by the waist and tried to work on the knot at the light with my free hand. I must have yanked, because, at that moment, the rope broke.

I've heard the expression 'dead weight', but wasn't prepared for the reality. He was unbelievably heavy. Try as I might, I couldn't hold him and he slipped through my hands to the floor, landing with a thump and hitting his head.

I bent down and turned him to check him. This was not my thing – I know nothing about medicine. I tried for a pulse, but couldn't find one. I looked at Eddie – what could I do? Anything was better than nothing. I had seen chest compressions done on the telly and thought I had nothing to lose. I couldn't make it any worse for him, so I got on my knees beside him and began a few chest compressions. Eddie grabbed his hand.

'I've got a pulse – keep it up,' he encouraged.

The prisoner wasn't breathing. Mouth-to-mouth resuscitation was a new thing to me, but I knew the theory. I had to give it a go. Holding his nose, I blew into his mouth. Nothing happened, so I blew harder. Still nothing. His airway was completely blocked. I began to blow in very sharply, hoping to overcome the obstruction. A stream of snot sprayed out of his nose, covering the side of my face. No matter. I kept at it, blowing away, feeling the snot run down the side of my face.

'I've lost the pulse,' said Eddie.

I switched to chest compressions again, pumping on his ribcage vigorously, then back to the mouth to mouth.

'Anything, Eddie?'

'Nothing. I haven't had a pulse for a while now.'

I was kneeling in the middle of his cell. 'What do we do now?'

Eddie just looked at me, then, after a few seconds, knelt beside me and began whispering a prayer in the ear of the dead man. I stood and looked around the cell. It wasn't difficult. There on the bed was a suicide note, addressed to the man's family.

I remembered him. He had been inside only a few days, on remand awaiting trial. It was so tragic. After a fight with his wife, he had thrown her out of the house. When she returned with the police, he had taken his mother-in-law hostage and was holding her against the upstairs window, a knife against her throat. He threatened to kill her if the police came in.

After a four-hour standoff, the man had relented, giving up his hostage and surrendering to the police. That had been less than a week ago. Now, he was dead.

The doctor arrived and told us officially what we already knew. The governor, who lived in the prison at the time, was also quickly on the scene. An ambulance was called. One came from the fire station down the road from the prison and removed the body. I knew one of the firemen – he went to the same scuba club as I did.

'This is my first time in the prison,' he said. 'How do you put up with the smell?'

'What smell?' I asked him.

He just looked at me incredulously.

After everyone was gone, I had to write up a report on the night's events. Then, it was back outside to complete my patrolling. I was on my own outside for the rest of the night and my head was spinning. It was all so sad.

Eventually, morning came and I drove home, glad to fall into bed for the day. That evening, I woke up and saw my wife's dressing gown hanging from a hook on the back of the bedroom door. The door was white and the dark fabric of the gown hanging there began to unnerve me. I got up and moved the gown to the wardrobe, then unscrewed the hook from the back of the door before going back to bed. My wife noticed the hook had gone, but I never offered an explanation. That was the way back then; prison officers never spoke about the job.

Meanwhile, life returned to its normal routine in the prison. The two Englishmen were transferred within a couple of days to a prison in Dublin. This led to problems – a rumour went around the prison that if you were in a cell and one of your cellmates took his own life, you would immediately be released, no matter how much of your sentence remained. We laughed at first, then the implications began to dawn on us. The prisoners really believed this rumour, and it was only a matter of time before someone decided to test it by hanging one of his cellmates. We went to great lengths to let everyone know that the two Englishmen had merely been transferred.

The Gardaí carried out a full investigation into the suicide, and of course I was interviewed. This was several weeks after the event, but I could still recall all the details. They went through my statement thoroughly, but there was one small detail they weren't happy with. Finally, it came out.

'This looks open and shut,' said one. 'But there is one small detail that we aren't happy about. Why was the prisoner wearing someone else's underwear?'

'How in heaven's name do you know they weren't his?'

'Because someone else's initials were on them.'

'Whose?'

'Someone called p.s.'

I burst out laughing. 'That stands for prison service.' Every item of a prisoner's clothing was stamped with p.s.

With that, the file was closed.

The inquest was held a few months later. It was my first time attending a Coroner's Court and it was more formal than I had expected. I was questioned by a barrister. Brendan Nix is a bit of a superstar in local legal circles, Limerick's own Rumpole. He has a razor-sharp mind, and if I was ever in trouble, he would be the man I would want in my corner. If I was ever trying to fudge testimony and get away with something, he is the last man I would want to face. Luckily, I knew the truth about that night in the prison and had nothing to hide. We had done our best for the suicide victim.

Just before I took the stand, a Garda told me that the two English prisoners had changed their testimony. They were now claiming that they had banged on the door for half an hour before anyone came to their assistance, and that if we had acted faster the victim could still be alive. I don't know what they thought they would gain by lying; it wouldn't shorten their sentence and I couldn't see that they were getting at anyone.

Pondering this, I was called to the witness box. I refused the Bible, which surprised the coroner, but he allowed me to take the civil alternative when I explained that I have no religion.

Brendan Nix took me carefully through my evidence. He put it to me that the two prisoners sharing the cell with the deceased were claiming that our excessive delays had led to his death.

'That's not true,' I said. 'We got there as quickly as possible, certainly within minutes.'

'Are you saying the prisoners are lying? What would they gain by lying?'

That was a route I wasn't going down. Instead, I explained that the two men were in a panicked state, they had no clock in the cell and their sense of time must have been distorted. But even if our response time had been slow – which it wasn't – why didn't they help the poor victim? Why didn't they try and take him down and save his life?

At this point, I looked at the two Englishmen and asked them directly: 'Why did you not help that poor man?'

They hung their heads and made no answer. In fact, they didn't look at me for the rest of my evidence. Behind them, I could see the mother of the deceased, her head in her hands as she sobbed.

The inquest rejected the evidence of the two prisoners, who were returned to Dublin to complete their sentences. Later, one of them succeeded in escaping from Mountjoy.

The inquest over, we went to the pub for a few pints and as the drink flowed, the sense seemed to flow out of Eddie. He felt I had let down the entire prison service by not swearing on a Bible, and he was quick to tell me so.

'Those bloody Brits spent eight hundred years trying to crush the Irish and our language and religion, and in your case they succeeded,' he said. 'I would die before renouncing my faith.' From this, he moved on to conspiracy theories. I listened to a couple of hours of rubbish from him – I even goaded him into more and more outlandish statements as the drink brought out the crackpot in him. By the end of the night, he was trying to convince me that the two prisoners who had lied on the stand were sent over to cause trouble for Charlie Haughey.

There might have been a bit of a crackpot in Eddie – there is in all of us – but there was no badness. I was glad he was with me on the night of my first suicide. He was a big, strong man who would flinch from no one, and if the two prisoners had been trying to escape that night, they had picked the wrong crew to try it on. But that isn't why I was glad he was there. It was humbling to see this gentle giant of a man kneeling down, head bowed, as he whispered prayers into the ear of a dead man in a dirty prison cell. I was glad that not everyone in the cell was a pagan like me.

I'm sorry that the parents and family of the deceased were never made aware of this act of Christian kindness shown to their son by a man some would see as a big, thick jailer. He was big, but he had a big heart to go with it.

He was one of many wonderful and life-affirming characters I met in my thirty years behind bars. Not all of those wonderful characters worked with me – some were locked up by me. But I'm getting ahead of myself. Let's go back to the beginning.

Chapter 2

Welcome to Limerick Prison

On a Saturday morning at eight o'clock while all my mates were having a lie-in with their wives, I was standing in front of Limerick Prison. It was March 1977 and the cold was biting. I stood before a big wire gate waiting for it to open, but nothing happened. Then a voice called from my left and an officer beckoned to me.

'In this way,' he said, and I walked over to him. 'Everyone comes in this way, except visitors. I presume you *are* the new officer?'

'Yes, starting today. What's the score?'

'I'll tell you while I search you. Everyone from the governor down is searched when they come in.'

I emptied my pockets onto a table and got a rubdown search.

'Go up to the main gate and ring the bell at the side. Welcome to Limerick Prison.'

The gate was a huge wooden structure with a small picket door on the right-hand side. A small hatch slid open and someone looked out, then the picket door opened.

'Come in. You're the new man. We're waiting for you.'

I followed him into a small office. The heat hit me like a furnace. There was a small fireplace, but it was packed with as much coal as could be crammed into it.

'Nice and warm in here,' I said, trying to make conversation.

'It's the only place in the prison that's warm,' he said, but he wasn't getting much time to enjoy it. In the few minutes I was there, he opened and closed gates, made entries into a huge book on the desk and made numerous notes in other, smaller books scattered around. An electric buzzer called him to the main gate, then someone was tapping on the inner gate. This guy was kept going.

'OK, the ACO is waiting to take you to the governor's office. Welcome to Limerick Prison.'

It took two men to open the inner gate, each with his own key. I had already met the main gate man. On the other side was the inner gate man. The gate opened and I stepped into Limerick Prison for the first time. Facing me was a large tower with two three-storey wings coming off the tower at an angle. On the left were rows of windows with bars on them. The right was similar, but with 'office' written in old Irish letters on the bottom right. A lot of the windows were without glass as far as I could see. A concrete footpath lined with flowerbeds led straight to the door at the bottom of the tower. This was the circle. The wings were D and C Class. A and B Class were wings running from the back of the circle.

'My name is Bill Black,' said the ACO (assistant chief officer). He had a single gold stripe on each shoulder. 'We'll go over to the governor's office and get you organised.'

We turned right. The inner gate man opened a picket gate and we stepped into the governor's small garden. At the end of the garden was a beautiful stone-cut detached house. It would have been stunning placed on a few acres of rolling countryside; instead it was crammed into a corner of the prison. The downstairs had been turned into offices. As we walked in a magnificent staircase faced us and the landing was dominated by a huge fifteen-foot window, arched at the top and with stained glass running down the sides. But the view it framed was of a grey prison wall, just six feet away.

Most of our jails were built by the British, as were our courthouses and psychiatric hospitals, most of our hospitals and many of our schools. I could imagine a request from the authorities in Ireland to their superiors in the colonial office in London to be supplied with the designs for a house suitable for someone of the rank and status of governor – and they'd sent over the plans for a country squire's house. It was a folly like the Royal Pavilion in Brighton, and about as out of place.

The governor lived upstairs. At that time, he lived there on his own while his family lived in Cork. Back then, a governor was required to live in. Previous governors had raised their families in this house and the chief officer had lived over the main gate with his family.

'Welcome to Limerick Prison. Sit down.' The governor was a small, neat, well-dressed man and he had a hat in his hand. 'I'm just on the way out, but I'm glad to meet you. If you have any problems, just let me or the chief know and we will work them out.'

I didn't want to start our relationship on the wrong foot, but I had something that I needed to clear up.

'Governor, you might put my mind to rest on a matter. My wife and I recently had our first child die at six months old. We're expecting a baby in July, and you can understand how worried we are. I know that there's an overtime issue in the summer and I wonder if you could allow me a few days off at short notice at the time of the birth?'

'No problem, Mr Bray. Just mention it to the chief, who you'll meet in a few minutes.' Then he shook hands with me and left.

The ACO brought me out of the office and up to the prison. We mounted the steps, pushed open a wooden door and entered a twenty-foot narrow landing. At the end was an officer standing beside a gate, the circle gate. He opened the gate and we entered the prison proper.

'Welcome to Limerick Prison,' he said.

I was in a large circle that rose nearly forty feet, with two landings stretching off on either side. That's where the cells were, in those three-storey blocks. It was eerily quiet. Looking at the building that hadn't changed since 1821, except for a couple of hanging light bulbs and the odd lick of paint, I had the disturbing feeling that I hadn't just stepped through a gate, I had stepped back in time.

'Where are the prisoners?'

'They're all out in the yards on exercise, but you'll see them soon enough.'

Then the smell hit me. It smelled exactly like the lion house in Dublin Zoo, that acrid, sharp smell of urine that caught in your throat.

'What's that smell?' I asked.

'What smell?' he replied. I thought he was joking.

The ACO offered to show me around. We turned right and went into B Class. The farther down B Class I went, the stronger the smell got. It was coming from the toilet at the end. But the cells also stank because piss was being spilled on a regular basis and had seeped through the floorboards. While working nights, it wasn't unusual to hear a muffled oath and a clatter as a prisoner stumbled over his piss pot and knocked it over in the dark. Body odour and stale tobacco completed the smell that was Limerick Prison.

We turned back and crossed the circle to A Class, which was just as bad. I looked into one cell with an open door. A prisoner who was sitting on the bed looked up at me.

'Hello, Officer,' he said.

I was a bit embarrassed to have invaded his privacy and I turned away. I was to become very used to invading people's privacy over the coming years. The cell was bare, cold and sparsely furnished and contained no personal items.

Then, we went out to the yard and I saw the prisoners. They crammed the yard because it was a Saturday and they had no work. They looked miserable. That was a bitterly cold winter. I remember it well because the water pump in my car froze on a number of occasions. The prisoners were walking anticlockwise around the yard in groups of three or four. Every group of prisoners I have ever seen – here, in Britain or in the States – have walked anticlockwise. I don't know why.

At that time, there were only two exercise yards, one for convicted prisoners and the other for remand prisoners. This was the first time I had seen anyone who had been in jail. All these prisoners were smaller than me, I think through undernourishment. They were all lean and thin and none of them wore shirts, even though they were issued with them. They all wore jeans, a vest (string at the time) and a v-neck pullover. Many of the clothes were ill fitting.

They were a dreary, cold, bored-looking bunch. There was one officer in the yard, on his own among them, standing beside what I was told was an alarm bell. In the centre of the yard was a bare patch of earth, not concreted over, and on that were several large tree trunks. Across the way was a lean-to shed where some prisoners huddled. There was a long bench along one wall, but most prisoners were on their haunches, playing cards. They were playing don, a card game I had never heard of before. The stakes were pinches of shag tobacco, which they placed on the ground to bet. Beside them, a couple of tons of wooden blocks were neatly arranged for firewood.

I was then brought down to D Class, where the remand prisoners were held. In theory, they were innocent and were awaiting either trial or sentence, or they were in contempt of court or were debtors. D Class was a revelation to me. It seemed more dilapidated, unkempt, uncared for and colder than any other part of the prison. The best way I could describe it was as an upstairs dungeon.

Stone steps led up to the second-floor landing. I could see something leaking from around the toilet, going across the floor and seeping down the stairs. That seepage remained there until they knocked D Class down twenty years later. The landings of D Class were like a maze, and it took me a long time to figure out where things were. There were a couple of four-man cells which originally housed debtors. A debtor was treated separately from other prisoners in that he could carry on his trade inside, employ other prisoners to clean and tidy for him and order out for his food and even for drink. He had a fireplace and some space. I could see the fireplaces were bricked, and four men shared the cell instead of one. A huge bolt and padlock secured those doors. I learned later that those bolts and padlocks were the original ones, from 1821.

Reception and C Class were next. Reception was on the ground floor of C Class. The upstairs in C Class was semi-derelict, and only two or three cells were used to house prisoners who were admitted late at night. Reception housed the only shower in the prison. There was a bath in D Class, but I never saw it used. There was a bath in the women's prison, and obviously I never saw that used either.

That first day passed in a haze. There was a bewildering array of different duties, different starting times and different knocking-off times. This was clearly no nine-to-five job. It crossed my mind that I would need a secretary just to keep track of what I was supposed to be doing. Instead, I got a diary. I still have every diary from my thirty years of service.

I was on A2 landing when the prisoners came in from the yards. A group of them came towards me. The landing was only a few feet wide and I stood frozen, expecting to be bumped around the place, but they all passed me without touching me. I couldn't believe it. It was like a shoal of fish passing a scuba diver. They would pass over you, under you and around you, but not one of them would rub off you.

I had been locked in the yard with the prisoners and there was no getting out. There were no toilet facilities for officers or any drinking water. If I wanted to get out of the yard, I had to go to the gate and shout into A Class to attract the class officer's attention. He would often be on business in the office, the tuck shop or reception. You wouldn't want to be in a hurry. The officers' toilet was in the officers' mess, a small detached house built inside the prison. A number of single officers had to stay in the mess, locked in each night with the prisoners. They got no extra pay for this; they were a free reserve force in case of trouble during the night. This caused havoc to their love lives and much disruption to the serious drinkers.

My general impression was that the place was filthy and I didn't know how long I would last.

What the hell was I doing and how did I get there? We have to go back a few months to explain that.

Chapter 3
Beginnings

It was a bleak December afternoon. I reached into my pocket and the day became bleaker. I had damn all to pay for Christmas with. This was success in the late 1970s. I had my own business and it was thriving – I was a skilled mechanic with a solid base of customers. But do you think I could collect the money from them? Not on your life.

I called in on a man who owed me a lot, and for a change he didn't avoid me. In fact, he gave me a cheque for the entire amount. I was delighted. It was the last business day before Christmas and I went immediately to the bank. But he had post-dated the cheque. By chance, another customer did pay that afternoon and Christmas was saved, but I knew my days as a mechanic were numbered.

I found a job managing the swimming pool in the National Institute of Higher Education, now the University of Limerick. It was great; I was paid to supervise a swimming pool and could take a dip any time I wanted, and I regularly used the gym. I would still be there but for my mother. She was getting fed up with me flitting from job to job and she was worried my next move might be emigration, which was on my mind. So, she applied for me to become a prison officer.

Because of her intervention, I swapped the pool deck for the prison landing. I worked thirty years among people others cross the road to avoid. I endured fights and riots, lousy working conditions, threats and long, hard hours among murderers and rapists.

Why? Because once I became a prison officer, it was never again a bleak day when I reached into my pocket.

Like many prison officers, I discovered my vocation when I got my first pay cheque. But don't get me wrong; it's not all about the money. Along the way, I have formed deep friendships, met fascinating characters and enjoyed a life less ordinary – a life behind bars.

———

I was twenty-nine when I joined the prison service. As the upper age limit was thirty, I was cutting it a bit fine. The lower age limit was nineteen and you could retire at fifty, but you didn't get full pension until you had done thirty years of service, so I knew I was in for the long haul. It wasn't that the prison service was a particularly attractive job – I don't think anyone ever grew up thinking, 'I know, I'll be a prison officer' – but it was the civil service, and my mother wanted me in something solid with a good pension at the end.

The recruitment process began with an interview at the Protestant Young Men's Association on O'Connell Street, and they asked me if I knew what a subversive was. Then, they asked me to stand up to see if I was big enough. I was six foot and eleven stone – if I wasn't big enough, they were looking for monsters. I must have met with their approval because I was asked to sit an exam in Dublin. Not everyone had to sit the exam. If I'd had my Leaving Cert or trade qualifications I could have skipped it, but I had no Leaving Cert and couldn't find my trade certificates, so I sat the standard civil service exam, with the standard test in Irish. I had been out of school more than a decade, so my *cúpla focal* were barely even that. But somehow I stumbled through and passed. The only excitement was a bomb scare in the test centre, which meant I had to go in through the rear entrance. Bomb scares were part of life back in the 1970s.

The exam I sat was primary cert standard – the standard that got you into secondary school. When I joined, only one prison officer in Limerick had been to university. Today, qualifications and degrees abound on the landings.

I think they weren't too fussy. They needed prison officers on the landings fast, and that was the bottom line. People today forget the turmoil the country was in back in the 1970s. The future of the state was in doubt and the Troubles were in full swing in the North, while in the South, some of our ministers had been accused of gun running

Some guys came out and they were dressed like models. They had obviously responded better to the inquisition 'about the GAA.

We were expected to wear blue shirts on the job, and to provide them ourselves. One experienced hand told me to go down to McGovern's on William Street and buy some light blue shirts. I went down and bought two shirts that cost me about £30. I was flabbergasted, as the average industrial wage at the time was around £36 a week. I wasn't going to spend half my wages on shirts, so the next time I needed a shirt, I passed McGovern's and went to Dunnes Stores, like a lot of my colleagues.

There was no uniformity in the uniform. Over the coming few years, I went through at least five different shades of light blue. We all would have liked to have had the same shade, but it didn't happen. Because of our hours, our wives were in charge of buying them and they all went to different places. The single guys didn't care what they wore – and weren't as well presented as the officers today; they wouldn't have been fussy about ironing or anything.

We had just the one pair of trousers and jacket, which led to problems when they got dirty. Some officers bought a spare pair of dark blue trousers, and they didn't match either. With the shirts and the trousers and an assortment of different shaped and coloured ties, we could look like a right raggedly bunch – a modern Black and Tan force.

None of the shirts had epaulettes, as they were civilian shirts. Eventually, the department issued epaulettes, but the epaulettes weren't attached to the shirts, so we paid a prisoner down in the reception five fags for each one he sewed.

At any rate, we were given the uniform and told to come back on Monday and report to the training unit. Our first day was over.

————

On Monday morning, I put on my uniform, kissed my wife goodbye and hopped into the car. I thought I was being clever putting on the uniform at home. I was sure to get respect in the traffic, and possibly shave a few minutes off the commute from Killiney. Not a bit of it. Dubliners don't seem to like Gardaí, not like down the country, where they commanded great respect, and obviously my uniform gave the wrong impression. No one cut me any slack on the road, but I still got in on time. That evening coming home, I drove down Sheriff Street and got glares of hatred for the first time, just because I was in the blue.

When I arrived, I was shown to the training unit. I thought that this was for officers, but, no, it was the prisoners' training unit and when they weren't using it, we got it. We sat there for a few dreary lectures on the theory and logistics of running a prison and we did some foot drills. We jogged endlessly up and down the Royal Canal with people sniggering at us from the windows of offices. Of course, we supplied our own gym gear. There was no physical contact training, self-defence or restraint training – nothing that would be of any practical use to us once we began on the job. A lot of what we were told was theory and the practice proved to be wildly different. But I did meet some training assistant chief officers whom I respected and I was getting to know my fellow recruits, starting to form the bonds that would last for the next thirty years. Thus passed our six weeks of training.

At one stage, I was sent to an open centre in County Wicklow for a day. That was fabulous. It was a converted seminary used to house trustee prisoners. There were no walls or wire fences and the officers wore civilian attire. There was a waiting list of up to seven years to get a post there.

Halfway through the first day, we were told we would have to go to the prison that evening and do a reserve. At that time, the job was eight to five, but the prison had to be fully staffed from five, when the officers knocked off, to eight, when the prisoners were locked up for the night. We raw recruits provided that staffing. That was doing the reserve.

I went to the circle hall that evening, the tower in the centre of the prison, the nerve centre. It was filled with loud, confident men in uniforms laughing and smoking. It was the first time I had heard a person in a uniform speaking with a Dublin accent. All the Guards I had ever met had country accents.

'There goes the bleeding overtime,' muttered one as he saw us walk in.

I spent the next thirty years being told that the overtime was going. In fact, the only flat week's wages we ever got were after holidays or sick leave.

The job I was given was to patrol the grounds. It was January and pitch dark. The night was freezing, and it rained frequently. An assistant chief officer brought me up to the area I was to patrol, but, first, we stopped by the grave of the executed 1916 men. Little did I know that almost thirty years later, one those heroes would be exhumed and reburied at his home place, and I would be one of the men asked to be in the guard of honour.

There was a high wall separating Mountjoy from St Patrick's Institution for Young Offenders. He pointed down along the wall.

'Down there is the officers' mess. Walk down to that and back again, OK?'

'Is that it?'

'That's it. About 7:45, make your way back to the circle and knock off.'

I spent the rest of the evening walking. The patrol was very badly lit and I couldn't see much. I would meet people and I wouldn't have a clue who they were. Some were in uniform, which was all right. Others were in civvies. They could be escapees for all I knew. I didn't ask, and they didn't ask who I was. We just passed in the night. I was glad to knock off at eight.

On Wednesday, we got our pay cheque, which was fantastic. We had arrived up for Saturday, and now it was Wednesday. We hadn't even done a week, but the cheque was for over £100. The guy ahead of me snatched his and ran, but I was older and wiser. I knew that if they had made a mistake in the cheque, they would discover it and come back for the money, so I decided I might as well get it over with now.

'You've made a mistake,' I pointed out helpfully to the officer who was giving out the pay.

'Did they not pay you enough?' he asked. Then he took my cheque and looked at me. 'You get paid for every hour you work after five.'

'But even at that...' I began, then the light went on inside my head. I went home to Jan that evening with a happy heart.

'You won't believe this,' I said, handing her the cheque. She didn't. I knew then that I was going to stick with the job.

I never fully understood how the wages were calculated. It is only in recent years that any sort of breakdown has been included in the pay slip, and pay was never the same from one week to the next, so I soon lost any interest in trying to find out what I was on. I just knew it was very good. I remember we got four rises during the first six months. Eight months later, we got £2,000 back pay – enough to buy a small car. The back pay was from some earlier agreement, and I didn't understand how it applied to a raw recruit like me. All I can say is that we had a fantastic union.

The union had linked our pay to that of psychiatric nurses, so that gave us an immediate 40 per cent boost. Add in the overtime, and we were singing. But there was a big difference between us and the nurses. Nurses had to have a good education before they could even apply, then do their basic nursing training, then pass a number of exams over the years before they got full pay. We got it from day one and we had several hours of compulsory overtime a week. You had nineteen-year-olds getting over £300 a week, which was big money back then.

The money was the hook. Very few left the job. The turnover was miniscule compared to any other job I have been in. Over the years, I have only seen a few who couldn't hack it, but even they stuck it for ten or fifteen years before they quit.

Three weeks into basic training, we did a full day of duty in Mountjoy, and after six weeks in the training unit and marching along the canal, our training was finished. We were all asked to fill out a form listing our three preferred prisons to be posted to, putting them in order of preference. I wrote down Limerick three times. I knew where I wanted to go.

I was called in and asked what I meant by not listing a second and third preference. I explained that I had a house in Limerick and my wife was pregnant, so I would be returning to Limerick that evening. If they wanted me to report to Mulgrave Street on Saturday, I would. Otherwise I was out.

I was lucky that they didn't take offence, which they would have been entitled to, but there was no way I would have moved my home. I got my way. Along with another male and three female officers, I was posted to Limerick. All the rest were sent to the Bog, as Portlaoise was called. This midlands town was universally unpopular, unless you were from there. It housed the IRA and was one of the most secure prisons in Europe.

Limerick Prison is one of two impressive Victorian limestone buildings on Mulgrave Street. The other is the psychiatric hospital. The prison was built between 1815 and 1821 and oozes history. A fence surrounds the high limestone walls and admission is through a narrow gate, with army sentries on constant duty and a Garda posted at each corner. Once inside, we reported for duty at the circle and found out where we would be posted that day.

The first day I passed the sentries and walked into the prison, I was terrified but excited. It was a good time in my life. I was beginning a job that paid unbelievably well and my wife, Jan, was pregnant with our second child. My only worry was that I didn't know if I would be tough enough, or brave enough, for the prison. I am not brave by nature, but I learned that people adapt.

———

Limerick was a small prison back then. Cork wasn't open, and neither was Arbour Hill. There were fewer prisoners to accommodate too – it was only one man to a cell. That was a Quaker tradition to enable prisoners to reflect on their wrongs, though I don't think many did. Few enough of Limerick's criminals were Quakers.

Back then, it was taken for granted that you were a Catholic. When a prisoner was admitted, he had to declare his religion, and it was an offence if he was a Catholic and didn't go to Sunday mass. He could be put on report. Officers were also expected to go to mass in the prison chapel, and they all did, without exception.

Until I arrived. This was the subject of one of my first clashes with management. I wasn't in the job a wet week when my lack of faith became an issue.

One spring Sunday, when I had only been on the job a month or so, the chief officer came down to the circle and asked would someone do mass guard. No one said a word. I foolishly asked what mass guard was.

'Someone to look after the prisoners when they go to mass,' he said. 'I'll do it.'

'You can nip down to St John's yourself at twelve for mass,' he said.

'It's OK, I don't do mass. I'm not a Catholic, so it doesn't make any difference.'

He looked at me askance and called me into the office. 'Are you a Protestant?'

'No, I have no religion.'

'No, listen to me. If you're a Protestant, that's no problem. You can go out for an hour or two hours or however long you like,' he offered. He seemed completely unconcerned with what religion I had, as long as I had one.

'I'm a nil,' I said. 'Do you understand that, Chief? A nil. I have no religion of any kind whatsoever.'

'I can't have that,' he said. 'Do you believe in God?'

'No, Sir.'

'Do you believe in any God?'

'No, chief, that's what no religion means. I don't believe in any God.'

Then, he threw in what he thought was the clincher. 'Who made the world?' he snapped.

I looked at this grown man with incredulity. 'Are you joking? I don't know who made the world. Do you?'

'Are you being smart with me?' he shot back.

At that moment, an assistant chief officer came in and asked what was going on.

'I'll tell you what's going on – this man has no religion,' the chief thundered, and it started up again.

'I'm not going around the dance floor again on this one,' I said and walked out.

It wasn't the first time that not having a religion got me into trouble. A few years before joining the prison service, I had been in the orthopaedic hospital in Croom for a knee cartilage operation. A young nurse asked for my religion when filling out my chart, and I replied nil. She scuttled away and fetched a more senior nurse, who got the same answer.

'I'll just put you down as Protestant,' she said.

'You won't,' I replied.

So she went off and fetched the big boss. The matron was a nun. She swept into the room radiating authority and without any preamble said, 'We demand to know what religion you are going to declare.'

'None. I have no religion.'

She then drew herself up to her full height. 'And who, Mr Bray, do we call if you get gravely ill during the night?'

To which I replied, 'Call a shagging doctor.'

My punishment for that insubordination was that I was placed under the loudspeaker which played the mass and the rosary during my six-week recovery. On Sunday evenings, the nurses would come through the men's ward with the sausages and rashers that the more genteel ladies hadn't eaten. On each occasion, I was passed by and never offered any. I had heard of taking the soup, but not taking the sausage was a new one on me.

At least the prison service had the decency to have a row with me and let it go. The upshot was that I got to be in charge of the prison every Sunday. I was the man on mass guard. Every prisoner had to be called for mass, and if they didn't come promptly, they could be put on report. (That was beginning to die out, though; I never put anyone on report for skipping Sunday service.)

The job wasn't as easy as it sounds. I had to know how many prisoners were in the prison and I had to do the rounds. I didn't know if there were two fellows or one in a cell. After mass, I'd tell the chief how many were in the chapel. I'd subtract the number left in the cells from the total in the prison and that gave me the number who went to mass.

This wasn't a great system. Surely they should have told me how many were in church and I could have seen how many were left. But that would have been too easy. So, after a few months, I invented my own system. I would stand outside the church, count the prisoners coming out, and tell the chief. He'd be counting them beside me and I'd just tell him what he had just counted.

But I got fed up with it all and with running around like a blue-arsed fly and seeing some of the other officers standing around smoking. One Sunday, I said I couldn't do prison guard. I was going to mass.

'You can't go to mass,' said the chief.

'Gee, Chief, you wouldn't stop me from going, would you?'

Of course, that was the last thing in the world he would do. He turned to an ACO and instructed him to get someone else to do mass guard. Naturally, I didn't go to mass. The next week I did the same thing.

After that, they rotated mass guard.

———

You might deduce from my experiences that I worked a lot of Sundays and got no time off in lieu. When I came down to Limerick after basic training, I worked the next thirty-six days without one off. And they were long days. I would go in at eight, expecting to be home at five. But, at five, I would generally be told to stay on until eight. And at eight I could be told I was needed until ten or twelve. Overtime was compulsory, and most days we were held on until eight. At least once a week, eight stretched to midnight.

I wasn't too many months in the job before the big day arrived and our son was born. The governor had promised me time off for the birth when I'd started in the prison. I had also asked the chief officer and I reminded them both of this every week for the five months before the child was born.

Jan was rushed into the hospital on a Monday night. On Tuesday morning, I rang the chief.

'I won't be able to come in for the next two days. My wife is just after having a child,' I said.

'Oh, Jesus, I can't spare you,' came the reply.

'I was under the impression we had an arrangement.'

'You have to come in. I'll tell you what – you can do four to twelve today. There's no need to be in until the afternoon.'

So I had to leave the hospital and go back to the prison. I worked the next twenty-seven days without a single day off. That included the weekends, and many of the days were twelve hours and longer. On the twenty-seventh day, I was reported to the governor for being twenty minutes late. My baby was a month old before I saw him awake.

I learned my lesson. When our daughter was born a few years later, I was struck by a mysterious virus and had to take a couple of weeks off sick.

Welcome to Limerick, my arse.

———

In my first months in the prison, a potential problem arose, but I managed to dodge it. Had I not, it would have dogged me throughout the rest of my career. The problem was my name. Not my regular name – my nickname.

Prison is like a schoolyard. Everyone has a nickname, officers and prisoners alike. We had Johnny One Ball, Twenty Major, Forty

Questions, Horse's Arse, Camel's Hole, Johnny Rotten, Evil Ali, Joey the Bitch, The Bull, The Horse, Boxer, Mick the Liar, Joe the Con, Hatchet, Gangster, Battery Head, the Golden Goose (so called because whenever he came into prison, he always had to go to hospital. When overtime was scarce, we were always delighted to see him coming because he laid the golden egg for us), and so on. Some people called trousers 'kacks', so if an officer showed up in an unusual pair, he could be christened Kacks. If another officer joined who looked like a smaller or younger version of Kacks, he could be Nappies. Imagine having that follow you for thirty years of service.

Boxer hated his nickname. One day, he lined us up and told us that the next man who called him Boxer would be put on report. A suppressed giggle rippled through the officers. It was as if he had tattooed the name to his forehead. There was no getting rid of it after that.

I didn't have a nickname when I joined, but I knew one would inevitably be chosen for me. Six months passed and I was still Mr Bray to the prisoners, Philip to my colleagues. Then, it happened. I was on night duty one summer night. Dawn was breaking as I walked down towards the main gate. Hearing a noise, I looked up and saw the most amazing sight – silhouetted against the pale light of dawn, a squadron of Luftwaffe fighter planes were skimming low over the prison, flying in perfect formation.

The army had a machine gun mounted over the main gate to shoot down any helicopter that might try to land in the prison and replicate the IRA escape from Mountjoy. The air above Limerick Prison was a no-fly zone. There were, I was told, only two others in the country: Portlaoise Prison and Charley Haughey's private island, Inishvickillane, off Kerry.

The soldiers on duty that day obviously decided not to start the third world war by bringing down German air force fighters. I returned to the main gate and began to write my night duty report. Because the event was so unusual, I decided to mention it in the report. I wrote: 'At 5 a.m. this morning, a flight of the Luftwaffe flew over Limerick Prison.'

Big mistake.

Over the next few days, everyone was reading the book and laughing. I walked around the front of the prison one day and Johnny One Ball shouted out the window at me, 'Luftwaffe, come here.'

I ignored him and kept going, but I knew I was on my way to getting a nickname, and not one I wanted.

I devised a plan to make my own nickname, and quickly. From that day on, whenever anyone asked me a question requiring a one-word answer, I tried to answer 'Fab'.

'How's the car going?'

'Fab.'

'Is the coffee all right?'

'Fab.'

'How was the golf?'

'Fab.'

I kept overusing the word and, eventually, it stuck as my nickname. It could have been worse. Like Horse's Arse.

The prisoners never called me Fab, though. They had their own nickname for me – McCloud. The reason for this was that I looked very similar to Denis Weaver, who played the part of cowboy detective McCloud in the series of the same name that was popular in the 1970s. McCloud was a sheriff from the West who came to New York and rode around on a horse solving crimes. Long after the series ended, the name stuck, particularly among the older prisoners. Years might pass without me hearing it, then someone who had been released years earlier and who was back in would shout at me, 'How's it going, McCloud?', inevitably followed by the same question: 'Where's your horse?'

'Over at your house taking a shit in your garden,' I'd reply. It was the standard answer, and we'd both have a laugh.

The younger prisoners, who had never heard of McCloud, would be bewildered.

The nickname had no malice in it, and once it even got me out of a bit of bother. I was in the yard supervising some prisoners when one fell badly while playing handball. He was rolling around on the ground in agony, and it was obvious even to an untrained eye that he had dislocated his shoulder.

I quickly ran over to help and tried to turn him over gently. But whatever I did, the shoulder popped back in. The prisoners were very impressed with my skill, though I knew it was a sheer fluke.

The following day, the prisoner went to the doctor as a precaution. The officer who accompanied him told me that the doctor was livid that a prison officer had carried out what he saw as a serious medical procedure.

'What officer put your shoulder in?' he demanded.

'Officer McCloud,' replied the prisoner.

With that, the doctor picked up the phone and gave the governor a bollocking for allowing Officer McCloud to interfere in a medical matter. The governor listened, then hung up in bewilderment. He knew there was no Officer McCloud in the prison.

———

One thing that intrigued me during my first weeks in the prison was the cell cards. Outside each cell was a card listing all the details of the prisoner inside: name, sentence, release date and religion (almost inevitably RC). What intrigued me was that some of these cards had a brown streak running down their centre. After a few weeks, I got to the bottom of the mystery. One of the officers was a bit soft towards prisoners and when he was on nights, they would beg him for a cup of tea. There was a tiny hole in each door. He would make a funnel out of the cell card and pour the tea in through that hole, and they would catch it in their jug. The more he liked a prisoner, the darker the stain on the card.

I was asked to supply tea some nights, but I wouldn't – you could easily scald someone pouring boiling water in at him.

Chapter 4

Trouble

B ack then, a film was shown once a week in a darkened recreation hall. The entire prison population was thrown into that one small hall, with five or six officers scattered around. We never had problems, despite being so heavily outnumbered. With rare exceptions, the prisoners were fairly compliant.

Real violence in the prison was rare. There was the casual violence that pervaded society – a kick up the backside or a clip on the ear, the same as in the schools. Back in the 1970s and early 1980s, corporal punishment was not just allowed in schools, it was expected. I was often beaten by the Jesuits when I was in school. The only difference between the Jesuits and the Christian Brothers was that when we were presenting ourselves to the priest in charge of beating children, we had to give him a slip of paper written in Latin listing our offence and the amount of slaps we were to get. That's posh for you. I learned to forge his initials – W.T. s.j., Willie Trodden, Society of Jesus – which was brought back to the teacher as proof you'd been beaten.

A certain roughness was to be expected. For example, guys would be pushed into cells if they weren't moving fast enough, but nothing more serious happened. That changed as the years passed and more violent men were locked up, but we learned to cope.

Each of us came up with his own strategy for dealing with a fight. You couldn't be caught off guard. Rules said that you couldn't respond until a prisoner had attacked you, so there were no pre-emptive strikes. But each man knew exactly what he would do after that first strike. I had my own thing, but all I will say is that it allowed me to protect myself when things got rough.

After your first few prison fights, you become blasé. I have seen officers and prisoners involved in ferocious punch-ups, and a day later the prisoners are running around the yard playing football. It's hard to really hurt someone in a fight, and once you realise that, you become less fearlful. If I'm honest, many of the bruises and marks I got in fights were on my back and weren't caused by the prisoners, but by my fellow officers rushing in behind me to help.

When the IRA came down a few years into my service, we were issued with batons, but in practice we tended not to use them, as we had no baton training and I quickly got fed up of carrying the thing. My older colleagues, men with a few years on the job, didn't carry them for one very good reason – if a prisoner managed to grab one from you, you were in trouble. They came to the conclusion that you couldn't produce a baton unless you were going to use it. After all, you couldn't shake it at someone and tell him to do something. If you didn't use it, someone would take it from you and use it, but if your baton was back in the locker room, that couldn't happen. I followed their lead and ditched mine.

I got to use mine once and decided I would never carry it again. Around the spring of 1985, I was in charge of D Class and two officers brought back a prisoner who had hit his wife in the mouth during a visit. He was agitated and violent, so they decided to take the furniture out of his cell for his own safety. As they were doing so, one officer held him against a wall. The prisoner was shouting out the window to the yard below that he was being killed by the screws.

'They're breaking my arm!' he shouted.

The prisoners in the yard were becoming agitated as he shouted and screamed. When they came in at tea time, they glared at me, and I knew trouble was coming. About fifteen prisoners gathered outside the door of the wife beater, who was now locked up. To diffuse the situation, I told them to come down and get their tea, but they told me to fuck off. They demanded that a doctor examine the man immediately. I assured them that his arm was not broken and that he was perfectly OK. But they were having none of it.

The landings in D Class were very narrow, and some of the archways were so low you had to bend to go through them. There was no way to react fast in the circumstances, and, in any case, there were only three of us on duty, myself and two assisting officers. The situation needed defusing. I made to go down the landing towards the gathering of prisoners, but someone shouted, 'The first screw down, I'll take their fucking eyes out.'

I took a step back and the situation ignited. Some of the prisoners ran at us, using bits of cell furniture as missiles. The two officers with me ran downstairs and I made what could have been a fatal error – I foolishly ran upstairs. I was now on my own in D Class at the top of the stairs while the prisoners below were breaking up furniture to use as weapons. I took my baton out, waiting for them to come up the stairs. But, in fairness, none of them came up after me, even though they knew I was up there on my own.

I looked at the baton. I might as well have had a match or a pencil in my hand. That's how useless it seemed to me.

After a few minutes' tense stand-off I heard the cavalry coming, officers in riot gear with shields, helmets and batons. Seizing my opportunity, I ran down to the second floor and joined my fellow officers. There were ten of us now facing their fifteen. I was heartened to see the new chief, who had just transferred down to us, in the line-up with his helmet and baton like everyone else. It was not often you saw a chief in the fray, and it reassured us that we had backing for what we were about to do. Bobby, a big galoot of an officer, came up beside me and said, 'Are you OK?'

'Fine,' I replied. 'Are you all right?'

But he misheard me. He thought I had said, 'Right.' Taking it as the signal, he charged forward. I had no intention of running down there. I was shitting myself, but I couldn't let him go on his own, so I followed him into a hail of broken furniture and other missiles thrown by the prisoners. The rest followed us down.

The landing was so narrow there was barely room for the two of us to run down side by side. We were being showered with all sorts of rubbish, but it didn't deter us; we got in amongst them. One prisoner popped his head up. He had a metal chamber pot in his hand and he swung it at us. How he missed in that narrow space, I don't know. In pure fear and without thinking, I hit him straight down between the eyes with the baton. He sat down suddenly. As the baton bounced off his skull, it crossed my mind that I wasn't supposed to hit anyone on the head, but I was so full of fear that I wasn't thinking straight.

We were surrounded by confusion. As we gained control of the situation, the prisoners who were already locked up and who didn't really know what was happening were shouting, 'Leave them alone, ye bastards! Leave them alone!'

Then, smoke started coming out of some cells as the prisoners inside started to set fire to things. The smoke began to fill the narrow stairways and landings. Then, prisoners who had nothing whatsoever to do with the protest found smoke coming into their cells and began to panic. They were shouting to be let out, and some were even trying to break the doors down. There were shouts all over the place for me because I had the keys. I was running up and down opening doors to let officers into some cells to quench fires and shoving prisoners into other cells to lock them up.

By now it was all hands on deck. Two officers were in the exercise yard with a big petrol-powered power hose. We were shouting down instructions to them, telling them which cells were on fire, though they could see for themselves the smoke billowing out of the windows.

Now some of the prisoners in A Class, on the other side of the exercise yard, were shouting out their windows, adding to the confusion. But a flick of the hose from the officers in the yard quietened them quickly. They didn't want their cells destroyed with water and to have to sleep on wet mattresses.

I was called down to one cell and opened the door. The smoke billowed out in a thick, toxic cloud. I knew there was a prisoner in there and I went in to get him. I took two steps and fell flat on the floor. It was an incredible feeling. In movies, you see guys manfully striding through smoke-filled rooms, but it simply isn't possible. I took one breath, and a second, and it was like there was no petrol in the tank. I went down. The officer behind me dragged me out by the heels and I came around almost immediately. He stepped over me and went into the cell, and he went down. I dragged him out by the heels. But he went in again on his hands and knees, and this time succeeded in dragging the prisoner out.

There was huge confusion – smoke dimmed the lights, flames flickered in some cells, water flowed from others and prisoners were begging to be released. We were running on pure adrenalin – or at least I was.

The prisoner whom we dragged out of his cell wasn't moving, and when I went over to him I could see he wasn't breathing. I knelt down and gave him a couple of puffs of mouth-to-mouth and he came around and was taken away. About ten minutes later, just as we were getting the place under control, an officer shouted, 'Look out, Fab, behind you!'

I turned and saw the prisoner who I had just given the kiss of life to coming at me with the leg of a chair. I stopped him from hitting me, but I remember thinking it was a bit unfair that he should have tried it at all.

I looked into one cell and saw a prisoner gathering newspapers together and lighting them. I got two fire extinguishers and put one in the spyhole and the other in the centre hole of the door and let them off together. A few days later that prisoner came to me and said, 'Mr Bray, you destroyed my cell with those fire extinguishers.'

I was unapologetic, but asked, 'How did you know it was me?' I hadn't spoken and had had a crash helmet on. I was amazed he could identify me.

'We all know who ye are,' he said enigmatically. But I doubted it.

The day after the riot, a prisoner came up to me and said, 'Any chance of bringing me over to the reception to get dry sheets, Mr Bray?'

I looked at him and did a double take. It looked like someone had taken a biro and drawn a baton on his forehead. There was a livid bruise, a perfect impression of the blow I had struck him. He never said a word about it, but that day I decided I would carry no more batons. A prison officer's best weapon is between his ears.

A few minutes later, I heard a voice: 'Did you enjoy kissing me, Mr Bray?'

I turned and saw the prisoner I had given mouth-to-mouth to the day before. He had gathered an audience.

'It wasn't too bad until you slipped me the tongue, you pervert,' I shot back. He stopped slagging me after that.

Funnily enough, I still have a copy of my official report on that riot, prepared on the night before I knocked off. The report, now twenty-two years old and on yellowed paper, was written while the events were fresh in my mind, then slipped under the chief's door.

The Governor:

Sir, I respectfully wish to report the following: at 5 p.m. on this date in D Class the following prisoners [I will not repeat the names] staged a protest outside – cell.

They said they would 'stab the first screw they could get in the eye'. Officer – rang in for the chief, who came down at once with ACO –. The prisoners were throwing bed ends at us and we were told to put them in their cells. This we did.

A very short time later, smoke and flames were seen to come from prisoner –'s cell. He was rescued by the officers, and as he had difficulty breathing, I applied mouth-to-mouth to him. He came round at once and was put in another cell.

Philip Bray, Officer

We all got into the habit of keeping our reports brief and stark. The less detail you included, the less trouble you could get into.

———

Eventually, most of us abandoned the batons. What wound up in the baton pocket instead was the newspaper. We weren't supposed to read on duty, and they could be quite severe about that. Newspapers were supposed to be censored so that all references to court cases were cut out, and prisoners couldn't have access to an uncensored newspaper. That was beginning to be phased out, but if I was caught with a paper, I just told the chief that I was censoring it before giving it to a prisoner, but, of course, he had used the same excuse himself over the years.

By the late 1970s, the only thing we cut out of the papers on a regular basis were the crosswords. These were very popular, as they could while away the time on a boring watch. But you had to be careful not to be caught, so some of us stuck the crossword inside our hat. We would take off the hat, solve another clue, then shove the hat back on again. There was no rush about the crosswords; in fact, we would string them out to fill the hours. We looked for the hardest crossword we could find.

Some of the prisoners started doing them too – you could have forty of us doing the same one. And, of course, there would be some needle between us to see who would solve all the clues first.

Chapter 5
Daily Routine

Thirty years ago, the prison wasn't overcrowded; we had just one man to each cell and you might have thirty men on a landing. The women's section had just two or three inmates. You only doubled up the cells if you thought a prisoner was depressed or suicidal and needed the company. That all changed a few years after I joined.

In the early 1980s, the justice minister decided to double up the cells, against the advice of the prison officers' union. Immediately, the prison population doubled. Cells are like a vacuum – if they are available, they will be filled. There is no such thing as an empty cell. But while the prison population doubled overnight, the number of staff didn't. Recruitment gradually increased through the 1980s, but we were under pressure a lot of the time and working crazy hours to cope.

Despite the long hours and the occasional bouts of trouble, the job could be unimaginably boring. I still remember the first day I was put on Number One Patrol, which was the patrol around the back of the women's prison. The women's prison had a few subversives in it, which was the reason for the army on the walls and the Gardaí outside. The place was full of people. The double gate into the women's unit was manned by an officer in a small shed who let people in or out. In addition, there was a sentry post at the back of the building, about the size of a telephone kiosk and without even so much as a seat. You could be there for twelve hours on the trot. I was brought around to this at four in the afternoon by a more senior officer.

'What do I do here?' I asked.

'You're here now until twelve o'clock.'

That was the end of any thought of knocking off at five.

'What about a meal break?'

'You'll probably get a meal break if we can send someone out to you for a few minutes.'

I would have rather got an answer a bit more definite than that.

'What if I need to go to the jacks?'

'Knock on that window over there, that's the female office.' I was to get the female officer to ring over to the male prison and ask for someone to come over and relieve me.

There were a lot of *ifs* about this: if there was a female officer in the office, if anyone answered the phone, if there was anyone free to come over, I might get a toilet break.

He brought me farther around the back and showed me a big pile of sand. There must have been a ton of it.

'Most of us use that, but it's up to you,' he said.

I did not intend to use it, but one night, after a number of failed attempts to get relief, I had to give in. Ten o'clock on a winter's night, my fifteenth day in a row on duty, tired, wet and frozen, with rain dripping off my nose, I pissed into the sand. *This is worse than the fucking Foreign Legion*, I thought.

Night after night, I stood watch for eight solid hours. I didn't even have a place to sit, though I did manage to find a stick that I could lean my backside on for a few minutes before it went too numb. Most of the Number One Patrol shifts were eight hours long. In the middle of winter, hail, rain or snow, you would still have to stand there. Your whole day or night shift could pass without seeing a soul.

At two minutes to twelve, the women's chief officer would return. She lived in the prison. Once I heard the *clip clop* of her shoes, I knew I could go home.

But if I did that shift, I was always put on nights the following day. The night shift was seven in the morning until noon, then back again at eight in the evening until eight the following morning. It was a split shift that screwed up your entire day. I would drive home, grab a few hours' sleep, then drag myself out of bed and back to the prison for dawn. Seven in the morning to midnight shifts, followed by a seven o'clock start the following morning, were quite common. Overtime was compulsory, so we had to put up with it.

The men I started out with stuck with the job. Over the decades, some of them rose in the ranks, modernising and bringing improvements as they went. The three women who joined with me left the service fairly quickly, though.

———

Looking back, a number of things stand out. The perception of prison officers is very skewed by the media. If there was ever a dispute, you could depend on the papers to trot out our earnings – you would always find some article moaning that we got paid £75,000 a year. What those articles never told you was what the officer had to do to earn that. I could have to report for duty at seven in the morning and not get home until midnight, seven days a week for five months on the trot. We earned our money. And the chiefs were the same as us rank–and-file officers – they worked around the clock.

I got used to the hours, but I never got to like them. I couldn't play any sport for the first fifteen years I was on the job. There were inter-firm tournaments in the city, but we couldn't enter them because we couldn't put a team together. When would we be off?

The overtime also put an end to me playing rugby. No one was involved in any kind of sport whatsoever. I had a young family and that is what I concentrated on when I did have time off, spending as much of that free time as possible with my kids. My days off were all the same – I would grab the kids and head off before the prison sent for me to do an extra shift.

After a number of years on the job, things eased slightly, especially when I went into the kitchen in the 1990s, which gave me regular hours. I took up golf and was one of the founders of the Limerick Prison Golf Society.

It was strange meeting people in the golf club. These would be fellows twenty or thirty years old who had grown up in my village. They would ask, 'When did you move here?'

'Thirty-six years ago,' I'd answer.

'Why haven't I seen you before?' they'd ask.

Where would they see me? I wasn't a Catholic, so they wouldn't have seen me in the church. My kids didn't go to the Catholic school, so they wouldn't have seen me there. I don't go out drinking in the local pubs, so they wouldn't have seen me there. I didn't play golf and I didn't follow GAA. I was stuck in a prison. My life revolved completely around the job, particularly for the first five years. That brought me well beyond thirty with no sort of a social life whatsoever.

Families suffered because of the way the job took over our lives. All marriages have problems, and not being there is a big one. I know of cases where children suffered from the lack of a male presence in the household. But there was a compensation – if you take away the money problems, it makes a big difference. That made relationships hang together that otherwise might not have.

At one time, there was a loophole that could break you free of the compulsory overtime and buy you some time at home with the family. If you took an uncertified sick day, you were punished by not being allowed to do overtime the following week. Of course, we'd be delighted – home at five. But after a couple of months, management copped on to this and stopped it.

Overtime wasn't just compulsory if management collared you in the prison. You could be gone home or be on a day off and get a call telling you to come back. And it was no use ignoring the phone. If the prison rang the house and you didn't answer, a squad car could be sent out to tell you that you were needed.

Management wouldn't tell you in advance when you would be needed so that you could plan your time off. It was almost as if they didn't trust us. Despite the money the overtime brought us, it wasn't our choice to work those hours.

The lack of time off did take its toll on families. Something that is rarely spoken of is the effect of a prison sentence on a prisoner's family. If a man is taken out of his home and put in prison for a long stretch, a vacuum is left in the home. Nature abhors a vacuum, and his place within the home will be filled, often by a son who might just be in his teens, or by a daughter. When the father eventually gets out, there is no place for him. His son, who was a child when he went in, is looking at him and thinking, 'Where were you when we needed to pay the rent? Don't think you can come swanning home and take up where you left off.' It can be the same with prison officers and their families.

I was talking to a colleague's wife recently and she said that her son's behaviour had suffered because of the absence of his father. And it suddenly dawned on me that I did nearly as much time in the place as any prisoner, with the one difference being that I slept for a few hours in my home each night instead of in a narrow bed on Mulgrave Street. A number of prison officers have told me that they had trouble with their children because they were never around. Thankfully, that was not my experience.

I don't want to moan; this problem is not exclusive to prison officers. There are doctors working long hours or truck drivers on the road day after day, and many others. It takes its toll.

Chapter 6
Beginning Your Time

I quickly learned that there was a strict routine for admitting prisoners. They could arrive at any time of the day or night, though it was often well after office hours, particularly if they were coming from distant Garda stations. If a man was arrested at seven in Tipperary, the Gardaí would often just leave him in the station until ten, when the next shift took over, rather than bring him in and risk being late home. But if they were coming from the district court, they often arrived when the court finished in the late afternoon.

The prisoner is brought to the gate of the prison and left in a holding cell there for us to deal with. The holding cell is a recent development; prior to that, the Gardaí brought the prisoner into a waiting room and stayed with him until an assistant chief arrived to do the paperwork. Occasionally, prisoners gave trouble to the Gardaí who brought them in, but they generally calmed down once the Gardaí left, as they knew they were going nowhere then.

The assistant chief officer had to check the warrants, which was an important job; some ACOs believed that the Gardaí could try to offload someone even though the warrants weren't in order. And the prisoner had to be in order as well. We weren't supposed to take them in if they were drunk or damaged. 'Damaged' sounds awful, but that's the way it was. We had to issue the Gardaí with a body receipt – a receipt for the body – that said: 'Received the body of the above prisoner, who was sober and correct.' Any marks on him after we issued that receipt were our responsibility.

Our first task was to ask the prisoner their name and if they understood why they were in prison. With the number of non-nationals in the country now, that is becoming increasingly difficult. Often the prisoners were drunk or stoned, even though we weren't supposed to admit them in that state, and that made the admissions process more difficult.

Every point on the warrant was checked, including that they had been sent to the right prison. Every court circuit had its own prison. If I was on escort duty and took a prisoner from Limerick to court in Letterkenny, I would have to return him to Mountjoy rather than Limerick if he was sentenced. That made for a long day. It could be 2 a.m. by the time I got out of Mountjoy, and 5 a.m. when I got home to Limerick.

After the warrant check, the prisoner was brought over to the reception and checked in, then it was off to the showers. Everyone had to strip off and take a shower, regardless of who they were or what they were in for. I suspect it's the same in the women's prison, but I don't know. There is a big book about four feet long and two feet thick that had to be filled in with the prisoner's name and their possessions. Everything was noted in that big book, right down to the brand name of their shoes. Many prisoners would chance claiming that their £300 pair of designer jeans had gone missing, but having the record proved the lie of that. Usually, they were in tracksuits anyway; I suspect some of them thought a tracksuit was a suit.

Some lads were shy about stripping, but we insisted. We would give the prisoner a towel and some soap and send him to the showers. All his clothes were put in his locker to be returned on his release. When they were finished, we examined them for any distinguishing marks of scars, which were recorded in a book. Quite a lot had tattoos, for example LOVE and HATE on the knuckles of each hand, a series of dots around the neck or wrists with CUT HERE written underneath, also the names of deceased family members and girlfriends names (sometimes crossed out) were common. A small blue dot under an eye was a sign that they had spent some time in a borstal. Almost all the tattoos were amateur jobs and looked it. Over the years, the scars we saw changed from marks in the head from sticks or suchlike to gunshot wounds. Most reception officers could tell the difference between the marks various calibre rounds would make on a human body. And many prisoners bore the marks of knife fights.

Our priority was to get them in, get them washed and give them their prison clothes. The standard of those has gone up enormously.

At least now they get a clean pair of socks, clean underwear and a clean vest. Back in the 1970s, they could end up with the mankiest, mangiest briefs, but, back then, many of the inmates didn't wear underwear anyway, so perhaps what they got was an improvement. Remand prisoners (those awaiting trial) were given grey trousers and jacket, while the regular prisoners wore denim. It might not have been the height of fashion, but it was clean and it came close to fitting.

The problem was the shoes. If you were size eight or nine, there might be no shoes for you because they would all have been given out, since those were the most common sizes. It was great if you were small or big; if you had size thirteen feet, you were in luck – there were loads of shoes to choose from.

In practice, you didn't have to stick to the prison uniform. After you were in a few days, you could apply to the governor for permission to wear your own clothes, and many prisoners did. They were allowed to bring in two of everything. The clothes were held by the Stores and dealt out on a regular basis. Many prisoners succeeded in smuggling several pairs of underpants into their cells so they could change daily. We didn't view this as a serious infringement, not like smuggling in hash. I wasn't going to raid your cell for a pair of undies.

When I started first, some fellows were slow to take a shower – to be honest, many had never seen one before. We got a lot of indigents in, and tramps and psychiatric patients. They weren't too keen to wash themselves. Plus there was only one shower in the prison, so weeks could go by before someone had a wash. If he wasn't too dirty, that wasn't a problem. Occasionally, we had to encourage someone to wash and, very occasionally, we'd have to force him. Back then, a lot of inmates had lice and nits in their hair, and sometimes we would have to shave their hair off, which was a job no one liked to do, as you could see their whole scalp moving.

By the time I retired, it was completely different. The prisoners were cleaner coming in, and they stayed cleaner inside. If someone gets his head shaved now, it's a fashion statement.

After they were issued with the prison uniform, the prisoners were given a pillow, a knife, a fork, a spoon, a jug and their crockery. They used to get razors, but not any more – that changed after an officer got viciously slashed across the throat. Today, they get an electric razor.

The cutlery used to be steel, but that created problems as we had to collect the knives and forks after each meal and distribute them before the next. You couldn't let a prisoner walk away with a knife. Today, everything is plastic – even the jug and plates are plastic. Why take chances?

Sometimes, a guy would opt to shave his head when he was admitted because he knew the hair would grow back by the time he was released. But the results could be comical. One prisoner cropped his scalp down to the bone and then discovered he had an appeal hearing coming up. He was ugly enough with hair, but without it he was ten times worse, and with the tufts beginning to grow back in odd places, he was worse again.

I had to bring him up to Dublin for an appeal and I asked him if he'd realised he had a court appearance when he shaved his head.

'I didn't,' he grinned. Obviously, his solicitor had lodged the appeal as a matter of form and thought nothing more about it. At any rate, the solicitor was nowhere near the court and the prisoner ended up having to represent himself.

The judge looked at this gargoyle and said, 'Why are you appealing?'

There are only two reasons you can appeal – either you're not guilty or you are guilty but feel your sentence is too long. In technical terms, you're either appealing against your conviction or against the severity of your sentence. My man didn't know any of this.

He stood up. The whole court could see the gears working slowly in this guy's head. He looked up and the light went on.

'I'm getting married, Judge,' he said.

'I wouldn't rush into anything if I was you,' replied the judge and sent him back down.

I took the same prisoner up to Dublin four months later. By then, he had a bit more hair and was in great form. He was about to hit the jackpot.

'I have a claim in for £1.5 million,' he told me in the van on the way up.

'You couldn't.'

'I do. There was a riot in Mountjoy and I was on the roof. When the officers came up to get me, they threw me down and broke both my legs.'

He said he had been dragged back to his cell after the rooftop riot, and it was three days before anyone realised both his legs were broken. Now, it was payback time for him.

He spent the journey telling me what he planned to do with the money. He wasn't gloating or anything; he just seemed genuinely delighted with his luck. We arrived at the Four Courts and he was rubbing his hands in anticipation.

But when the case was called, it transpired he was being charged with causing £1.5 million worth of damage to the prison. It wasn't a compensation claim, but a bill he was facing. He stood there and his jaw dropped.

'What about my broken legs?' he wailed. The judge didn't know what he was talking about.

On the way home I stopped in Newbridge and bought him a kebab, the poor devil. What else could I do?

———

It's not nice to be locked up. Nobody likes the sound of a door locking behind them. Occasionally, the Gardaí brought groups of teenagers around in an effort to deter them from a life of crime. Some of the trips were organised by schools, while others were organised by community Gardaí. Some rough characters took the tour. I didn't believe in giving them a fright, but in telling them the truth. Others took a different view.

One of my colleagues used to bring the groups down to the toilets, which were rough enough. There'd be a mix of these young teenagers, boys and girls. He'd pick on the biggest and toughest looking and say, 'You, where would you like to be raped? In the showers or the toilet?'

'I don't want to be raped at all,' the youth would protest.

'I'm not asking you do you want to be raped at all. I'm asking where you want it to happen.'

I didn't agree with those sorts of shock tactics, but I didn't mind turning the key and giving them a brief taste of confinement. I would open a cell and let everyone in to look around, and then I'd lock it behind them. They used to freak out. But, sometimes, the ones who freaked out most were the Gardaí.

'Let me out, you fucker!' he'd yell. I think it was the fear in the Garda's voice that scared the kids more than anything else.

Usually, there was a reliable prisoner, a long-term or lifer, who would meet the kids. We would leave them together in a secure place and I would go away. That was the deal – he could be straight with them without us overhearing or interfering. I don't know what he said to the kids, and, to be honest, I don't know if it made any difference.

————

When I joined the service, the prison was painted dark green with oil-based paints. There was no breathing through the thick coating, so the walls would weep with condensation. The walls were so thick that the prison never warmed up, even in summer. And the prison authorities, like the schools and the hospitals, ran the heating completely divorced from what was going on with the weather. The heating came on in October and stayed on until March, and that was that. If you got a sweltering day in March, you could roast alive inside the thick walls, but during a cold April day, you ran the risk of freezing solid.

Prisoners spent a lot of time inside those miserable, weeping cells. A lot of them told me that time didn't start for them until they were locked away at night. That was the roughest time for them. In the late 1970s, they were on their own. It wasn't good long ago, especially if you were on remand. The cells were very bare, and remand prisoners didn't get the cleanest cell as there was a constant turnover of prisoners. There was no radio, no television. You might have a book, but once the lights went out at 10 p.m., that was gone too.

In any case, a lot of the prisoners couldn't read or had limited literacy skills. They had been let down by every one. Often, their parents didn't have the skills or support to guide them. Judges had the power to send young children away for years into the Church gulags, many for offences that, today, look very minor indeed, like skipping school. And they sent plenty of them off. When these children complained about the abuse they suffered, they were not believed. The schools were unable to teach them to read and write which limited their chances of getting any kind of proper work. Anyway, their addresses alone could bar them from even an interview. They didn't trust the gardaí, the clergy, politicians – nobody in authority was seen as a help. They were treated like second-class citizens and they knew it. They were battered and had no support of any kind, no jobs and no influence. Ireland had a culture of pulling strings – I had to pull strings to get a phone because there was a two-year waiting list.

These guys had no strings to pull. They were ground down by poverty and ignorance. Ignorance is not stupidity. As a rule, the prisoners had limited education, but that didn't make them thick, so we tried to treat them with dignity.

I felt honoured if a prisoner asked me to read a letter for him or to write something. I felt it was a sign of trust and I was happy to help.

Chapter 7
Escorts

I wasn't long on the landings when I was introduced to one of the joys of the job – escorts. Prisoners don't spend their whole sentence inside the prison. They have to go out to courts and hospital appointments, or are transferred between institutions or up to the Central Mental Hospital. We escort them when they are outside.

My first escort was to Cork Circuit Court. I was really looking forward to seeing what went on behind the scenes. The officer in charge was a veteran of several years; I'll call him Paddy Murphy although that's not his real name. I was handcuffed to the prisoner in the back of the taxi. Back then, the prison didn't have its own van.

We left Limerick early to be at the courthouse before ten o'clock. Paddy was a good guy to travel with; he was calm and was one of the few officers I never heard curse. His easy-going nature made him popular with the prisoners and he always had time for them – too much, according to some officers. But I was glad I was with him and I knew things would be done by the book.

He was also one of the few officers who didn't drink. There was a terrible drinking culture in the service, and I soon learned that escorts were seen by many as a day on the tear. At that time, officers were expected to be able to down numerous pints at dinner time and tea time, then more back in Limerick after the escort before they drove home.

This was a great adventure for me – a break from the routine, a spin to Cork and my first glimpse of a circuit court. As most escorts were done on overtime, I was being paid on the double as well. The guy I was handcuffed to was elderly for a prisoner, about fifty-nine, and soft spoken. He was from a small village in County Cork and was on remand for arson. He told me his story – he was sleeping off a load of drink in a neighbour's barn and his cigarette fell, igniting the hay. He woke up smothered in smoke.

'I barely escaped with my life. I was beating out the flames when the people came running out of the house. They thought I had started the fire. I thought they were going to kill me, so I did a runner,' he said. 'I might have been a bit drunk at the time, but it was a pure accident.'

As we passed Mallow and neared Cork, he got animated, pointing out the places he knew.

'Look, Officer, that's the village I came from,' he said. I couldn't see anything except a small road.

'And there's the farm I worked on for twenty-five years. The son of the farmer got married and I was kicked out on my backside. I had nothing, nothing at all. I wasted most of my life there. After the bastards threw me out, I had to go to England to earn a crust.'

He went on to detail some of the scrapes he had got into in England, mostly through drinking. I suppose it wasn't an unusual tale for the times.

The court building was being refurbished and the holding cells in the basement were in bits, so we used a large room with a big table and some bare chairs to hold the prisoner. Paddy told me to remove the handcuffs, then he went up into the court to find out what was going on. The prisoner and I passed the time chatting.

'I'll see my brother today,' he remarked. That caught me by surprise.

'We're here for a court appearance, not for socialising,' I said.

'You wouldn't deny me a visit. We're so close to home.'

I was a bit green, but this didn't sound kosher to me. I was only a few months in the job and this was my first escort, so I didn't know the score. I thought that honesty was the best policy. I explained that Officer Murphy was in charge, and that when he came back we would see what would happen. First mistake.

'Are you denying me my right to see my family?' he roared. He had gone from Dr Jekyll to Mr Hyde in the snap of a finger. 'I've had enough of this shit. I'm going home. Get out of my fucking way, Sonny.'

I didn't know what to do. I stood and turned to see if there was anyone around to help. That was my second mistake. As I turned, he punched me in the head. It knocked my cap off and I took a step back. I was more shocked than hurt. My softly spoken friend was ranting and raving; he had really lost it.

'Get out of my fucking way or I'll kill you where you stand!' he bellowed.

I stood back and took stock of the situation. I was on my own, but he was about thirty years older than me. I thought he wasn't going to win a fight with me, and even though he said he was going to kill me, he was unarmed and he hadn't picked up a chair or anything. I didn't really want to hurt him. Our training hadn't covered a situation like this.

'Look, relax, man. You'll get your visit, I promise you. Just sit down and I'll take care of it personally, OK?' Honesty had just gone out the window.

He came at me again, swinging wildly. I moved round the table to avoid him and he came after me. When we were opposite each other, I made my move. I shoved the table hard, pinning him to the wall. He wasn't strong enough to push me and the table away, so he was stuck there. He kept flailing away at me, but couldn't reach me. We faced each other across the table like that for about fifteen minutes, he was fucking and blinding me at full blast.

I got fed up looking at this nutter and turned my back on him again. I was still holding the table with my backside and I lit a fag. I was on my third cigarette when Paddy sauntered back.

He was a few years senior to me and I knew he would know what to do. I moved across to explain the situation. My third mistake. The prisoner shoved the table and broke free. He came for us. He punched Paddy in the chest.

Paddy met him with a punch between the eyes and sent him staggering back against the wall, where he slid gracefully to the floor.

'Get him up, he's wanted in court,' said the voice of experience.

I helped him up. All the fight was gone out of him now. There was a trickle of blood running down one eye.

'Jesus, Paddy, he's bleeding. We can't bring him into court like that.'

Paddy got some toilet paper, spat on it, and wiped the wound.

'Now bring him up,' he said.

The dock was reached by spiral stairs. From the court, you would see a person coming up in stages, first the head turning as he climbed, and then the shoulders. It was like something on a stage. The whole place was looking at us. The prisoner was asked his name and who was representing him.

'I am representing myself, Judge.'

The judge threw his eyes to heaven. Judges hate people representing themselves because they don't know the rules of court, they don't understand the process and they get their law from the TV. They never show proper respect, and, on top of that, the judge has to ensure the defendant's rights are protected to the full.

He was allowed to enter the body of the court from the dock. He stood there, a solitary, unkempt figure compared to the smartly attired professionals, making his own defence. It quickly became apparent that the story he had told me on the way down was just that. He was charged with setting fire to no less than fourteen barns and sheds in his local district. He had the place terrorised. People were afraid it was only a matter of time before he burned a family home to the ground.

The judge urged him on numerous occasions to seek professional assistance, but he refused. Even to me, as a court novice, the whole thing was a farce. The prisoner was rambling and making crazy statements instead of cross-examining the witnesses. The judge was at his wit's end trying to keep him on track.

'You're a liar!' my man would shout.

'You may ask the witness questions, not make statements,' the judge would explain.

'What do you mean, Judge?'

'You can ask him if he is a liar, but you can't tell him he is a liar.'

'Fair enough, Judge.' He turned to the witness and asked, 'Are you a liar?'

'No, I am not a liar,' came the reply.

A look of triumph passed the arsonist's face. 'There, Judge. Now he's telling lies again.'

As this farce rumbled on, the prisoner kept rubbing his eyes. I was sure the blood would start running again and the judge would ask what had happened. I had visions of losing my job and posting back the uniform before the day was out. But the proceedings came to an end and the prisoner came home with us. He gave us no more trouble. The trial went on for a week, but I wasn't there for the rest of it. Life is busy and I didn't get a chance to enquire whether he was convicted or if his defence improved.

A few weeks later, I was sent round the back of the prison with two prisoners. Two new army sentry posts were being built and the prisoners were mixing the concrete for them. Not too bad, I thought. Lean against the wall for eight hours smoking, watching two men working. I can handle that.

As we came round the corner, we could hear a prisoner singing. It was coming from c Class. That surprised me, as c Class was almost derelict.

'Give me land, lots of land. Don't fence me in,' he sang at the top of his voice. Not a bad singer, I thought, as he went into 'Home on the Range'. As we came into his view, he stopped singing. He watched us for a few minutes to see what we were doing.

'Hey, you! The prisoner with the shovel! Hit the screw on the back of the head for me. Are you a man or a mouse? Hit the bastard! Kill him!'

I recognised the voice. It was my old sparring partner from Cork Circuit Court. He was at the window shouting down at us.

'Do I have to come down myself and do it, you cowardly bastard? And you, Blondie,' he shouted to the other prisoner, 'beat him into the fucking ground, you windy fucker.'

The two prisoners were embarrassed.

'Jesus, Mr Bray, he's a mad bastard.'

'Take no notice, lads. He's not the full shilling,' I explained.

He kept the threats up for about an hour, then returned to the singing. He only knew the two songs, but he sang them over and over. The prisoners with me were getting fed up and asked me to get him to stop. I went up to c Class to calm him down. I thought he had it in for me because of the trouble in the court, but when I spoke to him he didn't even recognise me. His posture seemed stiff and it took me a few minutes to realise that he was in a straitjacket. Till then, I had only seen them in the movies. I didn't even know we had them in the prison.

I watched him staring blankly at me, confined in a straitjacket, singing his two cowboy songs. He alternated between singing and the threats for the whole day I was there. We just had to put up with it. I never saw him again after that.

I think the thing that kept me in the prison service at the start was the escorts.

Escorts broke the mind-numbing monotony and boring cycle of duties. I loved the unpredictability. They could take place at any time and be to almost any place.

We did court escorts all over Ireland. Prisoners from different parts of the country doing their time in Limerick had to be returned to the court that they had been sentenced by.

I remember one remand prisoner was from Donegal, and I had to bring him up to Letterkenny for his trial. He was found guilty and the warrant was made out for Mountjoy, so I had to drive him from Donegal down to Dublin to execute the warrant. Then, I did the paperwork to get him transferred to Limerick, and we got back in the van and drove for another few hours. That day began at six in the morning. It was four the following morning when we trundled back into Limerick Prison. But it had been a full day of not having to stand guard behind the women's prison with a pile of builders' sand as a toilet. I got two hours of sleep and was back on duty at eight that morning.

Escorts brought me to every court, including the Supreme Court (where an extradition case was being held), the High Court (which dealt with bail applications for serious charges), the Central Criminal Court (which dealt with the serious cases of rape and murder), the circuit courts (which were scattered around the country and dealt with serious cases excluding murder and rape), district courts (in every nook and cranny of the country dealing with the more minor cases), the Children's Court and the *in camera* (or secret) hearings of various family courts.

But escorts also included visits that might not automatically spring to mind. My first visit to an STD clinic saw me handcuffed to a man who was having genital warts removed by a nurse. His genitalia shrunk through fear, and so did mine.

There were many different types of hospital visits, including prisoners going for x-rays or physiotherapy or getting patched up after rows. Occasionally, we brought prisoners out on humanitarian grounds. We might bring a man to the hospital to visit a sick child or an elderly parent. On one occasion, a prison officer attended in the operating room while a major criminal was having piles removed under anaesthetic.

Hospital staff were usually helpful and friendly. Many nurses were married to men in uniforms and would be helpful for that reason. Others were nervous of having handcuffed prisoners around for any length of time, so we would normally be accommodated as quickly as possible. No waiting for us – we often walked past queues of decent, respectable people to get treatment. Prisoners also usually got a private room with two officers constantly in attendance. I remember passing crowded wards filled with compliant taxpayers who didn't have the luxury of two people to chat to all day long while they were in hospital.

The hospital staff were trusting, not alert to the dangers of having trolleys filled with needles, syringes, scissors and scalpels, but we were at pains to keep these potential weapons away from the prisoners. A prisoner was normally treated while still in handcuffs, unless these absolutely had to be removed. Sometimes, we came across doctors who would tell us to take the handcuffs off. These doctors were normally foreign, often from countries where anyone in a uniform is seen as corrupt. We would take them outside and explain that we didn't have permission to remove the handcuffs. If they insisted, we insisted even more. More than once I had to say to a doctor that I would return the prisoner to custody untreated rather than remove the handcuffs. This was generally enough to get them to see things my way. I wasn't a cruel man; I just wasn't going to see an escape on my watch. Hospital visits were the number-one escape opportunity, and we knew it as well as the prisoners.

Other escorts included bringing a prisoner to a funeral parlour to attend the funeral of a parent or close relative. I hated those escorts, but there were some officers who were brilliant at it. They would stand with their head bowed in deep, respectful silence and seemed to be genuinely sad at the passing of the person.

Some long-term prisoners were brought to home visits for a short period as well. Again, certain officers were very good at those kind of visits and could be unobtrusive and still maintain security in somebody else's house.

Some escorts, especially those to the Central Mental Hospital, were particularly prized. The most important thing was to have enough medication to keep the prisoner calm during the trip. I remember dosing a guy with Largactol to keep him under control for the trip to Dublin. Halfway up, he fell asleep. I said to the officer who was assisting me, 'Isn't it great that he's sleeping? I gave him a bit of Largactol to keep him quiet.'

'Jaysus, I gave him some too. No wonder he's not doing much,' said my colleague.

Escorts to the Central Mental Hospital didn't begin early in the day. It was usually mid-afternoon before the documentation for committal to the hospital was completed. This meant it could be 5 or 6 p.m. before we left Limerick, and one in the morning before we returned. This meant overtime, but that's not the only reason those escorts were popular: the staff at the Central Mental Hospital went to enormous lengths to make sure we were catered for when we arrived. If we arrived while their mess was open, they would usher us to the head of the queue, have us order what we wanted from the menu and under no circumstances allow us to pay for anything. If we arrived after the canteen was closed, say, 10 or 11 P.M., there would be plates of ham and cheese sandwiches waiting for us. They also had pots of hot water on standby so we could make tea or coffee for ourselves. This happened on every visit to the CMH.

We got one opportunity to return the compliment when we discovered that three psychiatric nurses from the hospital were passing through Limerick on their way to play golf in the West of Ireland. They asked if they could see around the prison, and of course we were delighted to accommodate them. A row broke out between the governor, the social club and the Prison Officers' Association as to who could best take care of them and repay in some small way the kindnesses that had been shown to us. Naturally, they had a free meal in our mess, but we also had a collection on the spot amongst the staff, which we hoped would pay for their golf on some of the links courses in the West of Ireland.

———

As the governor used to live in the prison alone, he would often get bored after coming in from the pub at eleven or half eleven, and he'd walk around the prison, allegedly on duty but really killing time. Sometimes, he'd come across an officer like myself and stop to have a chat with me.

One night he said, 'We'll be getting a van soon, Mr Bray. You used to be a mechanic. You'd be an ideal candidate to drive it.'

I just nodded sceptically. We were as likely to get a couple of helicopters and a small plane, it was that outlandish. The prison service had nothing. We used taxis for all the escort duties. But, eventually, a van did come – though not much of a van. 'Heap of shit' would be the kindest description. That was around 1980.

Unbelievably, a priest came to bless the van. I rounded a corner and came upon the chief, the assistant chief officer and the priest sprinkling water on this ramshackle heap of junk. One of the chiefs had run up to the kitchen, got three commercial tins of beans, emptied them out, cleaned them and brought them down. They were put down in the middle of the van for ashtrays.

The first bump in the road or bend we came to and someone was going to get a lap full of butts. I looked at it and thought, *There's the prison service in a nutshell.*

But it ended once and for all the practice of using taxis for prison escorts. For the first number of years of my service, we phoned for a taxi when we had to take a prisoner up to a court or to the Central Mental Hospital. We used the one firm the whole time, and they must have made a fortune from us. But that doesn't mean it was easy money.

One of my taxi escorts involved bringing a big prisoner up to the Central Mental Hospital. He was huge, a bear of a man. If he started causing trouble, it was going to be hell on the trip up, so I went and got a dose of Largactol for him. He knocked it down and I went to sort out the paperwork. When I returned, I handcuffed him to the officer assisting me and we waited for the taxi to arrive.

'He'll be quiet today – he knocked back a good dose of the Largactol,' said my colleague. We had done it again: double dosed. But I said nothing.

The taxi arrived and we set out. The prisoner was quiet and docile to begin with, then his head fell forward and he began to snore gently. We were sorted. I was sitting up front with the driver and my colleague was in the back, still handcuffed to his charge.

But as we neared the Curragh, the prisoner began to stir. Within minutes, he had woken up fully and was howling like a wolf. I was a bit nervous of him because he was an aggressive enough man at the best of times, so I decided to get into the back and sandwich him just in case anything happened.

'Pull over here,' I said to the taxi man. 'He's getting a bit fidgety, so I'm going to get into the back. There's no need to worry, but if things get out of hand, I'll ask you to pull in again. Just get out of the taxi and walk away without turning back. We'll sort it out.'

With that, I got out of the passenger seat and sat in the back, wedging the prisoner between myself and my colleague. I was delighted with myself. I had been so accommodating to the taxi man. If he followed my instructions, he wouldn't be involved in anything and would be well out of any danger if the prisoner turned violent.

The taxi pulled back onto the road and we continued towards Dublin. The prisoner continued to give trouble, howling continuously. The taxi man kept glancing nervously in the mirror.

'Do you mind if I drive a little faster?' he finally asked.

'Drive as fast as you like, man. There's no problem,' I replied.

It was like I had asked Scotty to bring us up to warp speed. He dropped about three gears and the taxi took off like a rocket. He was driving like a lunatic, handbrake turns and everything, and we were in Dundrum faster than I'd ever done the journey before. We lodged the prisoner and went for our usual feast. The poor driver confided that we had scared the shit out of him.

'I don't think I was ever so frightened in my whole life,' he said.

Later, I heard that he moved to a different company and would never do another prison escort again.

But he needn't have bothered, as we got our own van shortly afterwards and could handle most escorts in-house.

Chapter 8
The Women's Prison

Limerick was classified as a high-security prison, meaning it was very difficult to escape from. In those times of heightened tension, we had the army and Gardaí on duty. We had a machine gun on the tower and anti-helicopter measures in place. Other prisons had a more lax approach and some were open prisons, where inmates wore their own clothes and could enter and leave with a degree of freedom. It all depended on what you were in for.

The sole reason Limerick had the high-security status was that the female prison housed a number of republicans. Two were particularly high profile: Rose Dugdale and Marion Coyle. At a later stage, they were joined by Rita O'Hare, also a republican. She was convicted in the South of smuggling a bomb into Portlaoise prison and was sentenced to three years. That was in 1976. Pamela Keane and Josephine Hayden were also held there, though much later. Ms Hayden didn't arrive until 1995, convicted of carrying weapons.

Rose Dugdale was an unlikely republican. The daughter of an upper-class British family, she had been a debutant in London, with all that that entails. In fact, the year she came out in London society was the last year that groups of debutants were presented to the Queen, so this firebrand had met Queen Elizabeth II. Pádraig Pearse would have turned in his grave.

Rose had a degree in economics and a PhD, but decided to turn into a violent republican to attain Irish freedom. She was convicted of stealing paintings from Sir Alfred Beit, a rich South African living in Wicklow. He was a famous art collector and some of the paintings, including a Vermeer, were priceless. She was also wanted in Northern

Ireland for hijacking a helicopter and dropping a milk-churn bomb on an RUC station. So she ended up as one of our guests.

As I have explained before, every prisoner who is admitted is searched and made to take a shower. There are no exceptions, so I am at a loss to explain how no one spotted that Rose Dugdale was four months pregnant when she was admitted. The first the prison authorities knew of the situation was when the contractions started and she went into labour.

That put the prison authorities in a quandary, and a decision had to be made whether she would be sent down to the local maternity hospital or whether the child should be delivered in the prison. Hospitals are not easy places to secure, so Dugdale remained in her cell and the baby was delivered in the prison.

The rules are simple: a new mother is allowed to keep her child while she is feeding it, but once the baby is weaned, it is removed from the prison. Thus, after a short time the child left the prison, but he was brought back regularly to visit his mother. I remember him as a very handsome, lively child when he visited.

Rose had been with us nearly two years when two other republicans, Eddie Gallagher and Marian Coyle, kidnapped Dutch businessman Tiede Herrema. He was the managing director of the Ferenka factory in Limerick, which provided employment for thousands of people from the area. Gallagher and Coyle demanded the release of Dugdale in return for the safe return of Dr Herrema. It was nice of Gallagher to be so concerned for Rose Dugdale and not altogether unexpected; after all, he was her boyfriend and the father of her child.

The Irish state was less moved than you might imagine by this touching show of affection from Gallagher. It reacted by having the Gardaí search every house in the country, even the attics, in an effort to find the hostage. He was eventually tracked down to the small town of Monasterevin in County Kildare, where a siege ensued. The siege ended without any loss of life, though I seem to remember a policeman got his finger shot off. Gallagher and Coyle were both convicted of kidnapping and served long sentences. Dr Herrema returned to Holland and Coyle came to Limerick to join Rose Dugdale.

Dugdale married Eddie Gallagher in Limerick Prison. It was an unusual event. They had sought a special dispensation and they were the first prisoners to be married inside a prison in the history of the state. The wedding took place on 24 January 1978, and, on that day, I was put outside the main gate to search the visitors coming in. I was under particular instructions that no camera was to be allowed in. The rumour was that big money would be handed over for a photo of the nuptials. No picture of that wedding ever appeared, so I must have done a good job. It was not the most romantic of affairs. For a witness, they used a solicitor. I spoke to one of those present as we were leaving the prison later that day.

'Well? What did you think of the ceremony?'

'It was a very cold affair,' he said. 'Like a Protestant wedding.'

Not too long after the wedding, another high-profile woman was sent down to Limerick. Marie Murray had been convicted, along with her husband, Noel, of killing a Garda in the course of an armed bank raid in 1975. Both were extreme left-wing republicans. Initially sentenced to death, which was commuted to life in prison, both served seventeen years, though Marie only served some of her time in Limerick. From the beginning, she was marked down as a troublemaker because she had been very disruptive during her trial. Things had got so bad that the two killers were confined to a holding cell for much of the trial, with a speaker relaying the court proceedings to them, yet they still made so much noise that they could be heard through the thick walls. But when they arrived in prison, they were the most polite, respectful and pleasant of prisoners.

When she was sent down to us, Marie was desperate to start a family. Facing life imprisonment, that might not seem to be a bright idea, but her heart was set on it, and, more importantly, her lawyer was set on it. The couple took a case to the European Court of Human Rights claiming that her constitutional rights were being denied because she was not allowed conjugal visits with her husband and she wanted a baby. That case dragged on for years and, in the end, she lost, but it sparked off a fear amongst the management, who had already been embarrassed by the birth of Rose Dugdale's son, that she might try to get pregnant surreptitiously. It led to some funny scenes.

One visiting day, I was called aside by the chief officer.

'I want you to keep a sharp eye on Marie Murray today,' he said.

'No problem.'

'Nothing is to be passed over to her. Look out in particular for anything like a hanky or a tissue.'

I was a bit surprised. 'Why is that, Chief?'

'Because the tissue could be covered in sperm, and she might use it to get pregnant when she gets back to her cell.'

I nodded and quickly turned away before an explosion of laughter got me in trouble. That man badly needed a lesson on the birds and the bees.

——

No male was allowed into the female prison unescorted, and that included the governor. I think it was due to the old, backward Irish way of doing things, with nobody trusting anybody. Back then, men and women were segregated in schools and even sat on opposite sides of some churches on Sundays, so it was no surprise to see the practice kept up in the prisons.

But while my colleagues and I never patrolled the landings of the women's wing, we did many a long, dreary night outside guarding the back of the block. Part of the duty of an outside night guard at that time was to supply fuel to the female block. I would collect a prisoner, get a wheelbarrow and bring a barrow full of coal into the female prison to fuel their small furnace, which was in a converted cell.

When we got to the cell, a female officer locked us inside – myself, the prisoner and the wheelbarrow. We would be left there while we got the furnace going and, after a while, she would come back and let us out. It was a nightmare job. We would get the fire going nicely, but the furnace was old and leaked smoke and fumes into the cell at a terrible rate. Within seconds, our eyes would be burning, then our lungs would be burning as the smoke and the fumes worked their way into our systems. Soon, we'd be coughing and spluttering and banging on the door to get out.

That went on for a long time, until an officer from Dublin with a bit more service than any of us was asked to light the furnace. As the female officer was locking the door behind him, he turned and planted his foot in the gap.

'What are you doing?' he asked her.

'Get your foot out of there. I'm locking you in.'

'You are not locking me in with any fucking prisoner.'

The end result was that the poor prisoner was locked in on his own to get the furnace going, and he had to cough and splutter on his own until the female officer came back with the key – we never lit the furnace again.

Another part of outside night duty that I hated was 'fishing for brown trout'. A more accurate way of putting it is shit patrol. It consisted of accompanying a prisoner around the side of the prison blocks and shovelling any mystery parcels we found into the wheelbarrow. The prisoners disliked defecating into their piss pots during the night, and who could blame them? No one would want that smell lingering in their cell until morning, so they would shit onto a couple of pages of newspaper, wrap it up and throw the bundle out the window. That was the brown trout.

But the worst part of patrolling behind the female prison was the isolation. There was a clock at the rear that we had to punch regularly, which proved we had patrolled the area. If you had to go around and punch the clock, you might as well be honest and do the patrol.

In winter, if there was a storm, the slates could be raining down from the women's prison. The place was falling apart. In that case, you were issued with a crash helmet, but you would continue the patrol. You could get wet through to your underpants, even through the thick coat and uniform.

I always disliked working in the female prison. I felt uncomfortable there and wasn't really sure of my role. Apart from guarding the back wall, the duty of the male officer consisted solely of standing around in the exercise yard while the females were on exercise.

The first task I had to perform each time I did exercise duty was to set up the tennis net. The male exercise yards didn't have that; our yards were solid concrete, not the manicured grass that was in the centre of the female yard. I would adjust the tension on the net, then get four rackets and a number of tennis balls and leave them on the grass.

At that time, there was no shelter or patrol box for the officer on patrol and we were there in all weathers, wet and dry, hot and cold, winter and summer. Some years later, the union managed to get a shelter in the yard.

I don't know why I bothered with the tennis net. The female prisoners just walked around the yard in an anticlockwise direction, the same as the men.

Another thing that struck me as strange was that in all the years that I was there, I never heard the voices of Marian Coyle, Rose

Dugdale or Rita O'Hare. Whenever they approached the officer on patrol, they stopped talking and only resumed when they were out of earshot. Also, Rose Dugdale wore the same beige duffel coat for her entire incarceration.

Those three women were our most high-profile female inmates, though there were others in for shorter terms – prostitutes, shoplifters and so on. At one point, an extension was built onto B Class and it encroached two or three feet into the female exercise yard. The republican prisoners were up in arms and refused to enter the yard until the extension was removed. But building policy within the prison is not dictated by the IRA and the extension stayed, so the three republican prisoners served out the remainder of their terms without exercise.

———

The republicans weren't the only women in the female prison. There were quite a few ladies of the night, usually charged with public order offences. Whatever drink does to a man, it destroys a woman. These poor wretches were beaten, battered and broken by the time we got them. The female drug addicts all had lives of unbelievable sadness and hopelessness.

Years later, when the Eastern European prostitutes came on the scene, we were treated to a parade of the most beautiful, graceful women passing the kitchen window and going to the female prison. We had to peel the prisoners off the windows whenever they passed. I think a few officers stole a glance too.

I remember one night, shortly after joining the service, being ordered to the main gate to collect a doctor and bring him to the female prison. I chatted to the doctor on the way around, but the mood of levity swiftly vanished when we arrived. We were confronted by the sight of a hysterical woman screaming and roaring and lashing out. The poor creature was obviously cracking up. Two female officers were doing their best to prevent her from harming herself. The doctor spoke to her for a few minutes, then said to us, 'Would you hold her down, please?'

We held her down as he lifted her nightdress and gave her an injection. She calmed down immediately. I escorted the doctor back to the gate and carried on with my duties.

A week later, I received the same instructions and went to the main gate to meet the doctor. This time it was a different doctor.

'I'll show you the way, you must be a new guy,' I said.

'No, I'm the regular doctor. The man who was here last week was a locum,' he explained.

When we arrived at the female prison, we were greeted by the same sight of the hysterical woman. The doctor spoke to the woman for a few minutes, then I said, 'Do you want us to hold her down now?'

He looked at me. 'What?' he said.

'Will we hold her down while you give her an injection?'

I could see the incredulity and disdain on his face. 'Do you think we're in fucking Stalinist Russia? There'll be nobody held down and injected against their will while I'm here.'

I slunk away, suitably embarrassed. I knew he was completely right. He was a kind and intelligent man and I was shocked when he took his own life just a year later.

At one point, the female prison was closed for refurbishment and the women were put into c Class. By then, male officers were trusted to work with their female colleagues, but c Class was a disgraceful place to put anyone, male or female. It was shocking. There was a frosted glass door on the toilet at the end of the corridor and the women had to use that toilet in full view of the male officers. We always cleared off the landing at once, but what a disgrace. The union complained bitterly about this.

The women spent most of their days in pyjamas and were bored out of their heads, as there was nothing for them to do. A lot of them were junkies. On one of the few days I spent there, a woman high on drugs began to spray the landings with a blood-filled syringe. We managed to get her into her cell, but she continued to spray blood out of the spyhole, filling the syringe from her arm when she ran out. Christ, I hated that place.

I remember the day Rose Dugdale was finally released. It was October 1980. She was entitled to several years of gratuity, which came to about £3,500, a lot of money then. It was offered to her in cash, the norm back then, but she refused it, saying, 'I don't want your filthy money.'

'Will you take a cheque then?' an officer joked. But she was in no mood for jokes. She left without it.

A car reversed up to the main gate and she ran forward and ducked into the back of the car. The door was pulled shut and they shot off to avoid the waiting journalists and photographers.

It was a different story when we released Marian Coyle in 1985. She had passed the entire decade of her twenties behind bars, as she was only twenty years old when she was convicted. We opened the main gate and let her out. There was no waiting car, no newspapers and no photographers.

After thirty minutes, there was a plaintive knock on the main gate and we opened it and let her back in. No one had showed up to collect her, so we brought her into the office and gave her a voucher for the train. We called a taxi, which drove up to the prison to bring her down to the railway station.

Looking at this young woman who had missed out on so much, I thought it must be as daunting to start your freedom as it is to start your incarceration. I don't know whether she took her gratuity.

It was many years later before Marie Murray came up for release. Going through thirty years of papers recently, I came across a souvenir programme for a concert held in the prison in 1986, starring The Fureys and Davey Arthur, with Mick Hanley. Some prisoners also took part. It was a huge success.

Marie Murray wrote a short story for the programme. It was beautifully written and told of a young girl being sexually abused by an uncle with whom she was forced to live. The aunt comes back from mass and catches him. The girl thinks that now she is saved, but the aunt pretends she saw nothing and the child realises that she has no hope. A chilling tale, written a quarter of a century ago.

Years after her release, I saw Rita O'Hare on television with a delegation of republicans, including Gerry Adams and Martin McGuinness, standing on the steps of Capitol Hill in America. I thought that was a fabulous leap forward and the start of the real change in Irish politics. She had learned to open her mouth and let her voice be heard by all.

Rose Dugdale went to ground after her release. The only reported sighting of her I have heard of was from a prison officer who was passing a Travellers' rights protest march in Dublin. There, waving her banner, was Dr Dugdale, still fighting the system.

Chapter 9
The End of the Fear

After a few years on the job, fear became a thing of the past. You learned to adapt and to sublimate the fear. It could come out in heavy drinking, or an aggressive attitude, or a vicious swing on the golf course (if you ever got the time). But it never came out in front of the prisoners, and, eventually, it wasn't there at all any more. If you pretend not to be afraid for ten, twenty, thirty years, it becomes the same as not being afraid. By the early 1980s, I was afraid of no one, even though I should have been.

I had been in a few fights, and then some. I had seen prison riots and had come out mostly unscathed. I often gave axes or hatchets to prisoners out in the yard, and I would be on my own. There would be forty of them and one of me, and many of them had bad records for violence. Logically, I knew I should have been afraid, but I wasn't. It reminded me of the old joke that if you aren't panicking, you don't understand the situation. So did I not understand the danger?

I've asked several prison officers why we weren't afraid and I've got hundreds of different answers. I think it boils down to an old cliché: if it doesn't kill you, it makes you stronger. We adapted to cope with the fear, and the fear disappeared. After your fifth fight, after your seventh riot, after the ninth time you drag a fellow from a cell, the twelfth time you make him take a shower, you no longer take any notice of the fear. It's not gone, but deeply hidden.

You learned to stand up to any challenge. You didn't back down from the prisoners, because the moment you did, you lost control of the prison. If there was a fight, you had no option but to go in. Even if you lost, you had to find a way to win. And you were dealing with some very dangerous customers, men like Pickaxe Collins.

'I hear you were in the Foreign Legion, Mr Bray,' Pickaxe called out one day. 'I hear you're a tough guy.'

'You got the wrong man, Pickaxe. I was in the Legion of Mary. I'm not tough,' I joked. A lot of prisoners thought that I had been in the Foreign Legion because I speak a bit of French. I always denied it, as having a reputation as a tough guy was one sure way of attracting trouble. Pickaxe walked right up to me, put his face in mine and repeated, 'I hear you're supposed to be tough.'

We were in B Class. I was in charge of B1, the ground-floor landing, and Pickaxe and a couple of other prisoners were lounging around, bored. They were supposed to be cleaning the landing, but you'd be better off doing it yourself. Pickaxe had obviously decided to entertain the others by giving me a bit of grief. A loudmouth from Cork, he had a reputation for violence, but I normally got on well with him. Not today, though.

He stayed in my face, repeating, 'I thought you were supposed to be tough.' He goaded me into making a mistake.

'I can take care of myself if I have to,' I said.

With that, he threw his head back as if to laugh, then suddenly launched a head-butt at me, stopping a hair's breadth from my face. He had a big grin. He could have split me wide open. He knew it, the other prisoners knew it and most of all, I knew it. The prisoners were naturally delighted.

Cries of 'Nice one, Pickaxe' and 'Boy, you could have busted the screw if you wanted to', assailed my ears. Pickaxe swaggered off, the man of the hour, leaving me shame-faced with a group of hooting prisoners.

I had lost without throwing a single punch and I was seething with anger at being stupid enough to have given him an excuse to show me up in front of the others. I was going on holidays at the end of that shift and I knew there was no time to rectify the situation. My authority had been compromised.

Later that evening, at lock-up time, Pickaxe was still swaggering with confidence. When I had to lock him in for the night, he lunged at me, making as if to grab me and pull me into the cell. I reacted instantly, chopping him on the wrist with the edge of my hand and slamming the door shut. He roared at the sudden pain and I stomped off. I didn't bother putting him on report.

Three weeks later, I returned to the prison and Pickaxe was waiting for me on B1, his arm in a sling.

'Fuck it, Mr Bray, you nearly broke my wrist,' he said with a laugh. 'The score is one all now.'

I threw him a couple of cigarettes, which he caught with his bad hand, and that was the end of the matter. But during the course of the day, a number of prisoners came up to me and said, 'I hear you broke up Pickaxe, Mr Bray.'

I denied it completely, but all B Class knew the score was now even and my authority was intact.

Pickaxe was a bully and a repeat offender. He could be an annoying bastard, and we saw enough of him down the years. He had a talent for causing trouble, like the time in the mid-1980s when a prisoner burned himself inside in his cell and Pickaxe put around the story that the officers had stood outside laughing.

The prisoner had demanded toothpaste and wasn't getting it fast enough, so he decided to speed up the whole process by lighting a fire in the cell. He barricaded the door with his stool and table, then went to the window and lit some fabric. The idea was that the smoke would set off the alarm and bring the officers running.

What he failed to take into account was that the prison was painted with an oil-based paint, and over the years some prisoners, especially the neat ones, would steal paint from the storeroom to freshen up their cell. To be honest, we never tried to stop them; we liked a nice, neat cell. If a prisoner decided to do a bit of housekeeping, we encouraged it, because his living conditions were my working conditions. But all the paint that was stolen was also oil-based, so there were several layers of this on the walls of the cell. Add to this the fact that the wooden floor was cleaned with a wax-based polish, and the guy was inside in a death trap.

The officer in charge told me that when the prisoner lit his bit of fabric, the whole cell went up in an inferno. He was standing by the window and he never had a chance. When the officers got there – and they got there fast – he was already dead. When they opened the door, he was blast-roasted. A gush of hot air came streaming out the door and that drew in cold air from the window, acting like a bellows. He was crisp and fried, a charred black statue standing by the window. The smell of roasted flesh was horrendous. There was scalp and hair melted into the wall by the window. It was there for a year and a half.

That happened just before Easter, and I remember there was so much trouble after that death. It was the first Easter in ten years that

I didn't spend down in Killarney at the Circuit of Ireland Rally.

Pickaxe Collins put the story out that the fire was the fault of the prison officers. Some prisoners were inclined to agree with him. Then, he started saying that we stood outside the cell laughing while he was roasting inside, screaming for help. That was a monstrous allegation and led to industrial action. We wouldn't let the prisoners out of the cells until it was sorted out. That's the sort of guy Pickaxe was.

Inevitably, he went too far. After his release, he picked on a young man from his hometown in County Cork and gave him a very hard time. This was a respectable lad who worked in a local factory. He had a gorgeous girlfriend, and Pickaxe had his eye on the girl. Pickaxe harassed him every day, shouting at him in the streets and the pubs. He told the man that he would ride his girlfriend while he was working a night shift. One night, in the middle of this terrible abuse, the young man stood up and walked out of the pub. A few minutes later, he returned with a shotgun under his coat. He levelled it at Pickaxe and killed him stone dead. He put down the gun and sat and waited calmly for the Gardaí to arrive. He could take no more.

Whether he realised it or not, Pickaxe had broken an unwritten rule – you don't slag someone's wife or girlfriend, either a prisoner's or an officer's. If someone said something nasty about our wives, we would react instantly, and that would be the last time he made that mistake. And the prisoners knew that. There were other things you couldn't tolerate either.

One officer on D Class told me that a prisoner kept calling him a homo.

'I had him before in Mountjoy, and he broke my fucking heart,' complained the officer.

'I can't give you any advice, but if I was in that situation, I would put it up to the prisoner, because I couldn't allow that,' I said helpfully.

'I can't do that because I wouldn't be able for him.'

'That doesn't make any difference. If you can, put it up to him the first time, and also the second time he says it. It doesn't matter even if he beats you, set off the alarm. He won't say it a third time. He'll start picking on someone else.'

But the officer didn't have the guts to do it.

A month later, the prisoner was carted off to hospital with a big gap in his skull. I met the officer.

'I took your advice on that little problem,' he said.

'You clocked him?' I asked, horrified. The last thing I had intended to advise him to do was hospitalise a prisoner.

'No. Another officer told me an easier way. I gave another prisoner twenty fags and he busted his head with a piss pot.'

I looked at him in disbelief. 'How does that solve your problem? He doesn't know he got his head busted because he was calling you a queer.'

He looked at me blankly, then the penny dropped.

'I never thought of that,' he said sheepishly.

I think he went to the governor after that and got the prisoner moved to another prison.

————

That story illustrates the danger of giving advice. I tried not to, and I didn't take it either. One prisoner on D Class was a terrible nuisance. He was always giving other inmates advice. He was always complaining; nothing was ever right. I used to tell him to do his time and stop whinging.

'We didn't send out for you. If you don't like it here, it's optional. Just go straight,' I'd say.

Eventually, I had to start playing mind-games to protect my own sanity. When he said it was bad, I would say, 'It's going to get worse. They're knocking the cells and replacing them with smaller ones.'

One morning, I was giving out the breakfasts on my own and he complained that there was no porridge.

'What do you want me to do, go and make you a special pot?' I asked.

'They have porridge on B Class. Why don't you go and fetch it?'

'No. You have the choice of whatever is here.'

'I want porridge.'

'You're not getting porridge. I am giving you a direct order now to get out of my face and up those stairs, with or without your cereal.'

'No,' he said and sat down on the floor.

'What are you doing?'

'Peaceful protest. If you want me up those stairs, you'll have to carry me.'

'It's Sunday morning and I want to go and get my breakfast. I'm not carrying you up those fucking stairs.'

In the end, I got him the porridge. It was the easiest solution. His peaceful protest had worked. I took the hit that morning, but it's a long game.

Chapter 10
Industrial Relations

T he first meeting of the Prison Officers' Association took place in Limerick Prison in 1948. Fifteen attended that first meeting and three of them were female wardens – or wardresses, as the minutes referred to them. Warder Thomas Hoare was elected chair, while P.M. Kelly was secretary. Edward Fitzmorris controlled the purse strings and two women made it onto the committee.

A letter was drawn up to be sent to the branch secretary in Mountjoy Prison.

A meeting of this branch of the above association was held here on this date.

Assistant Clerk Sean O'Riordan
Warders Patrick Walsh
Daniel Renihan
Richard Dunne
Thomas Hoare
Edward G. Bond
Charles W. O'Doherty
Michael Hayes
John Ryan
John Murphy
Edward Fitzmorris
Thomas P. McGovern
Wardresses
Margaret E. Brady
M. Mullany

Julia Cotter

The following offices were elected.
Honorary Chairman Warder Thomas Hoare
Treasurer Edward Fitzmorris
Secretary Warder P.M. Kelly

Committee
Warders P. Walsh and J. Murphy
Wardresses A.G. O'Rourke and C. Frawley

The members present expressed satisfaction that the association had been established and hoped that their existence would be of benefit to the prison service.
The following resolutions were proposed and passed unanimously.

1. *That the uniform that at present applied to the Male members was in the opinion of the members unsuitable and that a different pattern and material be issued. It was further suggested that the uniforms be tailored by some outside firm. In support of the resolution it was pointed out that under modern prison conditions the maintenance of discipline becomes more and more dependent upon the individual officer and that it is difficult for an Officer now attired in the uniform now supplied to command the respect and obedience of those in his charge. It was further submitted that the uniformation of materials is a subject of the greatest importance and that a staff of Prison Officers attired in well-tailored uniforms in good material would automatically tend to inoculate in prisoners a respect for the officers themselves and thereby a respect for the state whose servants they are, and for the laws of the state. It was further stated that members of the public are inclined to base their opinions of prison officers on the uniforms the latter wear and for this reason the average officer and his family sometimes find it difficult to find their places in the social life in the city or towns in which they may be living. In this connection it was also urged that it is the duty of each prison officer to maintain both inside and outside the prison a living and conduct that will entitle him to the respect of his fellow citizens and the trust and confidence of his superiors.*

2. *That the uniform supplied to the female officers is in the opinion of*

the branch of a drab appearance and that a uniform of more attractive design be issued.

3. *That an adequate yearly supply of black stockings which must be worn by the female officers on duty and the outlay for the purchase of which is at present borne by the officers themselves be put on issue.*

4. *That the practice of the withholding of the rent allowance payable to officers who are absent from duty owing to illness for a period of longer then 6 months, in the opinion of the members of this branch, is unfair. This is a hardship that does not have to be borne by officers occupying prison cottages. In conclusion, members present express the hope that the formation of the association will see the birth of the new tradition in the prison service. A tradition of devotion to duty, loyalty to each other and our authorities and honourable conduct on the part of every prison officer at all times.*

Signed P. Kelly

In the intervening years, nothing much had changed. Prison was not a great work environment, with its long hours, dingy conditions and primitive work practices. We blamed poor management for much of the poor conditions we endured, such as patrols in the cold and rain outside the back of the women's prison, long hours of night duty when there was no need and compulsory overtime. I was a few years on the job and it was obvious that these conditions weren't going to improve in a hurry. The doors and locks on the cells were the same ones that were put in 1821 when the prison was built. We were working in a nineteenth-century building with an archaic managerial system. The system should have been perfect, because management were promoted through the ranks. They should have known the problems and tackled them.

The 1947 rule book that governed our working life was a relic of the time of British imperialism. The rules were Victorian: no talk between prisoners and officers, meals to be restricted as punishment and so on. We were in a time warp. The management were in a time warp as well. We wanted a change. We wanted some place to sit down rather than stand for ten hours; we wanted some heat; we wanted light; we wanted raincoats. So we fought for these things. We fought for years.

Our main weapon was the Prison Officers' Association. The POA is our trade union, and a very strong one. We were constantly at loggerheads with management, and we knew how to fight our corner. There were some things we couldn't change, such as the long hours, but we made sure our wages made up for that.

Almost every officer was in the POA. Management consisted of the governor and the chief officers. Assistant chief officers and class officers weren't management, they were with us. At various times, I served as secretary and chair of the POA, and that gave me a direct line to both management and Department of Justice officials.

Some issues may have changed slightly over the years, but the union has never lost its strength, and I was more than happy to play my part. I threw myself into the fight with management. They won a couple of rounds and we won a couple, but industrial relations were never smooth.

In 1980, I was invited to go to the Department of Justice for a meeting. At the time, Limerick Prison was referred to as the Lebanon of the prison service because of the constant war between management and staff. I was one of the representatives of the POA. We were meeting with department officials and Limerick management to see if we could reconcile our differences.

I outlined the conditions in the prison and gave some suggestions about how they might be improved.

'I have worked at a number of jobs. This is just another job. Our only interest is in doing it to the best of our ability, then going home to spend some time with our families,' I said.

The governor sneered at me.

'There's no need for that,' I said. 'I've been around, worked in a number of places. I'm no virgin.'

'Don't use that language,' he snapped.

'What language?' I asked.

'I won't have any bad language used before me under any circumstances.'

I looked around blankly, trying to figure out what word had caused this outburst. None of the faces looking back at me could help. I looked at the governor.

'You used the word "virgin",' he complained.

'That's not a dirty word. Did you ever hear of a virgin forest?'

'There he goes, using it again.' He turned to the department officials. 'Now you can see what I'm up against.'

I could well have said the same thing.

'We're wasting our time here,' I said. And we were; the meeting didn't advance anything. We still had to deal with archaic conditions. At one stage, things got so bad that the department had to launch an investigation into the prison.

That investigation arose from complaints from officers against the management and, as a result, some changes were made, but it was like moving the deckchairs on the *Titanic*. It wasn't solving the real problem.

———

Disputes were a constant in Limerick. Management and the union almost never got on. We were hard to rule. It was confrontation all the time rather than co-operation. For a long time, the management felt aggrieved. They felt the union had the ear of the Department of Justice officials, and sometimes even the minister, and we quite often went over their heads. I can't blame them for being upset, but we had to advance our cause by whatever means we could.

Even though we had a very strong union, there were problems within the prison service and we felt some of those problems were caused by management.

Industrial action was not uncommon. Looking back, I remember lots of stoppages and works to rule. In 1982, there were five stoppages. One was because we felt the car parking and canteen facilities weren't up to scratch. One was for new overcoats for female officers on escort duties. One day, we refused to wear our hats – at this stage, I haven't a notion why. In 1983, there were also five disputes – we banned visits, closed the craft shops and banned evening recreation at various times. Every year had something, though the first five years of the 1980s were the worst, when the 'them and us' attitude dominated. Things didn't improve for another ten to fifteen years, when a new breed of management gradually took over – mates who had joined the service with me and who were promoted through the ranks. Things slowly got better then.

But even in the bad old days of the early 1980s, it wasn't all doom and gloom. There were funny moments too. Once we had an ACO who had forty officers on parade, and someone farted. Unerringly, he picked out the farter and put him on report.

Quite apart from the fact that farting is an involuntary bodily function and should not have been punishable, how the hell did he pick the exact source of the offence? There is no way you can look at forty men on parade and know which one let off a stinker. We had some laughs with that one.

———

I still remember the ructions when the women's prison closed and the female officers were transferred to the male prison. It's a funny thing – we weren't allowed on the women's landings, but, overnight, the women officers were allowed on the male landings.

Some of my fellow officers were concerned.

'What will happen if we're together on the landings and I leave her for a minute and she gets raped?' one officer moaned to me, his union rep.

'And what will happen if I leave you now and you get raped?' I replied. It was an unlikely scenario. Women worked out well in the male prison; most of them could do the job as good as most of the men. Perhaps they balanced the testosterone overload. But having the influx of women did cause some concerns – 'problems' is too big a word. The union sent word down that we needed a Sex Equality Committee and I was the man they nominated to set it in motion.

I let them know straight away that I had no interest in chairing this committee, but there was no way that the chalice could be taken from my lips. I felt it was a purely political device that wouldn't be of any use whatsoever, particularly in Limerick Prison, but I carried out my instructions.

I cajoled three men and three women to come on the committee with me. Straight away we had a gender imbalance, but what can you do with a seven-person committee? Getting three men, any three, was difficult. They were reluctant. But, group formed, I went to the governor, who was most co-operative, and he provided me with an office in the single officers' mess. These rooms were often available, as the single men were being snapped up by eager women.

In order to make the best of a bad thing, I secured a kettle, some cutlery and biscuits and convened the first meeting of the Limerick Prison Sex Equality Committee.

The room was a converted bedroom and I sat with my back to the window behind a desk. The six officers then sat facing me with their backs to the door.

I opened the meeting and had a general discussion on what our aims were and how best to achieve them. The talk dragged on without any great enthusiasm on anyone's part. My eyes began to wander. Half an hour or so into the meeting, I noticed something odd in the left-hand corner of the room. It took a minute for me to realise what it was. Somebody had used the loops on a sanitary towel to hang it with drawing pins in the ceiling. It looked like a tiny hammock.

In the hammock, peaking out at me with the face of a mouse drawn on it, was a tampon. The string hung behind as the tail. It looked exactly like a mouse in a hammock. I couldn't take my eyes off it, but I knew if it was discovered there would be hell to pay. You could not have come up with less appropriate decoration.

I spent the next three-quarters of an hour bricking it as I tried to bring the meeting to an end before anyone else noticed it. Thankfully, nobody did. As soon as the last officer cleared the room, I made an excuse to run back in and I tore it down. From then on, I thoroughly inspected the room before I convened any meetings.

———

Although the physical environment we worked in gradually improved, some things were slower to change, including attitudes.

A bone of contention with the union for many years was the fact that a photograph of the Pope was on the wall in the office. I'm a nil when it comes to religion, but a tolerant nil. Some of my colleagues, however, were annoyed enough about the picture to ask for its removal, though, really, I think it was mostly out of mischief. There was a second picture on the wall, a photograph of a priest, Fr Jones, and one of our prison officers. The picture had been clipped from a newspaper and was up there for more than twenty years. Fr Jones had robbed a bank above in Dublin. I presumed he was in the IRA.

'What were you doing behind the priest?' I asked the officer one day.

'I was bringing him to court.'

'Where are the handcuffs?'

'You don't put handcuffs on a man of the cloth. No way.'

That double standard when it came to the clergy always surprised me. Apart from teachers, I don't think any other profession was as well represented inside. Then, there were the ones who got away with it, like Eamonn Casey. One prisoner was obsessed with the bishop. 'I didn't mind him riding your one,' he would say, 'but what about the £150,000 that went missing from the diocesan funds? He never faced prosecution because a rich person replaced the money. I'd like to see someone like me from Southill get away with that.'

The governor had no problem with the picture, though, and didn't remove it. This was a bit of a storm in a teacup – you found shrines and the Virgin Mary in just about every Garda station in the country at the time. I think the issue wasn't really religious tolerance, but rather was more a case of the union looking for something to have a go about. The POA decided to have one more shot at it.

'Philip, we need you to write to the governor saying how offended you are by that picture,' I was told.

'Why me?'

'Because you're a heathen, so he'll have to take your complaint seriously.'

'Listen, I have no problem at all with the picture. Leave me out of it.'

So the POA went ahead without me and had a meeting with the governor. It didn't go well; they got a stormy reception and the picture remained on the wall. A few days after the meeting, they wrote a letter to the governor. Even now, I still laugh when I read that letter. It shows how, twenty years into the job, we were still no closer to agreement with the management. The letter read:

Sir,

With Ref to our meeting with you yesterday I am instructed by the Branch Committee to inform you of our deep hurt and resentment at the manner in which you reacted to our genuine request to have the Pope's picture taken down and replaced with a picture of our President.

To stand up and start berating us and calling us non-believers while at the same time allowing —— to howl at us like a mad man was totally uncalled for, as was the manner in which you threw us out of your office.

Once again, may I explain that there are Officers in this prison who are of a different persuasion than that of the Catholic Church and putting up a picture of the Irish President in place of the Pope's picture would assist in showing those officers that we work in a non-denominational workplace.

The picture was never removed. It stayed on the wall until the day the building was knocked down.

Chapter 11

The Velvet Trap

In compensation for the long hours and poor conditions, the money for the job was very good. The only other saving grace was the holidays. You applied for your holidays, and you knew well in advance when you would get them. Management didn't play games with that – holidays were sacred. We got about six weeks a year. The idea was to take two in spring, two in summer and two in autumn, but in practice you could run them together. Some officers got others to work for them so that they could take a few extra days. With a bit of judicious swapping around of hours, you could get up to two months off a year.

It preserved our sanity.

Unfortunately, we didn't benefit from the normal public holidays. For many officers, Christmas was just another date on a calendar, as was New Year's Eve a week later. There was no guarantee that you would be home with your family for these special days.

I worked two Christmas Days, and I swore I would never do one again. That was a day I wanted to be home to see the joy on my children's faces as they opened their gifts. I didn't want to be doling out food in a cage on B Class, so I arranged it by always working on Christmas Eve, doing nights, but a friend would come in and relieve me at six and I would be home before the kids got up. Religion or no religion, Christmas morning was sacrosanct to me. Not to others, though – I have heard officers boasting that they worked thirty Christmases in a row. Greed (triple time on the day) can be a great motivator, but that is carrying it too far.

It wasn't just the public holidays; Saturdays and Sundays were a haze to me. My rugby-playing days were a distant memory. We couldn't get together a sports team because we couldn't get off to play. Our wives were wandering around the villages and city streets like widows. I called it the velvet trap – we were working like rats, but the money was too good to walk away from. The proof was that any single prison officers were quickly snapped up and didn't remain single for long.

I was told a single officers' mess was being built in the early 1980s in Portlaoise to handle the influx of newly recruited prison officers to the town. By the time it was up, there wasn't a single officer left – they had all been marched up the aisle – so the single officers' mess was turned into a training unit.

It was only when I got into the kitchen in the 1990s that I escaped the velvet trap and got regular hours, seven to five with every second weekend off. My quality of life shot up. So did that of my family.

Then there were the emergencies. Back in the 1980s, it was normal to have just one car per household, so if a child got sick, who would bring her to the doctor? We weren't in a normal job where you could go to the boss and say, 'I need an hour off. I'll work over lunch to make it up.' You were locked in, just like the prisoners, until your shift ended.

Luckily, we were civil servants and, like all other civil servants, we had up to five uncertified sick days a year. And you better believe most of us used every one and didn't feel bad or dishonest about it. You could say that we were using the sick days as a preventative; we needed some time with our families or our sanity would have suffered.

In my final year, I was in a prison up the country talking to a colleague who had been promoted to management. I said, 'Hold on a minute – I've got to phone in sick for tomorrow.' I needed the day off.

My colleague – poacher turned gamekeeper – looked at me and said, 'Philip, you look well to me.'

'I'm very well. Couldn't be better,' I said, puzzled.

'So why are you phoning in sick?'

I couldn't believe what I was hearing. 'Don't give me that crap. You did it often enough yourself. You did it once to play rugby with me.'

He blushed and didn't mention it again. Deep down, he knew that the few uncertified sick days were poor compensation for the hours and hours a week of compulsory overtime.

The position on overtime was clarified in the early 1980s, when I was about five or six years on the job. It had been a bone of contention between the Prison Officers' Association and the management would finish at five, but invariably be ordered to stay on until eight. Three hours a day of double time means a lot to the pay packet, but plays havoc with family and social life. Throw in a few days a week of staying on until midnight, plus weekend work, plus escorts that could keep you out until three in the morning, and the pay just didn't compensate.

The chief once told me to get a haircut.

'Fine – can I slip out for a half hour?' I asked.

'Haircuts are on your own time,' he replied.

'Do you know any barbers that are open at midnight?'

'Not my problem,' he said, and walked away.

Through effective lobbying, we got the matter raised in the Dáil. It must have been a quiet day and perhaps someone who wasn't fully briefed was handling the questions. In any case, when the question was asked, the reply came back: 'There is no compulsory overtime in the prison service. No officer is forced against his will to work longer than eight to five.' That was now down on the Dáil record and we made the most of it.

At five, many of us would go out to Jerry O'Dea's pub, next to the prison, for a break, which always included a pint or two. Then we would troop back through the gates to finish our extended shifts. Suddenly, we didn't have to troop back through the gates.

Sometimes twelve men would go out and only three or four would return. The chief would be in a bad mood.

'Mr Bray, where is everyone?'

'I think they're in O'Dea's, having a coffee.'

'Would you go and tell them to get back here?'

'I think I'd prefer if you did that, Chief.'

The only reason the whole prison didn't collapse in disarray was that we knew our fellow officers would be left in the lurch if none of us came back. Plus there were always a few lads who sided with management and worked all the hours that were asked of them.

The trip to Jerry O'Dea's was a regular pilgrimage in the 1980s. The service suffered from a hard-drinking culture back then. We hit the bottle often and we hit it hard. O'Dea's is a large, comfortable, old-fashioned pub on the corner of the prison and was a natural haunt for us. Payday would see it packed. We would all finish work and have to wait for our cheques, so we would nip next door and have a pint. One led to another, and by the time the cheques arrived we could be half-cut.

The cheques didn't come from Limerick; they were issued in Dublin. At one point The General (Dublin criminal Martin Cahill) robbed a pile of Garda pay cheques, and after that security on payment was stepped up, so one officer would drive to Dublin each Wednesday and return with the cheques. If he met any delays on the road then the cheques would be late and we would remain quite contentedly drinking. We would be four deep at the bar by the time he arrived. Then there would be £700 coming across the counter to one man, maybe £650 to another. We must have been an obnoxious lot to land in the middle of.

Jerry O'Dea told me that he had to go to the bank each Wednesday to make sure he had enough cash in to cover all our cheques. He would often walk back from the bank with enough money in his pockets to buy a house. If only the criminal fraternity knew (of course, that doesn't happen any more).

Once the cheques arrived, we were in the money. Jerry would cash them for us and we would put a dent in the bundle of notes during the course of the evening. Then, when the pub finally closed, we would stagger out, climb into our cars and drive home. Drink driving was the norm back then; anyone who could walk out of the pub unaided was his own designated driver.

That all changed with the years. Eventually, our money was paid directly into our bank accounts, but those hours in the pub were still important; they were our bonding time. The pub held us together. We were loud and raucous. It was our debriefing.

It also served another purpose. We knew that if there was trouble in the prison, we were being watched by our fellow officers. And afterwards there would be twenty or more guys analysing our behaviour during the trouble. Had we held up our end or did we bottle out? No one ever bottled out. Our behaviour was governed by peer pressure, and the pressure was to back off from no one.

Some officers had a pint at lunch time and at dinner time, and escorts were just another excuse to get in a load of drink. Occasionally, we would go to O'Dea's and we wouldn't come back. We would just say to hell with it and stay drinking. There could be twelve of us out on a break, all supposed to be back at five. Eleven might return back at quarter to six with a load of drink taken. There was very little discipline for a while.

The two months coming up to Christmas were just flat out drinking – into Jerry O'Dea's and have as much drink as you could handle, then into the car and home. Then, show up the following morning for work again. Most officers did it.

Escorts could also be crazy. I often had to bring a prisoner up to Blacklion, on the border, and there would be a lot of driving involved. On today's good roads, it's a five-hour trip. Back then, you could add a couple of hours to that. But the huge hours meant huge money too. Because of the money, no one suffered from binge drinking seven days a week – except us with our health, of course. But we were young and fit and that didn't count for too much.

Some officers became alcoholics along the way, but so many of them dried themselves out that they were an example to the rest of us. They were great blokes, those guys who managed to straighten themselves out. There is that old Irish thing of enabling people – let the drunk have a drink. You didn't lose your job because you were drunk, but perhaps you should have.

We had officers you couldn't send on an escort because they wouldn't be able to stand at the end of it. We got to know who they were and we didn't want them because they were useless. Escorts were a great opportunity for liquor, but if you found yourself up in Cavan after a twelve-hour day with six hours of driving ahead of you, you wanted someone beside you who could do more than snore and belch alcoholic fumes.

Chapter 12
The 1980s

Back in the 1980s, a typical day began in the circle. I stood there with the rest of the officers and the parade was read out. That would tell me where I was for the day. Let's say I was in charge of A3, which is the third floor of A Class. I would go away and get the key to A3 and spend the day there. There would be twelve or fourteen prisoners and I would check them. I would also check the night report to see if there had been any problems.

Normally, prisoners were doubled up in the cells, which were designed for one man. There was a window high up so that you couldn't see out. There were just the bare brick walls, a little wooden stool, a flimsy table and a piss pot, and nothing else. There was an iron-frame bed and a mattress that I don't know how many people had slept in before, a blanket that dozens had used before and probably no pillow because someone would have taken it.

If a prisoner needed assistance, it was difficult to even draw attention to himself. It wasn't like a hospital, with an alarm button by the bedside. There was a handle inside the door that was attached to a flag outside by a bit of string. But the string was often broken and patched up with a shoelace or something. If I didn't spot the flag going up, I had no idea someone wanted me unless he banged on the door. But banging on the door could annoy officers, and if you annoyed the officers, you were on a hiding to nothing. Now that has changed and there is a button in the cell that lights a bulb in the guard room.

Sometimes, a prisoner would bang on the door and then sit down so we wouldn't know where the noise was coming from. But we would catch them – we put coins on the ledge of the locks of the doors, and when they banged the coins would fall to the floor of the landing and tell us who was making the racket. Then we could get them to knock it off.

Prisoner welfare could be hit and miss. Even with the best will in the world, I didn't have time. I had too much to do.

In the morning, I would check each cell and count to make sure everyone was in order. I checked both bunks. Escapes were unlikely, but prisoners could be sick or could have harmed themselves. Then, the cells were opened so that they could go down for breakfast. About half of them did go down. When they were doubled up, one fellow would usually collect the breakfast for the other, and I always encouraged that. It halved the number of prisoners wandering around the place.

All the cells were thrown open and they all went down in whatever order they liked. Because only half of them came down there was no system for breakfast. For dinner, they were let out in groups because everyone came down for dinner.

Breakfast was a pint of milk. Despite the country having gone metric, it is still a pint today, because the outside contractors are from Northern Ireland. You got a packet with bread, jam, butter and teabags in a sealed bag. There were usually four or five slices, but if you wanted extra that wasn't a problem. There were always lots of the basics. Obviously, we wouldn't allow them to take whole loaves, but they could have as much as they wanted within reason. Some fellows would try to take a pile and throw it out the window or store it up for the exercise yard to feed the pigeons. It wasn't my job to provide bird feed.

The prisoner also got cornflakes or whatever cereal he wanted, and orange juice. There was the option of porridge. After feeding the prisoners, it was time to feed myself. The officers usually went to the officers' mess for their breakfast. We normally opted for a fry, which we paid for ourselves. Officers were back on duty at nine o'clock. That was a great start to a day: show up at eight, open the cells for the prisoners to have their breakfast, then disappear for your own at eight thirty. On Sundays, we got an hour for our breakfast.

It's not that the authorities were doing us any favours. Prisoners were locked in the cells for their breakfast. What were we supposed to do, stand outside their cells while they ate? Officers were back on the landings at nine to let prisoners out for their daily routine, which varied. There were classes, work activities and a gymnasium that prisoners could take advantage of. How an officer spent his day varied according to where he was on duty.

The school options were quite extensive. I'd say there were between thirty and forty outside people coming in, between vocational education teachers, the senior college across the road on Mulgrave Street and outside civilians who gave the various craft workshops. There was plenty to occupy the prisoners, though some spent the day standing in the yard doing nothing.

Our job was to get them off the landing and shut all the doors. Our duties decreased by a huge amount once they were all off the landing, though you could never get them all off; there were the top cats whose duty it was to clean the place up, though they lounged around all day with brooms and didn't do much.

The upholstery class was confined to prisoners on B Class. We had to stop moving prisoners from one class to another to prevent fights. The school did domestic science, which was hugely popular. The prisoners cooked their own food in the kitchen and they loved it. They would say to the civilian teacher, 'What will we have tomorrow?'

'What do you want?' she'd ask.

'Steak,' they'd reply, so she'd go out and get them steak.

Those classes did something for the prisoners. The first time I saw a class in action, I was greatly impressed and very happy to see a group of prisoners sitting around a table with civilian women teachers. They were enjoying a meal together, chatting in a civilised way. This was a new experience for some of them, to sit down to a meal and be polite. I thought it was brilliant.

I had nothing but regard for the teachers. Some officers weren't too keen on them, but I admired them. They mastered that trick of walking the line between the prisoners and the officers. If they were too friendly with one side, they were out with the other. It was a delicate balance, but they managed it magnificently.

The school normalised people, as did having women officers around. I think it was a good thing, as it was in such situations that rehabilitation could take place.

We used to bring in experts for the various jobs, but it is in the nature of the prison service to train our own. That is how I got trained. I entered the service without a Leaving Cert; all I had was my mechanic's qualifications. But I was sent out to University College Galway first, then the Limerick Institute of Technology and the University of Limerick. I qualified as a trainer in catering, and I did that education on full pay. Others got trained in a variety of different disciplines, again on strong pay thanks to a strong union.

When I began, there were very few occupations for prisoners within the prison. There was a mat shop that made mats from coconut fibres and which were used in all the golf courses around the region for teeing up in winter. The mats were made in a shed out in the A yard. There was a small pot-bellied stove in the yard so you could be warm in the winter. I would be in that yard on my own with thirty prisoners and I would open the tool shed and hand out axes, saws and hatchets and try to get them to them work.

Once, a guy responded to an order by saying, 'You wouldn't say that if we were outside.'

I said, 'Would you ever look around you? All I have is a biro and a whistle. You have thirty-nine of your mates here and I'm on my own. You'd never get an opportunity like this outside, so if you're going to do anything, do it now.'

Of course, he didn't thankfully.

Another occupation in that yard was splitting down big logs for firewood. They would use wedges and mallets and two-handled cross saws. The norm for them was to saw with just one hand on the handle, no fear of breaking a sweat, and one hand nonchalantly in their pocket.

I only remember someone coming to pick up the logs twice. I don't know what the wood was cut for. There was a huge pile there for years. I used to shove a bit of it back to cock my backside on it and get a bit of a rest. I'd be out on my own with armed prisoners, no radio and a just a whistle in case of emergencies – not even a baton, as they hadn't been issued yet. No one ever used the whistle. I remember one time I heard one blown, but it was no emergency – an officer was using it to referee a football game between the prisoners.

At twelve thirty, the prisoners came in for their dinner. For a few years in the early 1980s, I worked in the kitchen. Out of curiosity, I checked the menu back in 1980. Here it is, day by day. On Sunday, they received one pint of soup, eight ounces of roast mutton or corned beef (with white sauce), twenty ounces of potatoes, eight ounces of cabbage and two ounces of bread, followed by a tub of ice cream.

On Monday, it was Irish stew, followed by rice pudding. Tuesdays, they got roast beef and peas, with apple or rhubarb and custard. Wednesdays, they got soup and chicken with turnips or parsnips, followed by prunes and custard. On Thursdays, it was soup and roast mutton with cabbage, followed by tapioca pudding. Friday was the bugbear; it was fish day. The fish was served with chips and either carrots or sprouts. Dessert that day was bread pudding and custard. On Saturdays, they got bacon or corned beef with cabbage and a bowl of rice pudding.

That menu was set in stone; you could tell the day from the food. Portions weren't too big either, though you could fill up on bread. The stew was very popular, a white stew with the potatoes mixed into it. Occasionally, someone with a bit of skill would come into the kitchen and there would be a brown stew, but they didn't like that as much, as it was just a stew without the potatoes mixed in. Whatever it was about the white stew, it put the prisoners into a coma and they would be docile for the afternoon.

There was never much to eat on a Sunday for tea. The tea, served a few hours after dinner, consisted of bread and butter with a slice of cheese, or an egg. The egg was to be put on at two when the officer came back on duty, and could be on the boil for two hours. It was rock hard and I'm sure it was good for you, but it was never appetising. So when Monday came, the prisoners would be hungry enough to eat the Lamb of God. When the stew arrived, they stuffed themselves.

They got their dinners and went back to the cells, where they were locked up to eat. Then, at 12:45, the officers would head off for our dinner. The prisoners stayed locked up until we came back at two to unlock them. Then, we had the job of collecting all the plates and making sure they all came back began. It was always a hassle.

The afternoon was spent like the morning, in various classes or workshops or lolling on the landings pretending to sweep. We continued to patrol wherever we had been assigned. Then the prisoners returned to the landing at four thirty for tea. Tea consisted of sausage and beans, or bread and an egg, with tea. Later, it became burgers and chips.

Today, the menu has changed beyond recognition. The food is prepared in a superb kitchen with top-of-the-range equipment. The prisoners are on a twenty-eight-day menu, which probably gives them far more variety than they ever got outside. And if that isn't enough, they can always stock up in the tuck shop.

Pot noodles and packet soups are popular, but when we see a prisoner stocking up on soups and pot noodles, we begin to smell a rat; is he planning a hunger strike or a demo? That's a dead giveaway. A sensible man won't attempt a hunger strike without a stock of food hidden in his cell.

When someone goes on hunger strike, we measure all the food going into his cell and keep a careful diary of it. Food is delivered at every meal, then taken away later. This is not to tease him, but to ensure that if he decides to come off the hunger strike, there is food available for him immediately. A hunger and thirst strike is more serious but rarer. You'll survive months without food, but only a week or so without water.

The last hunger strike that I remember was called the Pot Noodle Strike, because every one of the protesters went up to the tuck shop and bought over £100 of pot noodles before they began. They had cream eggs and cuppa soups and everything. It was the best hunger strike they ever had.

Fifteen prisoners were involved in the dispute. They demanded more access to the exercise yard, better food from the canteen and a rescheduled gym roster. The prisoners ranged in age from eighteen to late twenties and included some hardened convicts.

There was a lot of media interest initially, but then some smart wag leaked it to the press about the amount of food that was stockpiled. When word got out that the prisoners were growing fat on their hunger strike, they were laughed out of it. They ended the strike the following day.

We could see them stockpiling, so we knew something was up. You often got advance warning of their intentions. For instance, you would see a fellow in the yard with two or three pullovers and guess that he intended to stay out there or perhaps get out onto the roof. We weren't stupid.

Because of the tuck shop, a prisoner can now feed himself without ever coming down for dinner. I could prepare 120 dinners and have thirty left over because it might be tuck shop day for c Class so a lot of guys were fending for themselves.

After tea, there was recreation for two hours. Each wing had its own recreation hall. There was only one television and one channel when I started. Then there were two channels, and the officer would decide which would be on. In fairness, he generally called for a show of hands.

On Sunday evening, every prisoner would be brought to the one hall for a movie. After the prisoners trooped in, the whole room was full of smoke within minutes. You could see the flickering lights of the picture coming through the fog and you would come out of the hall stinking of cigarettes.

The ability to play the projector was a closely guarded secret among the officers, only three or four knew. This meant that every Sunday they could sit on their backsides and watch films. The pictures were supplied through a company called Reject Pictures. They were shite. They came in three reels, and so there were two breaks while the reels were changed.

Packed into this hall was every single ruffian in Munster and just three or four officers sprinkled around, yet there was rarely any trouble. Occasionally, someone would throw an apple core at an officer, and that would bring the film to an end. But I don't think many of the prisoners were too upset when that happened.

Apart from Sundays, recreation was television in winter or back to your cell, as there was no floodlighting in the yard. In summer, recreation was the yard or back to your cell. There was no choice between yard and television.

After recreation, they got late supper – tea and a bun. The buns were rarely fresh, but that didn't seem to matter. The currant buns were a particular favourite. And there was more tea. The amount of tea the prisoners got through in a day was amazing – they knocked back copious amounts of it. Then, they were locked up for the night, and that was it. If they needed to go to the toilet, they could use their pot.

The cells were locked with one master key and the officer on the landing didn't have that, so, even if I wanted to, I couldn't open them. If there was an emergency, I had to run to the guard room for a key.

That was a typical day a few years into my service. I would see great changes as the years progressed.

Of course, you mightn't be on days. There were two types of night duty: inside and outside. Outside meant standing in the cold and rain, though inside wasn't much better. We sat out in a landing with a small table and a one-ring electric cooker. We would sit at the table with our coats over our heads and huddled over the one ring, trying to trap a little heat. The windows leaked and the walls dripped. The Church of Ireland chapel would be broken into occasionally because there was a radiator there, but a lot of officers wouldn't do that because it was a Protestant church and as good Catholics, they weren't allowed to go in. I went in occasionally, but you had to be careful not to leave a mark on the wall with your shoes when climbing in the window.

There were two sixty-watt bulbs hanging from the ceiling of A Class, forty feet above us, illuminating an area 120 yards long, so it wasn't just night duty, it was dark night duty. D Class was a maze, with noises and creaks and coughing and moaning. And if you heard a noise, you had to go towards it. You couldn't run away. I walked down there a couple of times with a baton in my hand, not knowing what was around the corner. It could be four in the morning and freezing and I would be shaking with the cold. I often hoped the noise would be someone who had got out of a cell because I could warm up by capturing him.

There was one prisoner on D Class who, they said, could get out of his cell. He was doing life for killing a woman in Cork. He blocked up the window of his cell so no light of any kind could get in and he asked us to take away the bulb, but we couldn't do that, as we had to be able to observe him. He would often stay in the cell for days at a time, not even coming down for food.

At the time, they tried to modernise the wing and put in a more effective heating system. There was one big pipe that ran along the length of the landing in through the back of the cells. This fellow had an end cell and it was said that he could crawl around the pipe and out into the landing. I don't know if was it true. Personally, I don't believe it, but many men said they could hear him walking about at night. He is still serving his sentence – I think he's the second longest-serving prisoner in the state.

A Class and B Class are still the same as they were back in the early 1980s (or should I say the early 1880s), though C and D have been completely modernised. C is light and airy and prisoner friendly – and officer friendly too, as prisoners' living conditions are officers' working conditions.

Chapter 13
Feeding the Prison

Feeding a prison full of felons was easier than it seemed. Everyone thinks they know what goes on: all the prisoners get their slop, then sit down at long benches. Someone begins beating his fork off the table and soon there is a riot. Or perhaps someone jumps on one of the long tables and begins to dance the jailhouse rock as the entire prison stamps appreciatively.

That's the movies. The reality was different. For one thing, the food is good now – a hell of a lot better than you would expect, and, in many cases, better than the prisoners were accustomed to. And no one sat at long benches. Prisoners queued up in the serving area, or servery, of each wing and got their food on a tray, then made their way back to their cell, where they ate it with their cellmates or on their own.

The food was served on plastic and the cutlery was plastic. This was a prison, a Limerick prison, and no one was going to be given a knife. Each prisoner got a plastic jug, which he brought down for tea or coffee or whatever he wanted to accompany his meal. It was done quietly and efficiently, but that didn't mean that there was no fun. It depended on what was on the menu.

Every Friday, the dinner was fish. A relic of our Catholic past that lingered longer inside than out, it alternated between battered cod and smoked haddock. No one minded the cod, but the prisoners either loved or hated the haddock. When the hot food trolleys were being wheeled out of the kitchen to the service areas, the prisoners on A Class would call down from the landings, 'What's for dinner, Officer?'

'Fish.'

'What fish? Battered?'

'No, haddock.'

'The red smelly stuff?'

'Yeah, smoked haddock.'

'Oh, Jesus! Not the smelly stuff again.'

'What did he say, Eugene?' a voice from higher up would shout.

'He said fish.'

'What fish, Eugene?'

We moved across the circle to the B and C servery. As the lift with the trolleys moved down, the same scene was repeated on B Class.

'What's for dinner, Officer?'

'Fish, Jimmy.'

'What fish, Mr Bray?'

'Jimmy, don't ask.'

'Jesus, not the smelly stuff. I can't eat that, Mr Bray. You know I can't eat that shit. I'm dying here. Are you are trying to kill me?'

'I have a veggie for you, Jimmy.' We usually had four or five vegetarians at any time on B and C and accommodated them, but some days – particularly fish days – this number rose dramatically. I would bring over up to twelve veggie meals for those who just couldn't stand the haddock.

Jimmy came down to the servery with his pullover yanked up over his mouth, like an extra from a cowboy movie, all the while elaborately miming gagging at the smell.

Jimmy grabbed his meal quickly and made a dash for his cell.

The next prisoner gleefully took his place. 'I'll have his fish if you don't mind,' he kindly offered.

'Sure, man. White sauce?'

'Yeah, but only over the spuds. Careful – don't let it touch the fish, Officer.'

Other prisoners would see Jimmy getting his vegetarian meal and some would decide to chance it. Anything for variety. But this was a prison. Aside from anything else, I didn't have the facilities to cater à la carte but, over the years, I got good at sussing out who wanted novelty and who really couldn't hack the haddock. The chancers got the fish.

Sometimes as the diet was changed, some new food would be introduced. We were trying steak for the first time one day and the prisoners didn't know it.

'What's for dinner, Officer?' would float across the air as we crossed A class.

'Steak.'

'No, really, what's on tonight?'

'I told you, steak, gravy, mash and peas.'

'Eugene, what did he say was for dinner?'

'He won't fucking tell me.'

Steak was a big hit with the inmates. Even the vegetarians turned carnivore that day and I didn't need to bring along any veggie options. But there were still chancers.

'John Hickey says I can collect his dinner for him, Officer.'

'That's all right. I'll drop it up to him in a minute.'

All the old hands in the food queue smiled – they knew an officer never brings a dinner up to a cell for a prisoner. Waiter service is not included in the price. What the chancer didn't know was that every morning, we would check the discharge docket which lists all the prisoners who were leaving the prison that day, whether they had reached the end of their sentence, were on court escorts, visiting hospital or whatever. It was far too long to commit to memory, but the mention of a name usually sent up a red flag. I knew John Hickey had gone down to Cork District Court that day.

But my friend tried again. 'It's true, Officer. He said I could bring it up to him. I'm not lying. You think I'm a liar,' he challenged.

'Not at all. I would trust you with my life. You have an honest face. It's OK, though, I'll bring it up to him. You don't think I'm a liar, do you?' I responded.

The prisoners behind him were smiling as he shuffled away, muttering under his breath. They knew the score.

Suddenly, there was a call from up the landing. A face popped around the corner, beckoning and trying to get my attention.

'Give him my dinner, Officer,' he called across.

Our friend comes running back, saying, 'I'll take his dinner now.'

'Look, he has his own dinner on his tray. He has it hidden round the corner.' Which was true.

'Ah, keep the fucking dinner then. You'll probably just keep it for the hairies.' The other prisoners 'yup, yupped' him back up the stairs.

I just nodded pleasantly. The hairies, or sex offenders, were always the last down, so they occasionally got a bit extra if any was left over.

As his face disappeared around the corner, he shouted, 'You can't blame a man for trying.'

Fair play to him; he had a sense of humour at least. It wasn't the first time someone had tried to con me out of an extra dinner. Some had even succeeded. I had been caught a few times with the tray-around-the-corner trick, but I had never taken it personally. I always felt it was up to me to be on the ball, not up to the prisoners to be honest when it came to meal times. Sometimes, if we were well up on food, I would let a prisoner think he had got one over on me. It entertained us both.

It wasn't always the tray-around-the-corner trick, either. More than once, a fellow would get back to his cell and change his clothes, then come back and try for another dinner. As it was usually the same guys coming down night after night, we would generally recognise who had been down and who hadn't and we usually rumbled that one.

Sometimes, we had pies for tea, and the prisoners generally liked these. The pie filling was minced meat and vegetables, with a ladle of baked beans on the side. Occasionally, we had steak and kidney pies instead of meat and veg ones. In either case, it wasn't a bad tea.

One night, the first prisoner strolled up with the usual question.

'What pie is it, Officer?'

Before I had a chance to answer, the prisoner who was serving with me on the left jumped in.

'Pies on my side are mince.'

The other prisoner helping with the serving on the right then added, 'My side are steak and kidney.'

'I'll take mince, so,' said the prisoner, and before I had a chance to explain that all the pies were the same, he took his pie and departed, delighted.

'I'll have the mince as well,' said the next man. He went off happy.

'Give me the steak and kidney,' said the next man. I gave him a pie from the same tray.

'Mince,' said the next in line.

And so it went on, man after man, until we reached the end of the tray, with thirty men each stating his preference and getting a pie from the same tray. It had gone too far to correct it, and I was standing there waiting for someone to pull me up on how I knew which pie was which, as they all looked the same.

I reached down to bring up the last tray, again filled with identical pies. One of my two servers leaned down too. 'Mr Bray, they'll fucking kill us when they realise the pies are all the same.'

Inside Man

'We're nearly finished. Stay cool.' We carried on and no one came back to say that he had received the wrong pie.

———

Throughout the early 1980s, I continued to work in the kitchen, despite my complete lack of culinary skills. I think I only survived because of the universally low standards at that time. But I enjoyed the craic, and the regular hours. It meant I could plan my time off with my family.

I had a good relationship with prisoners in the kitchen and there could be a bit of fun. One evening, I was chopping liver with three inmates, preparing the tea. The prisoners hated liver, perhaps even more than they hated the smoked haddock. I often looked at the plates after tea and thought that we were taking back more than we had given out. But we persisted in serving it.

'Do you know a funny thing, Mr Bray? Liver never dies,' said one prisoner.

I had a big knife in my hand and blood from chopped liver was everywhere. I looked down on the chopping board.

'That looks fairly dead to me,' I said.

'Not at all. Liver doesn't die. It's just like eels. They don't die.'

I dug my knife into the big box of liver and poked it.

'Look in there. That's dead. You can't really believe that this load of meat in this box is alive.'

'It is alive, and I can prove it,' he insisted.

Another prisoner joined the debate. 'He's telling the truth, Mr Bray. Liver doesn't die.'

All three were adamant on this point. I played along.

'How are you going to prove it?'

The first prisoner went over to the stove and heated a frying pan. When it was hot, he threw a piece of liver on it and the liver moved around the pan as it sizzled. 'Look! It's alive.'

'Rubbish.'

'You're a hard man to convince, Mr Bray. But there is one more proof.'

'And what's that?'

'Put the liver on a shelf and a saucer of milk on the other side of the shelf, and the liver will walk across in the night-time and drink the milk,' he declared, with all the confidence of an expert.

I was incredulous that anyone could believe this, but decided to have some fun. 'We'll have an experiment. Pick out a bit of liver and get a saucer of milk and bring them over to my locker,' I said. As the officer in charge, I had a steel locker with a padlock in the kitchen. I cleared some space. 'Put the liver and the milk wherever you want.'

The prisoner organised them to his satisfaction, with the bowl of milk on the right and the liver on a plate on the left.

I secured the locker. 'No one is to go near that,' I ordered. 'In the morning, we'll see whether the liver has moved. And I'm telling you now, it won't.'

'How much do you want to bet?'

'Half an ounce.' Half an ounce of tobacco was the usual bet back then.

At the end of the day – after most of the liver we had cooked had been returned to us – I took the prisoners back to their cells and locked them up.

'See you in the morning – and you'll owe me half an ounce,' I said.

But before going home, I slipped back down to the kitchen. Opening the locker, I put the liver in the centre of the saucer of milk, then locked it again.

At seven the next morning, four prisoners were waiting outside the kitchen. I let them in.

'Open up the locker, Mr Bray,' said one.

'Don't be annoying me. That liver hasn't moved,' I said. I wanted more people to be in before I went near the locker. As more and more inmates showed up for work, the pressure kept mounting on me to open the door and resolve the dispute one way or another. Finally, around 9:00, there were fifteen men calling for the locker to be opened.

'OK – it's obvious no work will be done here until I show you that liver isn't alive,' I said as I threw open the door.

Without looking in, I addressed the prisoners.

'I told you it wouldn't move,' I declared.

'But it has, Mr Bray. It's in the milk.'

'It's not,' I said, but I turned around to look. I acted surprised when I saw where the liver was.

'One of you bastards came down and moved it,' I accused.

'We were locked up. We couldn't have,' they pointed out.

'Where is my half ounce? I won it,' said the first prisoner.

So I gave him the half ounce. I got a bit of fun out of that morning.

Six months later, the prisoner who won the bet was killed in a car accident. He was a passenger in a stolen car when it crashed at high speed. It's strange to think that he went to his maker in the sure and certain knowledge that liver got up and crawled across the shelves in the middle of the night.

But, by that stage, I had left the kitchen. Regular hours are all very well, but one thing was getting on my wick: the attitude of some of the big Dublin crime bosses.

At the time, we had some big drug dealers in. And they were demanding. I don't know why they were allowed to get away with it, but they had special privileges. For example, they could buy in their own food, and I, as the man in charge of the kitchen, had to cook it. So my day would end at seven, then I would have to turn around and spend the next hour cooking omelettes and steak for these guys. One night, they had a rabbit sent in and they ate it with a non-alcoholic wine. It was the final straw. I didn't join the prison service to be a lackey for anyone.

I sat outside a cell in 1988 when Ireland was playing England in Stuttgart and we triumphed one nil. The prisoner had kindly left a stool out for me to sit on and listen to his radio. I shook hands with him when I was leaving in 2007. That's how long his sentence was.

———

Getting up to do prison work doesn't happen so much any more. When I started first, you had to work to get your gratuity, which is the couple of pounds a week the state gives you for the tuck shop. If you didn't work, your name went down in the book and you didn't get the gratuity that week. Today, everyone is entitled to the gratuity from the state whether they work or not, so there's no incentive to work.

That change flies against common sense, but it works. For fellows who need to work – ordinary fellows who find themselves behind bars – we have work for them. But the guys who have never worked a day in their lives don't have to pretend they want to work as they huddle around a kettle smoking, with nothing getting done.

I had fellows who would work seven days a week for me in the kitchen. A man approached me outside Todd's on O'Connell Street and shook my hand the other day. I had him for three years and he was a bloody good worker. He was in at seven each morning. He would pester the night guards to let him out so that he was waiting for me at the kitchen at five to seven. And the days I wasn't there, he was still there, working as hard for whoever was in charge. I wondered why they did this, but there were perks to working in the kitchen. The biggest benefit was that you didn't have to hang around the yard listening to eejits. The day flies if you're working, whether it's in the kitchen, laundry or upholstery shop.

The big perk in the upholstery shop was that the sofas and armchairs sent in from the outside to be repaired had to be searched. The officers had to watch out because there could be anything behind someone's sofa. They've seen some strange things come out, but it was usually coins, and the coins were collected and put in a big jar. At the end of every week, that paid for the prisoners' biscuits and coffee and so on. Occasionally, a prisoner would steal the jar, but there was nothing that they could do with the money, and the others would make him return it. In the upholstery shop, like a lot of other workshops, you got a few who could work and a lot of dossers. There might be two who could upholster and a pile hanging around making tea. They would drink gallons and gallons of tea – their insides must be tanned – but it killed the day for all of them.

I had stopped working in the kitchen in the early 1980s and had gone back on general disciplinary duties. Then, in 2000, I had the opportunity to return to work in the kitchen. I applied for and got the post of Assistant Industrial Supervisor. There were a number of advantages to being back there. Most importantly, it was regular hours. I was getting a bit long in the tooth for the long escorts and the night duties. The kitchen hours were perfect for me, in at 7 a.m. and out at 7 p.m., missing the traffic coming and going. The kitchen team consisted of the four of us working under an Industrial Supervisor, Bill Fisher, who insisted on the highest standards. We all got on very well with each other and had some good laughs.

The kitchen had undergone a huge change in the fifteen years I had spent on the landings. It was no longer a dingy hole at the back of the prison; it had been knocked down and a new state-of-the-art, air-conditioned, fully kitted out kitchen replaced it.

The other big difference was the training. I was obliged to become qualified if I was to remain there. I attended courses in the management of food hygiene, Hazard Analysis and Critical Control Point training (HACCP); and a three-year course in professional cookery at the Limerick Institute of Technology. The days of me not being able to boil an egg were gone forever.

We had up to twenty prisoners working for us at any one time. There were no passengers in the kitchen; everyone had a job to. The prisoners were trained in all aspects of modern food production under FÁS certification, they put in a full day starting at 7 a.m. and finishing at 6 p.m. I came across some great workers in my time there, and, regardless of what they were in for, I came to respect many of them. Most had worked hard outside but had succumbed to the easy money to be had from selling or transporting drugs.

More and more responsibility was handed over to the prisoners as the years went by. One or two would be in charge of the vegetarian meals or the sauces or what have you, and they took it seriously. All the information and instructions they needed were there on charts and in pictures, and they followed them diligently.

The standard was very high. You couldn't feed 300 people and get 300 satisfied customers, but every single prisoner who took up his dinner knew it had been properly cooked. No one had spat in it or interfered with it in any way. They trusted it because it was of a high standard. Plus, we had different diets – fat free, vegetarian, even a full-fat option (this was for AIDS sufferers, to build them up and maintain their strength). You could have three different types of stew on the go – one regular with meat, the next one with the meat stripped of fat and the third one with extra fat added. Then you had the diabetics, the gluten sensitive, the Muslims who needed halal food and so on. We keep a stock of halal food in the freezer because we do try to respect everyone's needs – within reason. We were fully HACCP compliant.

No kitchen on the outside could possibly compete with the standard we set. We had one man full time on paperwork and nothing else. All the food was probed three or four times for temperature, and the same when it was being served. We were able to do this because we had an unlimited workforce.

If you wanted to work in the kitchen, all you had to do was go to the governor and ask. We had a simple admissions policy: we didn't ask what you were in for. We took in everyone and we got good results from everyone. They wanted to be in the kitchen because working in the kitchen was a perk. You could have all the food you wanted, whenever you wanted, and you came out qualified. It was a win–win situation.

We had a couple of guys who walked out and got jobs in catering after their time in the prison. I say this with all modesty: the kitchen was the only place in the prison where I saw rehabilitation. We gave people responsibility who had never taken responsibility before. We began everyone on the wash up and we would be watching them, assessing them. If you had any interest or any ability, you would be moved up the line. I have seen fellows blossom in the kitchen, particularly Travellers. I always had two or three Travellers in the kitchen. If you got one of them switched on, they were great workers. I was impressed by them more than anyone else.

Sometimes, my first instincts on a prisoner could be wrong. One sex offender spent the first three days roaring and crying in the corner. He had been convicted of abusing his neighbour's child. I said to Bill, the kitchen boss, 'He's useless. Will we get rid of him?'

'Give him another day and he'll switch on.'

The following day, he did switch on. From that point onwards, he ran that kitchen. He could do everything, and he never forgot anything. He took a big load off us. Quite a few prisoners took the load off us and were interested and committed. Bill had the theory that if you gave people a chance, many would take it and step up to the mark. He was proved right time after time, much to our delight.

The facilities in the prison kitchen were better than in any hotel. I did a number of courses with chefs all over Munster. When I told them about the facilities we had, none of them believed me. For example, we had four combi-ovens – few hotels had that. We had more and better equipment than any professional kitchen. Plus we had an unlimited workforce. If someone in a hotel kitchen gave a bit of lip, they had to accept it, as they had no one else to come in. If someone gave us lip, he was gone in ten minutes. There was a queue waiting to get into the kitchen and the guys in the kitchen knew that as well as we did.

The first time someone began mouthing off, threatening that he was out of there, we might instinctively panic, thinking that we would be in trouble without his contribution, particularly in the case of hard workers. But your mindset is different than that of the head chef in a big hotel. What we had to do was do the opposite of what you did on the outside.

So I would say, 'OK, if you want out, head off now.'

'I didn't mean today,' he'd protest.

'I mean today,' I'd reply and that would be the end of it. There was no room for blackmail; the prisoner just went. We would have to suck it up if we lost someone good and I'd have to get up off my backside and work until he was replaced. That was the standard we set ourselves.

But the surprising thing was that when we set standards, the prisoners rose to them. A lot of the prisoners really impressed me. Almost everyone who worked in the kitchen impressed me.

Because the kitchen had the name of being a good place to work, we got the best volunteering to join us. But we also got the worst, guys who were sent in by their mates to smuggle out extra food. We would suss them out quickly. We searched people coming in and out at the start of their time with us until we learned to trust them, though sometimes we would throw a wobbly and tell them that, that evening, we were going to search everyone.

A lot of guys do bring out food at night. Usually, they are allowed to make a sandwich or a snack for themselves which they can bring back to the cell. If they work hard and play the game, we turn a blind eye to a little bit extra for a cellmate or a buddy. I would often say to them, 'How many cigarettes will you get for that load?'

'Ah, stop, Mr Bray, I wouldn't do that.'

But we knew the score. We allowed a certain leeway in return for their great commitment to work for us. If the worst he was doing was bringing up two sandwiches at the end of the day instead of one, where was the harm? If he was up at seven and working hard all day while other prisoners dossed in their cells pressing buttons on a PlayStation, who's going to begrudge him that?

What I always remembered was that the prisoner would be there the next day at seven even if I was off playing golf. He was going to provide that service, sometimes for officers he didn't like.

They had their own reasons for working, but those reasons didn't matter to me because we got the benefit of it. And I felt proud of them. I see a lot of those fellows outside and I will go out of my way to wave or blow the horn. They do the same to me. I love it.

Chapter 14

Relationships with Prisoners

O ne thing about working in a kitchen is that it puts you in the way of frivolous temptation. We have been known to make a cake for a prisoner's birthday. It's stupid, I know – we're grown men – but, occasionally, we'd go to the tuck shop and buy a box of sweets or a pack of biscuits. The prisoners had their own room in the kitchen for their meals, and we would leave it there, particularly if a prisoner was liked or there was a special occasion. If we remembered, we would make an effort for a birthday. Some female officers were great for that. I've done it myself, walked down the landing carrying a cake and a candle. It was a small gesture, but the prisoner appreciated it. They would often say months later, 'Do you remember that day, Mr Bray?'

I remember lots of things. I remember lots of prisoners. Some who spring to mind were really fabulous fellows: very capable, very competent and brilliant in their own way. To be able to operate inside prison and not get into trouble takes some ability, as it's very easy to get into trouble in prison. Someone will say, 'I heard John talking about your girlfriend in the visiting box,' and, suddenly, that poor unfortunate was in trouble. John would get a dig in the back of the head and had no idea why while the guy who started it all was laughing in a corner.

I've met six or seven prisoners who have really impressed me down the years. I'm sorry I don't see them on the outside now that I've retired. I would love to meet them. I bumped into one the other day and we shook hands. He had been a drug dealer, but I still liked him. He did the business inside in the kitchen. He showed that he had ability and could shoulder responsibility. He made a mistake dealing with drugs, but we all make mistakes.

I liked a lot of prisoners, though I had to remain as aloof as possible for my own safety. I could give out no information about myself, but, occasionally, something did get out. Like the fact that I had a new car ordered.

That was back in 1979, and I decided to get a Mazda MX5. They weren't available in Ireland, so mine was on special order and was being shipped from Japan.

On the wall of the cell where the officers were stationed, they had hung a huge map of the world. The map had been in the prison school but had been stolen when the school was closed for refurbishment. On the map, the officers had stuck red pins tracking the progress of my MX5 as it travelled from Japan to Ireland. I had ordered it from Frank Hogan and had to wait six weeks for it to arrive. Every day, there was a new pin on the map, showing it coming from Japan to Korea, across Asia, into the Mediterranean, up through Gibraltar and so on.

I arrived on A Class one morning and an officer said to me, 'Your car is here now, Fab.'

'What are you talking about?'

'I was passing Frank Hogan's last night. They took your car off a loader.'

'Will you shag off? What would you know about my car?'

Two hours later, I got the call from Frank Hogan's saying it had arrived.

That car seemed to fascinate some of the prisoners. One, a sex offender, spent most of his time glued to his PlayStation. He had a game where you pick a car and race around famous circuits. One morning he come up to me and said, 'Do you know where I was last night, Mr Bray?'

'I hope you were in your cell.'

'No. I was in Monaco.'

'I'm glad to hear it.'

'I was in Monaco with my PlayStation.'

'It kept you off the streets.'

'It kept me on the streets – and I was driving an MX5. And I bashed it off every fucking wall and every fucking tree, and I reversed it into the crowds.'

'Ah, Jimmy...'

Most mornings started like that.

'I was in Nuremberg last night.'

'You were not. You were locked in your cell.'

'I was not. I was in Nuremberg in an MX fucking 5, and I bashed it off every tree and wall.' Thankfully, the damage done was only in his head.

≠≠———

Once I left the kitchen, I was back on regular duties, walking the landings. I walked down landings surrounded by men most people cross the street to avoid. Many of their neighbours were delighted they were inside, and, in some cases, their wives and children were equally delighted to be rid of them for a couple of months. Yet, they didn't hassle me.

The relationship between a prisoner and an officer is different than other relationships. The Gardaí have them for only a short time – a few hours at the most, if they are interviewing them. I have them for years. And, in the prisoners' minds, a Garda takes things off them – their liberty, their dignity – whereas we give them things. We gave a prisoner his food, a letter from his girlfriend, a book. I was a giver, and no matter how thick he was, he quickly realised he had to conform. If you were aggressive and unruly, you might not see the inside of a library or have to wait a long time to be brought over to reception.

That's why I can walk down the centre of town now and can meet prisoners who will have a friendly wave for me. I was on William Street on a Saturday just before Christmas and I almost bumped into a very big guy, a bodybuilder who ran one of the biker gangs. He could have told me to fuck off – he was brave enough to do that inside or outside the prison – but he didn't. He gave me a friendly salute. We are not always the bad guys to them.

I had great sympathy for some of the prisoners. Most of them conform within the prison in order to survive, but, sometimes, a prisoner did have difficulties. I remember one knocking on his door at one in the morning and shouting that he couldn't take it any more, he wanted to go home. He kept this up for a while and there was no talking to him. I could have told him to shut up, that he was stuck there, but, instead, I told him I would call a taxi. He could go to bed and I would wake him when it arrived. He did go to bed and, in the morning, he was over it.

Another fellow thought he was the King of Ireland. In the beginning, this was funny and there was a great temptation to take the piss. But after talking to him for a few minutes, I realised there was nothing funny about it. This poor soul was in agony. About one in four prisoners has a psychiatric condition, and perhaps prison is not the place for them. I had tremendous sympathy for people like that.

Other delusions were harmless. There was a sex offender down on D Class who said he was a sailor. I don't know whether he was or not.

'Were you ever on a boat, Officer?' he asked me.

'I have a big boat over in Killaloe,' I lied.

'Can you navigate it for me?' he asked.

It went on like this for weeks, with the prisoner talking boats and me spinning imaginary yarns about my craft. Then, the governor called me over to his office one day out of the blue.

'I have a request here for early release for a prisoner because he is navigating a boat for you,' he said.

'I don't think that man is the full shilling, Governor,' I said.

The IRA was the one group that removed itself from the relationship between officer and prisoner. They regarded themselves as political prisoners, though we never recognised that.

We weren't completely unreasonable to deal with. Their method of having one person in charge made life simpler and there was a bit of give on our side. Life doesn't work without a bit of compromise.

But that method of having one prisoner represent the others only worked with the IRA because they were organised and disciplined. We wouldn't tolerate it in other contexts. For example, one guy came up and said that another guy was looking for a pillow.

'Tell him to come up and ask himself,' I replied.

'He's a bit shy.'

'I don't care. If he's shy, he's not getting a pillow.'

You couldn't allow a third party to represent people because you were giving that man too much power. And some of them were clever people and good organisers.

Rossi Walsh was one of those – a prison barrister. He was famous.

Rossi came staggering out of the ruins of a pub he had blown up in Dublin and straight into the arms of the Gardaí. Quick as anything, he claimed he was walking past and had been sucked into the pub by the force of the explosion.

He was a clever guy, a bit on the small side and unkempt, but knowledgeable. He got a lot of changes made in the prison service, such as getting the vote for prisoners but, in the 2007 general election only twelve out of 300 prisoners in Limerick voted. He tortured the governors and the lawyers and barristers hated him.

He thought he was Robin Hood. He would give elderly women a few bob, give out tracksuits and so on. Or at least that's what he told me.

I liked Rossi. He was one of those guys who, if he had been born on the other side of the tracks, could have done a lot with his life. We respected Rossi Walsh as a character and a player. While his legal knowledge gave him a status among prisoners, we never let it make a difference to us, as we couldn't treat any prisoners differently. But Rossi was a cheery guy who always had a joke and got on well with the officers. Some prisoners can resent that, but he got away with it. I didn't care whether it was sincere or not – I would much rather a guy tells me to have a nice day and not mean it then tell me to go fuck myself and mean it.

―――

A lot of prominent and successful criminals were polite. Every prison runs with the acquiescence of the prisoners. I couldn't walk into the middle of forty men and ask them to do something unless they were agreeable. I've thought about it, and everyone has a different agenda. If you went into a recreation hall, some guys might want to start trouble, while others wanted to mind their own business. The troublemakers might be shouting and moaning about things and threatening violence and, soon, there would be a stand-off: thirty convicts at one end of the hall and three or four officers leaning against a wall at the other end. I noticed that the greater the distance between us, the louder they got.

After a while, if it wasn't quelling, we would ring the alarm. The men in black would arrive – the guys in suits of armour and protective clothing. They were ready to rumble.

An officer would step forward and say, 'Anyone who doesn't want to be involved in this, get out of here now.'

People would start thinking. You could almost see the wheels turning in their heads. One would realise he was only in for another three weeks and didn't want to screw up his release. Another might be hoping to get temporary release for a wedding. The guys who were doing twenty years didn't care, but the others did, so we give them the chance to walk away.

It was difficult to get the first to move, but the officers kept circulating around and there would be a bit of movement in the room. One would shuffle off and you'd take no notice. Then someone would brush past, saying, 'Get out of my fucking way, Officer. I'm going back to my cell.' And that started the avalanche.

Thank you, baby Jesus, I would think. Suddenly there were just the three or four diehards at the end, on a hiding to nothing, and they would start trying to negotiate.

'Here's the bleedin' deal, right...'

But you gave them nothing. They would often just back down then, but if they didn't, we could deal with that too.

Chapter 15
Invisible Water

War stories are a great way of keeping your sanity on a long watch. If you're standing outdoors for six, eight or ten hours with nothing to relieve the boredom except the scintillating conversation of one of your fellow officers, a lot of tales will get told.

Prison officers spend a lot of time together in halls and yards and in huts outside that are no bigger than two phone boxes shoved together. I often spent more time with some character from the job than with my wife. I would spend ten hours with this guy, come home at eleven and go to bed, and be back at seven the following morning with him again. We were stuck up on top of one another, so we'd end up swapping yarns. That's how men communicate; they avoid the personal.

There was great camaraderie among the officers. You would never see a crack between us. Prisoners hated it. We called each other Mister on the landings and never used first names in front of prisoners. Theoretically, an inmate could do three or four years and not know my first name. I always found that peculiar and was against it, as I thought it should have been the other way around – they should only know our first names, not our last. That's basic security. But I didn't make the rules.

We were also a united front. If I refused a prisoner something, the next officer had to as well. We backed each other up. There was a lot of socialising, beforehand in the pub and after the job in the pub. Even if we didn't like each other, we had to dive in when there was a row.

After thirty years on the job, there were only two officers I didn't get on with, but I shook hands with one of them on the day I left and I would have shaken hands with the other too, only he retired before I did.

I served with many men who became very close friends. I would trust them with my life and lay down mine for them, but I couldn't even tell you how many children some of them had. I never opened up my personal life to them and they never opened theirs to me.

Men aren't like women in that; the female prison officers knew each other's birthdays, their children's birthdays, details of every sickness and how their kids were doing at school. In contrast, we sat around and swapped stories.

I'd be telling the other officer about this fellow who attacked me last month and he'd butt in, saying, 'Listen to what happened to me down in the court.' And it goes on and on like that, hour after hour.

Some of the stories were legendary. Some were true; some were not. The invisible water was one such story.

Back then, none of the officers supervising the gym had the slightest training in the field, including the officer who was on duty when a particular prisoner got injured. I worked in the gym for years and I never got any training. I worked there because it was a chance to do a workout on the state's time and to pick up some free gear. I was never the new Mr Motivator, and what I knew about gyms, I had picked up by training in other gyms myself.

One of the prisoners hurt himself in the gym quite seriously – he had to have his knee rebuilt. But the prisoner – let's call him Alan – was not the brightest bulb in the chandelier. He could have told the truth and that would have got him the compensation he was due, but he thought that he could strengthen his case, so he concocted a story to explain his injury. His plan was simple: he would claim that he had slipped on water outside the toilet near the kitchen cage on A Class.

He set it up carefully. He had a couple of witnesses in place, and they would tell of his dramatic fall as he went down for his breakfast the day following his real accident in the gym. But that morning, an officer was on duty outside the kitchen cage, so he couldn't go through with it – no point in claiming he had slipped if a prison officer could refute it.

He didn't even make it down for breakfast – I suppose he couldn't move. He stayed in bed and asked another prisoner to go down for him. That isn't a problem; an officer would be delighted to give two breakfasts to one man, because that meant there would be one less prisoner milling around the crowded servery.

Nothing more was thought of the matter. Alan went to hospital and had his operation. His knee was repaired and he returned to the prison. But six months later, Bill, the officer on duty in the kitchen cage on the day in question, was handed a slip of paper. He read it with surprise. He was being asked for a report on this prisoner's supposed fall outside the kitchen cage.

Bill kept his report simple and to the point: 'I wish to state that I was on duty on the date in question. I saw no prisoner falling and I saw no water on the ground.' That's the way to do a report – keep it short and don't over-explain.

Two years later, Bill was summonsed to court as a witness in the compensation claim. By this stage, the prisoner had a prominent city solicitor on board and they were expecting a big payout. In fact, the solicitor was so sure of his case that he wrote a letter for Alan's girlfriend to a bank saying they had a case they were certain to win and she managed to draw a couple of grand on the strength of that. The good times were about to begin.

On the day the case opened, it did look good for them. The state wasn't disputing the medical evidence. It was accepted that he had been injured and that the injury was very serious. He had suffered damage. In fact, he was offered a settlement of £100,000 before the case was called, but he refused it. They were going for the big one.

Alan was the first witness. He did well – he described his fall in pathetic terms. Next up were two fellow prisoners. They both gave the same evidence – they had to wade through water that morning on their way to the toilet and it was a wonder only one prisoner was injured.

The legal team were rubbing their hands, anticipating the big bucks. How much would they end up with?

Bill told me he was the first witness for the defence. Standing in the freezing cold of the yard several months later, he admitted he was as nervous as a kitten, because it was his first time giving evidence before a court. He had been in the court often enough on escort duty, but never as a witness. On the morning of the case, he went to check his diary, just to refresh his memory. We all keep a diary in which we keep small notes, usually what duties we were on or any unusual occurrences. Bill couldn't find the right diary and that added to his nerves, but he took to the stand and prepared to face the barrister.

Alan's barrister was one of the dramatic guys. He swept to his feet and turned and looked all around the courtroom with a swish of his big black cloak. Slowly, he looked at everybody, then straight back at Bill.

'Mr Clancy!'

'Yes.'

'You're a prison officer.'

'Yes,' admitted Bill.

'You were on duty at the kitchen cage and A3 that day?'

'I was on duty that day.'

'Is there a record of you being on that duty?' asked the barrister.

Bill told me he was shitting himself because he thought they were looking for his diary, but he played it cool. 'I suppose there is a record,' he conceded.

With a dramatic flourish, the barrister produced a sheet of paper. He waved it at the crowd and then turned back to Bill. 'This is the record!'

Bill asked to see the record and took it from the barrister. It was the detail sheet for the day; a mundane list of who was on duty and where, nothing more. Bill realised the barrister was making a big deal out of nothing. Perhaps this fellow wasn't as sharp as he thought?

The barrister kept pounding away at the same point – Bill had been in charge of the kitchen cage/A3 on the day of the accident. Bill didn't deny this.

'Now the essence of this case is that the floor was wet,' thundered the barrister.

'No,' said Bill.

'No?' asked the barrister.

'Yes. I mean no. The floor wasn't wet.'

'Was the floor moist?' he asked.

'No, it wasn't.'

'Was it damp?'

He went through every word in the dictionary for 'wet' and Bill kept saying no, the floor wasn't moist, damp, dripping, sodden or sopping. It was dry.

Finally, the barrister produced some photographs and showed them to Bill.

'Look at those photographs. Do you recognise where they are?'

'I do. It's landing A3. There was no water on A3. I was on A1. The kitchen cage is on A1, two floors down from where these photos were taken. I was on duty on A3 that afternoon, but, in the morning, when the accident was alleged to have taken place, I was on duty at the kitchen cage two floors below. That's what being on duty A3/kitchen cage means.'

Slowly, it dawned on the barrister that his legal team had taken the wrong pictures. They had taken photos of the cage on A3, not the kitchen cage. He sat down muttering furiously to his instructing solicitor, the man who had written the letter to the bank guaranteeing a compensation payout. He could see the jackpot receding, but he had to carry on. He stood up again and tackled Bill once more on the crucial puddle of water.

'Could someone have spilled water when you weren't looking? Is there any possibility it was there and you couldn't see it?' he asked.

'Oh yes, there is,' said Bill.

'At last! At last, my Lord, an admission. There was water there,' he practically bellowed in triumph.

'No,' said Bill. 'There was no water. You asked me could it have been there and I couldn't see it. Yes, if it was invisible water.'

A wave of laughter rippled through the court. The barrister just looked at Bill. He was baffled. He had been caught out on the A3 photos and now there was the possibility that the water was invisible. A short recess was called and that was it – they never went back in. They withdrew the case and poor Alan got nothing. And I don't suppose the bank ever got back the money they advanced on the strength of an invisible puddle of water.

After the case, everyone went over to the pub. By this time, it was after three o'clock and no one was going back to work. Bill and the other witnesses were delighted. The management thanked them for saving the state millions, well done and all that sort of thing. I was out in the yard with Bill as he was telling me all this.

'Jesus, Bill, I've never got thanked for anything I've done here,' I said.

'You haven't heard the end of it yet,' he replied. 'Do you know what the bastards did? We were finished in the court at three o'clock and I was supposed to knock off at five that day. They docked me the two hours' pay.'

Months later, and he was still livid. He had saved the state one hundred thousand at least, and they docked him the two hours. But that's the prison service for you.

———

I had my own war stories and, again, they often revolved around court duties. One of the first court cases I was involved in was at the Cork Circuit Court. When I say 'involved', perhaps that is a misnomer. The case had nothing to do with me, I was merely escorting a prisoner. It was an unusual case.

A patrol boat had caught two Irish trawlers that were dragging a net between them. It was the first time I had seen a naval officer in court. He was prosecuting the case. Generally, prosecutions were brought by the Gardaí, so this one stood out. The two captains opted for separate trials. The first captain was found guilty, his nets were taken off him and fines were imposed – the whole nine yards. The second captain got off and I suddenly began to realise that this law thing was like a game of bingo. So much depends on the judge, how good your barrister is and on the jury.

The jury is the big unknown. They are so unpredictable and they vary from place to place.

As well as the juries, judges can have their little eccentricities. The district court judge in the south was an original. On one occasion, I was in front of him when he was presiding. The courthouse was being renovated at the time, so the court was being held in a hotel ballroom. There was a huge crowd that morning. The first three cases to be called were sexual offences. After the third case was called, a strange hush descended on the court. The judge was just sitting there, saying nothing. That silence seemed to stretch into four or five minutes. That's a long time in a court, and everyone was looking at the judge. Finally, he raised his head and in a weary and exasperated voice said, 'Men of Tipperary, will you leave your children alone!' Around that time, over 60 per cent of sex offenders we had were from County Tipperary.

A thing that infuriated this judge was seeing prisoners in handcuffs. Now, as prison officers, we had to be security conscious, far more so than the Gardaí. I would often see a Garda strolling down the street with a prisoner in front of him, but no prison officer would ever be that casual – I could see my job walking away from me.

One morning, I was bringing this fellow down to court on a charge of breaching a barring order, and I suspected there was a sex offence involved as well. I tried never to judge – I didn't want to know what someone was in for and I treated everyone the same way. If you gave us no trouble, we gave you none.

That morning, I had an officer with me, who hadn't done much discipline duties. He was a mad bastard who had no control over himself a lot of the time. He was handcuffed to the prisoner and I was in charge, so I took him aside and explained some of the judge's peccadilloes.

'I know you don't like this, but the minute we get into the courthouse, take the handcuffs off because the judge will go crazy if he sees the prisoner in them,' I explained. 'He will start this rant about how the British had us in chains for centuries and sent us off to Australia, and he'll just go on and on. He doesn't see them as handcuffs – they are chains and shackles.'

'Ara, fuck him,' he said.

'Look, please, this judge is notorious and you'll do what I'm telling you or we'll be in big trouble.'

We got to the court and settled in our seats. There was a sergeant in front of me and I got chatting to him. We had met a couple of times and were swapping stories of the mad things that the judge had done when the court hushed and the man himself entered. I nudged my fellow prison officer and whispered to him to remove the cuffs. He hesitated, but he did take them off.

Our case was called and our prisoner stood up.

'Is anyone representing this man?' asked the judge.

A young solicitor stood up and asked for the case to be adjourned because the prisoner wasn't present. 'He's in Limerick Prison at the moment,' explained the solicitor.

'Who is that behind you?' asked the judge.

The solicitor turned and looked, then said, 'I don't know.'

'That is your client. Are you telling me this man has been locked up in Limerick Prison awaiting a visit from his solicitor, and you don't even know who he is?' the judge thundered. He tore into the unfortunate solicitor. In front of me, the sergeant's shoulders were rising and falling in silent laughter.

Finally, the judge turned to the prisoner and asked him if he was pleading guilty or not guilty. I took out my notebook to record his plea. Wrong move.

'You down there! Who's writing in my court?' bellowed the judge.

I looked around to see what eejit was aggravating him again. Then, I realised it was me he was talking to. My colleague was sniggering.

'Sorry, Judge. I'm in charge of the prisoner and I'm writing down the man's plea.'

'Well that's all right, carry on.' Nothing happened. We were cool and got away with it.

The sergeant was the first to give evidence. He told the court that the prisoner had a barring order against him and that he had breached it. The offence had happened some time back, but the warrant had only just been served for his arrest.

This didn't please the judge. 'Does every Garda have a warrant in their back pocket that they haven't bothered to execute?' he asked. 'Why didn't you execute this warrant and arrest this man sooner?'

'Because he was in England, Your Honour.'

This brought on another rant from the judge and now it was my turn to snigger. The sergeant sat down with a grumpy look. Then, the judge turned to me.

'I'm adjourning this case until tomorrow. I won't be here: I'll be sitting in the next court venue. Can you have that prisoner there?'

'That's no problem, Your Honour,' I said although it was fifty minutes away.

A few more cases were called and then the judge looked at me again.

'Officer in charge of the escort, I'll tell you what I'll do,' he said. 'To save you having to travel that distance, I'll meet you in the courthouse here at 9:30 a.m. tomorrow. How does that suit you?'

'I'll be here,' I promised.

The sergeant looked at me and then whispered, 'I bet you're off duty tomorrow.'

'Indeed I am,' I replied.

To this day, I don't know what happened the following morning, or how the judge reacted to being stood up. He probably put it down to 800 years of British oppression.

Chapter 16
The IRA

The IRA changed Irish prisons. I knew I had been recruited to combat them and, in the early 1980s, they arrived in Limerick. Most IRA prisoners were sent to Portlaoise, which had massive security and was geared up for them. But we were also a high-security prison because of the republicans in the women's prison and we got the overspill. If a republican prisoner got into trouble in Portlaoise, he would be sent down to us for his own protection. We also got dissident groups who didn't get on with the main blocks of Stickies and Provos.

To give you an idea of the potential problem, the composition of the prison population in Portlaoise in 1980 was as follows: there were eighty-two members of the Provisional IRA, with twelve dissidents, seven Official IRA men, eighteen from the Socialist Republican Alliance (Group One), eleven from the Socialist Republican Alliance (Group Two) and four dissidents from the Social Republican Alliance Group Two. And they did not get on well together.

But the overspill of hard men who began appearing on the landings in the early 1980s weren't the first republican prisoners we had seen – that honour goes to three fellows from Galway who were locked up for a month or two each spring for the crime of selling Easter lilies and copies of *An Phoblacht*, the IRA newspaper.

They considered themselves political prisoners, but we didn't recognise that status, ever. What I remember most about them was their contrariness. They didn't recognise the state and wouldn't co-operate with its agents – us. Back then, we made all the prisoners line up in groups according to where they were going to work for the day, but these three fellows wouldn't line up. They just leaned against the wall.

The first time it happened, the chief ordered me to get them lined up, so I hustled them into position. But the next morning, it was the same thing. The chief was barking. I was bustling around trying to move them into line, but then I got a brainwave: I lined them up under the stairs, where the chief couldn't see them. I didn't give a hoot after that. From then on, they lounged under the stairs away from his glare – an Irish solution to an Irish problem.

One day while I was giving them a rubdown search, I asked one of them to remove his hat.

'What do you think I could hide under my hat, an AK47?'

'You wouldn't know how to use it,' I said.

He looked straight into my face and said, 'Don't be too sure, Sonny.'

I realised that he might be right.

Those were the first republican prisoners. Now, we were preparing for the real thing.

The first thing we had to do was make the prison escape proof. We had the army on the walls and the Gardaí outside standing guard. No place is escape proof, but we were close. All the landings on A Class were reinforced. There were cages at the gates into each landing, a cage outside the kitchen door and a cage in the exercise yard. The cages weren't for the prisoners, they were for us – it was the officers who were locked up in cages for eight hours a day. At first, we did eight hours in the same cages – mindless, boring, soul-destroying days. The union made a fuss and the regulation was changed. We were still in cages, but we moved between them, so at least we got some variety.

Regular prisoners don't often try to escape, but you can't trust the IRA to be so obliging. They had used a helicopter to lift a number of people from Mountjoy, so we installed a steel wire from the circle to the front gate and another from the circle to the back of the women's prison. It was supposed to stop a helicopter, though I thought it wouldn't stop a wasp.

The traditional escape you see in the movies, with prisoners dodging searchlights in the dead of night, rarely happened. Escapes from cells were quite rare. I remember just one attempt. Most of the escapes were on work parties outside prison or on the way to court or hospital. They took place outside the prison.

We had a couple of escapes that defied belief. Two inmates got over the wall of the exercise yard in broad daylight. They went over another wall past a guard who didn't see them. They strolled up Carey's Road and got away.

There was another escape about three years before my retirement. A tall prisoner lifted another fellow with the help of some items left behind during some building works that were being carried out on the walls of the prison and hefted him over the walls. The man went home to his Garryowen house, where the Gardaí were waiting for him.

Ordinary prisoners on the run had no place to go. They hadn't money or passports, so they pretty much stuck to their old haunts and were taken back quickly. The IRA was different; they had a support mechanism on the outside. The drug lords were different too – they had money to make a go of life on the run, or even relocate abroad.

But escapes were rare and we expected to be able to keep the Provos inside as well.

I was sent to Portlaoise Prison at the request of an official at the Department of Justice. The idea was to see how the republicans were treated and get a feel for the sort of people we would be dealing with. The atmosphere in Portlaoise was completely different from Limerick. The officers never spoke to the prisoners and had very little experience outside of the humdrum patrolling of landings. The prisoners didn't talk to the officers either. The only one who would talk to them was the IRA OC, or officer in command. He would speak to a class officer if there was a problem, but never to an ordinary officer. I knew that wouldn't work in Limerick.

The official said to me, 'The IRA will probably be coming down to Limerick on hunger strike. They will be naked and will be on a dirty protest.'

'Who the hell are you sending down?' I asked disbelievingly.

'These are the fellows the IRA have rejected.'

'That's like getting kicked out of the Gestapo for cruelty. What are we going to be up against with these guys?'

I was working in the kitchen when they came down. It was my first time in the kitchen, and the facilities were poor. So was the food. I couldn't boil an egg, yet I was the chef. But I didn't have to be able to cook. I formed the theory that if you heated food until it was edible, it was cooked. No one got food poisoning, so perhaps I was right.

I depended on a number of prisoners to do the work, but they weren't allowed to cook. They had to prepare the food and I had to do the actual cooking. The food was very basic and there wasn't a great amount of it. Deficits were made up for with lots of bread and tea. When I started, there was one officer in charge and about three prisoners on preparation and wash-up. Then, someone was appointed as relief to help if I wasn't there. No Michelin star application for us!

Sure enough, the IRA came to us on hunger strike, but, thankfully, they weren't on the dirty protest (when they smeared themselves and the walls of their cells with their own excrement).

Considering that I was doing the cooking, the hunger strike made my job easier – a few less mouths to feed. But we don't look on things that cynically. One or two of the new prisoners wanted to come off the hunger strike and we treated them with great dignity. We didn't slag them or anything. I gave them a bit of toast, maybe some scrambled eggs. I got the same wages whether I got on with them or was constantly fighting them, so it was as well to get on.

For all the talk, the IRA turned out to be the easiest bunch of prisoners we ever had. If we didn't fuck with them, they didn't fuck with us. They conformed and we met them halfway. These men wanted education, they wanted to work in the workshops and they were committed to their future. I had never seen that before in prisoners.

But their arrival did bring changes. No longer could we patrol on our own. Up till then we had guarded the recreation yards walking round on our own and walked three landings without assistance. Now we went in pairs. Staff increased to meet the demand. But instead of recruiting, management brought down officers from Portlaoise. They looked for about thirty volunteers to come to Limerick on full subsistence, which was a lot of money. Of course, some of them went wild. They were mainly single fellows, but even some of the ones that weren't went mad – they practically drank Lough Derg dry.

We called them the Third Force. Around that time, the Reverend Ian Paisley had gone up to the Glen of Antrim with all the unionists and brought their firearms certificates with them. They told the British and Irish governments that if the police didn't take care of the IRA and the army didn't take care of the IRA, then they were going to be the third force and would do the job. They waved the firearms certificates into the air rather than rifles, which would have been illegal.

The Pentonville design. Most Irish prisons were built when Ireland was under British rule. This design of a central tower with the cell blocks radiating off it was first used in building Pentonville Prison in London. In theory, the chief officer could stand in the circle and observe all parts of the prison. Single cells were used to cause the prisoners to reflect on their crimes and repent. Major J. Jebb was the designer and it became the standard pattern in Britain and throughout the British Empire.

This is one of the few photos of me in uniform. My good friend Séamus Enright is holding the flag. It was taken at the reinterment of Paddy Maher. Paddy was court-marshalled and executed in Mountjoy Prison, Dublin, by British forces in 1922 and was buried inside the prison walls for eighty years. Paddy was a member of his local IRA, but he was innocent of the crime he was charged with and protested his innocence to the end. In 2002, he was removed from the prison and reinterred in the Republican plot in his local graveyard in Glenbrohane, County Limerick. The Government allotted him a state funeral with full military honours and I was part of the prison officers' guard of honour. Kevin O'Connor, who was also part of the guard of honour, took the photo.

A shot of the old D Class. I took this photo from the tower of St John's Cathedral. It shows the sandbags on the gate roof. Also, note the cast-iron green bridge which allowed the remand prisoners to attend Sunday mass out of sight of the other prisoners. The man at the main gate is Mike 'Blackie' O'Neill, RIP, the then governor.

The opening of the new D Class. Staff and prisoners were delighted when the old D Block was knocked down and replaced with this new building. It had in-cell sanitation, which put an end to the practice of slopping out, in D Class at least. The old D was similar in appearance to the building on the right, C Class. The females were housed in this block for some time. The Minister for Justice Nora Owen opened the building. Michael Noonan, the then Minister for Health, was an invited guest. As he was on the way to the governor's office to take a phone call, he was attacked by a prisoner. The prisoner was a large, violent man and he punched Mr Noonan a few times before the staff overpowered him. We were impressed when the Minister shook it off and carried on; he was a lot tougher than he looked. The prisoner had no idea who his victim was – he had just lashed out. He was sentenced to life some time later for murder.

(*Press 22*)

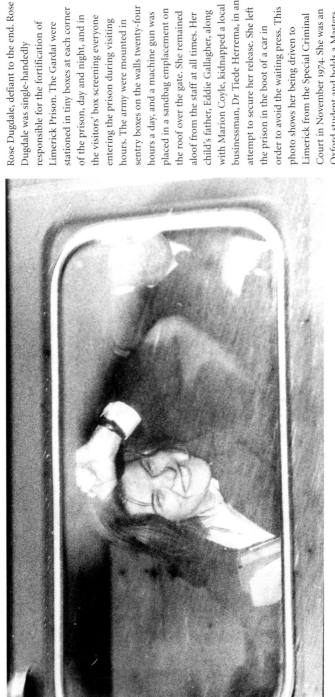

Rose Dugdale, defiant to the end. Rose Dugdale was single-handedly responsible for the fortification of Limerick Prison. The Gardaí were stationed in tiny boxes at each corner of the prison, day and night, and in the visitors' box screening everyone entering the prison during visiting hours. The army were mounted in sentry boxes on the walls twenty-four hours a day, and a machine gun was placed in a sandbag emplacement on the roof over the gate. She remained aloof from the staff at all times. Her child's father, Eddie Gallagher, along with Marion Coyle, kidnapped a local businessman, Dr Tiede Herrema, in an attempt to secure her release. She left the prison in the boot of a car in order to avoid the waiting press. This photo shows her being driven to Limerick from the Special Criminal Court in November 1974. She was an Oxford student and holds a Masters degree in philosophy and a PhD in economics. (*The Irish Times*)

The Army Explosive Ordinance Disposal Unit enters Limerick Prison. This was the first visit of the bomb squad to the prison. Two pipe bombs were thrown over the wall from the jail boreen and landed at each side of the kitchen. This was an escalation in the lethal and long-running Limerick feud. We evacuated the kitchen and a local chipper supplied almost 300 fish and chip meals without any bother. We ferried the food in relays in the prison van. The prisoners were delighted with the unexpected change to the prison diet. (*Press 22*)

The old and the new. The modernisation of the prison carries on apace. The new blocks are a huge improvement to the living conditions of the prisoners, and therefore the working conditions of the staff. The old block on the right is B Class and is mirrored on the left by A Class, hidden in this photo behind the new D. There is, as yet, no in-cell sanitation in these wings and the unsatisfactory practice of slopping out with chamber pots continues to date. (*Press 22*)

Alan Kavanagh leaving Limerick Circuit Court. Alan survived a murderous attack by three prisoners on D Class. After the trial of one of his assailants, Paul Dixon, a member of the jury was threatened. A note was placed under the windscreen wipers of his car, telling him that he would be got for sending down one of ours and that they knew where he lived. Dixon, who did the actual slashing while the others held Alan, was given eight years. The judge, Seán O'Leary, said that law enforcement officers were to be protected in a special way from these sorts of attacks. He said that if the case had not involved a prison officer, he would have given five years, but because it did, he handed down eight. The two other prisoners had already pleaded guilty. (Press 22)

The last day on the job and my last day in uniform, a civilian once again. (PA Photos)

. . . And Best For PICTURES

BATTLE ON JAIL ROOFTOP

● PICTURE 1: One of the prisoners lets fly with a slate as gardai in riot gear and shields close in. A second prisoner is being dragged into the hole in the roof by two other gardai.

● PICTURE 2: The prisoner runs at the garda and is grabbed by the arm.

● PICTURE 3: He is then held and dragged down the slates to the escape hole.

(Irish Press/Photos by Brendan Crowe)

Quick-acting warders snatch food and wreck plans for long siege

**PICTURES:
BRENDAN CROWE**

PRISONERS who broke onto the roof of Limerick Prison yesterday had intended a long protest against conditions in D Wing.

The four Limerickmen, described as dangerous by one source, took plenty of food and built a barricade behind them after breaking through a steel cover that led to the attic.

Staff immediately locked up the rest of the inmates before breaking through the barricade, climbing onto the roof, and snatching the prisoners food parcels.

The protest began at 3 p.m. About an hour after the food was grabbed from them two prisoners surrendered. And at about 5 p.m. a snatch squad ran at the remaining two and bundled them back inside.

Meanwhile, the protesters had damaged the roof and hurled slates down on staff. There were no injuries and no disturbances in the rest of the prison, according to the Department of Justice.

Justice Minister Ray Burke praised the governor and his staff for their "prompt and effective" action.

D Block houses inmates from the Limerick area. The prison holds some of the country's most dangerous criminals and is guarded by gardai, warders and soldiers.

During yesterday's protest, gardai took two rolls of film from photographer Kenneth O'Halloran of the Press 22 group. The Garda Press Office said the Defence Act forbids photography of property occupied by the defence forces.

The protest follows an attempted break-out at Cork Prison on Sunday, April 15, according to sources, and that the Strangeways, Manchester, siege is encouraging imitators.

Limerick Prison was "quiet" last night.

Most of the Third Force were cracking young fellows, off their heads and out for a good time. A few were middle-aged men taking advantage of a break from the Bog to let their hair down. We also had the Army Rangers walking the prison for the first time. They wouldn't talk to anyone. They patrolled in fours, two going forward and two back. You knew when they were around because you were sure to hear someone call out, 'You are going the wrong way, lads. Look out behind you!'

The regular army were on the walls. I don't think they took the Rangers any more seriously than the prisoners did. Back in the early 1980s, we got back pay of £1,600, which was a lot of money, and it followed a similar payout a few years previously. The money was great. At the same time, the army were in sentry boxes on the walls of the prison because of the IRA influx and they didn't have a penny. A private would shout down to ask the time because they couldn't even afford a watch. You'd throw them up a fag every now and then. I felt sorry for them. Then again, at least they were in shelter. They weren't walking around in the rain without even a seat to rest on.

To be honest, considering the behaviour of the republican prisoners, the army, the Rangers and the Third Force weren't needed. The IRA had its own internal discipline, and, as a result, they behaved as ordered by their leader. I remember often hearing them being called to order and ordered to fall in of an evening. Then, the order would be barked, in Irish, for them to fall out and go to their cells. Another order would be barked out and the cells would all slam shut, saving us the trouble. But we always double checked; trust is a great thing, but not in a prison.

Just like in Portlaoise, their OC was their spokesperson. He would come down to the kitchen cage and he would be on one side, me on the other. He would say, 'Mr Bray, there are a couple of things we need to talk about.'

He would explain their grievances and I would tell him my side. I would explain some things, reject others. Then, we would reach some agreement. He would ask, 'Is that the deal?'

'Yes, that's the deal.'

Depending on whether or not he was happy with the outcome, we could expect peace or trouble but, nine times out of ten, matters were resolved and there were no problems. We weren't completely unreasonable to deal with. There was a bit of give on our side as life doesn't work without a bit of compromise. It was so easy to deal with one man. In contrast, if there was a complaint on B Class, I might have had to talk to thirty-two prisoners individually, then go back to the first and start again because he would have forgotten what we had agreed upon.

Occasionally, there was trouble with the republicans, but you would see it coming. The tension would be there for a few days, and then there would be the big blow-up. But it wasn't personal. People on the outside don't understand that. We got a couple of digs, they got a couple of digs, but it ended there. No one was sneaky about it either.

The IRA prisoners tended to come in waves. The first came in the very early 1980s, the spillover from Portlaoise. The second wave, a few years later, consisted of the Official IRA, who found themselves more and more at odds with the Provos as the years went on. The final wave, in the late 1980s and early 1990s, were the dissidents. As they weren't aligned to either the Provos or the Stickies, they weren't being taken in by the IRA in Portlaoise, so they had to be shipped down to us.

While we appreciated the organised way the IRA went about their business inside, other prisoners didn't organise because we didn't let them. Neither did they have a shared ideology like the IRA and an organisation to back it up. The IRA could get you, either inside or when you got out.

An IRA rat was treasured by the prison authorities. He would usually go as high as he could before giving information. I wouldn't get it, and neither would the class officer who was in charge of the landing. The information would go straight to the top and we would know nothing about it. Even if they acted on the tip-off, we were never told the source of the information. The management played mind games with us as well. We would be told to search a landing, thinking we were acting on a tip, but all we were doing was shaking up the inmates. We would have been the tools – in both meanings of the word. But if an informer was caught by the people he was betraying, the consequences were deadly.

In addition to the regular informers – you find them among the general prison population as well as among the republicans – we once had a supergrass in our custody. That was in the mid-1980s, and it was all very cloak-and-dagger. None of us were supposed to know his name. He wasn't signed in at the reception.

Ironically, the supergrass was locked up on the same wing where the deputy leader of the Democratic Unionist Party, Peter Robinson, had been incarcerated. Mr Robinson had been on remand on a public order charge after he and some of his followers had crossed the border and protested outside a Garda station. I remember him as a very pleasant and polite man, but he had one peculiarity: he refused to drink tea because he thought it might have been Barry's Tea. Peter Barry, Minister for Foreign Affairs at the time, was a big tea importer in Cork. I saw him being interviewed on TV and being asked what it was like in the Republic's dungeons. He always had nothing but the best of praise for us. He said Limerick was like a hotel.

Like Peter Robinson, the supergrass was only with us a short time. He spent a week in Limerick, and every morning at six the Gardaí came and collected him. They brought him to Shannon, where he was put in a helicopter to point out arms dumps on the west coast. He was a cocky bastard, enjoying all the attention he was getting and the slack he was being cut by the Gardaí and the management.

I was chatting to the class officer one afternoon when he returned. The supergrass approached us and began making demands. He thought he owned the place. He stuck his fingers into the class officer's chest, isssuing threats. The class officer very casually flicked him in the balls with the back of his hand, dropping him to the ground, moaning. He then turned back to me and kept talking.

'What was that all about?' I asked.

'The Garryowen uppercut,' he replied.

'But why?'

'Because no one likes a rat.'

Another thing we didn't like was the searches we did when the IRA men were admitted. We did anal searches of them all. It was disgusting. We would tell them to strip, then we would tell them to drop the pants.

The management insisted we do this. If a guy co-operated and dropped the trousers and flashed the backside, we left it at that. But if he said no, we dropped him and pulled the underpants off him. It wasn't nice for the fellow it happened to, but it wasn't nice for us either. He went off to the cell unhappy, but we were going off to the pub unhappy as well. We rotated it so everyone had to do it. We would be very wary of an officer who wouldn't do it.

Recently, I was out with a couple of mates and I recalled these searches. Their wives looked horrified and the guys tried to hush me up – they didn't want their loved ones to know they looked up backsides for a living – but it brought something home to me: we didn't share much of our jobs with our wives. When I came home each night, I left the prison behind me. Apart from a quick 'How was your day?', 'Grand, and yours?', I never spoke openly about my job to anyone.

Chapter 17

Dublin Mafia

The Dubs began to arrive down in the mid-1980s. They were hardened criminals, many with a history of violence and they were referred to as the Dublin Mafia, though that's a bit of a generalisation. They weren't all like that, and they weren't a Mafia, at least not in the American sense. They weren't members of one criminal organisation, but rather came from many different gangs, all engaged in the drugs trade in the capital. They were tough men.

It began with one family. They were the first of the big drugs operators and, for a long time, they seemed to have luck on their side. They kept getting off; they claimed it was mainly through Garda inefficiency. The investigators made huge mistakes which allowed them to walk. After a few narrow squeaks, they started believing in their own mystique. They thought they could get away with anything.

Then it changed; they were caught by undercover Gardaí posing as buyers and three brothers were sent down to Limerick. The undercover Gardaí were young guys, straight out of Templemore, so they weren't known to the criminals or even to other Gardaí. They went around Dublin for two months buying drugs. Their work broke the back of this family's drugs empire.

The three brothers took to prison well. They gave no problems and got no hassle. I often noticed that the guys who were higher up the command chain in the criminal world were far more polite and co-operative than the foot soldiers. They would never tell you to fuck off. Instead, they would pay a guy to fuck you out of it, and they would maintain the smiling face the whole time.

One brother got fifteen years, which was a big sentence at the time.

I remember looking at his cell card and seeing that his release date was 2001. I was stunned. The only time I had ever encountered a year beyond 2000 was in the film *2001: A Space Odyssey*. It seemed a long, long time into the future.

'How are you going to do that length of time?' I asked.

He looked at me and lay down on the bed. He put his two arms behind his head and said, 'Like this, Mr Bray.'

And he did it like that, on his back. He didn't give it a thought. He never caused any trouble, but he could deal with it if it came his way. There were a couple of lackeys who did whatever he wanted done. I noticed that about a lot of the bosses.

I think the best way to look on those drugs lords is that they were the best transport managers ever, and they were able to enforce a contract without the aid of the civil law or the Gardaí. Some of them were quite good at handling people, including prison officers. When dealing with people like that, I made an effort to appear completely in control. So did my colleagues. We weren't dealing with these people for a few hours, like the Gardaí and the barristers – we could be stuck with them for twelve or fifteen years. It was a completely different relationship. We always tried to be professional but decent. We were as laid back as it was possible to be – certainly a lot more relaxed than some of the other prisons. This was not softness, but sense. The carrot is more effective than the stick when it comes to controlling people.

Limerick lads rarely took advantage of this, but some of the Dublin Mafia made the mistake of confusing politeness with weakness. They began pushing their luck, which swiftly led to the incident that has gone down in prison lore as the Apple Crumble Rumble.

It began innocently enough. A number of high-security gang member prisoners were transferred down from Dublin to Limerick. They fit in reasonably well, but they had an attitude. They didn't want to do time and they thought they had a right to everything.

We are an easy-going bunch and we treated them well, but they began to take liberties. It came to a head one evening when a number of prisoners demanded apple crumble with their dinner. They insisted and, suddenly, from all around us, the chant rang out: 'Apple crumble or we'll rumble! Apple crumble or we'll rumble!'

Some of the officers didn't even know what apple crumble was, but we knew what they meant by rumble. We were ready. One of the inmates shoved an officer, and that was the signal we were waiting for.

We threw ourselves into the battle with gusto. Furniture and beds went flying and radios were smashed. They barricaded themselves into a cell but came out peacefully after we started knocking through the wall of the cell next door with sledgehammers.

It had been a hard evening, but no one was hurt beyond a few superficial bruises that are gone in a day or so. And there were no hard feelings on either side. It wasn't personal and the prisoners knew that, but they lost a lot of privileges that they never got back.

A lot of the Apple Crumble Rumblers were in for long stretches. Some were doing twenty years, though they didn't spend the full term in Limerick. I met some of them years later. I was up in Dublin doing a course, and there were five of them in a line on one of the landings. They were surrounded by about fifteen officers, who were there for security.

Suddenly a voice rang out, 'Hoi, Mr Bray!'

'How are you doing, Tom? Nice of you to remember me,' I replied.

'Of course I do. Didn't I beat the shit out of you in the Apple Crumble Rumble?' The five of them were laughing; no hard feelings.

————

Prison escapes, as I have said, were rare. Most prisoners would have no place to go if they did get out and no money to get there. The Dublin drug lords were different – they had the resources to go on the run properly. Some even had the funds to quit Ireland entirely and move to the so-called Costa Del Crime in Spain, so we had to be alert to the possibility of an escape attempt.

Fortunately, there were always informers who kept us abreast of what was happening. An informer was a valuable asset and his identity was protected at all costs, so whatever information he gave to a senior officer was often filtered down to us in a very distorted fashion.

Once, I was on nights when an assistant chief officer told me that there might be an escape planned in A Class and I should look into the matter.

'How do you know that?'

'I can't tell you. You'll have to get another officer and search the cells, but make it look routine. I've got to protect my source,' he said enigmatically, tapping his nose.

'No problem. Which cell should we look at?'

'I don't know,' he replied with a straight face.

I just looked at him. 'If you know there's going to be an escape attempt, just tell us which cell to search and don't be wasting our time,' I said.

'I'd recommend you search all of the cells, so you'll probably need some help,' he said and walked off. I got the message – the tip-off came from a source that needed to be protected, so I was going to have to wake up dozens of prisoners and search lots of cells where nothing was going on.

I got the officers from the other classes together and we began the work. One of the officers with me was Eddie, the guy who had been with me many years previously on the night we found our first suicide. He was a good man to have with you in a tense situation.

The ACO did have the grace to tell us to concentrate on A2, the second floor, so we began going through the cells. We arrived at the cell where a well-known Dublin drug dealer was being held. Bingo!

We caught the man in the act of breaking through the wall. This obviously had been going on for some days, because when we lifted his bed we found a pile of debris, little bits of brick and mortar and stone. At that point, the hole wasn't big enough for him to get out, but he was very nearly there.

Two of the officers took him away and locked him up in another cell. Meanwhile, I searched his cell. I found a rough map of the prison with his escape route marked. Had he got out of his cell, he could very well have made his way to freedom. There was one security weakness which several prisoners thought they had identified. Being a high-security prison, Limerick had army men posted on the walls, Gardaí outside and prison officers patrolling inside. They believed that this was our Achilles heel – what too many people are responsible for, no one is responsible for. The army assume the Gardaí are keeping watch, so they sleep. The Gardaí assume the army are on the alert, so they daydream. The prison officers assume that the army and the Gardaí will catch anyone trying to escape, so we wouldn't be paying attention. What they forgot was this: if there had been an escape, it was our backsides on the line, not the Gardaí's or the army's, so we were always on the alert, no matter how well guarded we thought the prison was.

As I looked at this prisoner's escape map, I marvelled at how well thought out it was. There was a large x on the map outside the prison where a blue car would be waiting for him, keys in the ignition.

That prisoner got an unmerciful slagging over the next few days over his failed escape attempt and we got several prisoners joking to us, 'Well done, Officers. We're glad you stopped that bastard. He was keeping us awake all night with his quarrying.'

Joking aside, it gave me a fright when I saw the hole in the wall; this was serious stuff.

In contrast, the Limerick lads could be easier to deal with. They had no problem doing their time. They settled in and, generally, gave us a quiet life and we gave them a quiet life in return. It wasn't that they were any softer than the Dublin Mafia – they just seemed to have a more mature attitude to custody.

The truth is that Limerick lads were every bit as hard as the Dublin lads, and then some. As the 1990s progressed, the Limerick criminals began to form into their own gangs with ruthless leaders who fought viciously for control of the drug trade, with the Limerick feuds costing several lives. And we had all the gangs in the prison.

It used to be the tradition in the city that all feuds were suspended inside the prison. That doesn't happen any more. There are no truces, so we had to try to segregate prisoners. We had to be very careful not to allow rival members to meet on the landings if we felt there was the danger of a flare-up. Then, the gangs began to organise themselves, but we couldn't have that, so we tried to identify the leaders. Once a leader was identified, he was quietly transferred to Cork or Dublin. This would quieten down the rest of the gang, as they wanted to serve their sentences in Limerick, where they could get visits from their families.

It occasionally happened that someone from one gang would end up in a landing full of the other gang. It was also a problem in the visiting area, where there were fights when the families of rival gangs clashed. Some of these fights became quite vicious, and the Gardaí made more than one arrest at the prison gates. But it was the same in the courthouse – there have been several vicious incidents on the steps of the court itself as respect for authority has been steadily eroded by gang warfare.

It is quite a sight to see a major criminal trial in Limerick. The courthouse can be ringed by up to fifty armed detectives, like something out of Palermo or Bogota. Obviously, we couldn't have fifty armed detectives surrounding the visiting room of Limerick Prison, so how we handled the situation was simple: different gangs have different visiting days.

A lot of intelligence gathering goes on, trying to find out who is on which side. Sometimes, it's difficult to figure out, and the gangs don't always help. They often want someone on a different landing to infiltrate a rival gang, but more often they want all their people together. By putting them all together, you create a power block, but you also avoid potential assaults and riots.

One gang – and I won't embarrass them by saying which one – made our job of intelligence gathering childishly simple. They asked the governor to try to ensure that all their people were together. He surprised them by saying yes.

'Just give me a list of the people you want and I'll try to sort it out,' he said. They then gave him a full list of their members.

It's a pity they couldn't all be like that. The Limerick feuds show no sign of abating. I was chilled when I heard one prisoner shout at another, 'What have you ever done for the feud?' It was as if progressing the senseless murder and violence was a badge of honour.

Chapter 18
Jury for Sale

As the criminal gangs become more organised, more ruthless and more violent, they have also become more devious and cunning. Over the years, I have heard some incredible things about the way criminals organise themselves, but one story stands out. If true, it paints a frightening picture of justice in modern Ireland.

I was coming back from the Four Courts in Dublin in the prison van one Tuesday. There were seven of us in the van, four officers and three prisoners. There should have been four prisoners, but one of them had been found not guilty that day, much to everyone's surprise. He'd had a two-day trial and all the evidence seemed to be against him. Nobody who had been at the trial for even half an hour could understand how he had been found not guilty, and it was the main topic of conversation on the road back to Limerick that night amongst both the officers and the prisoners. After about half an hour of settling in, the prisoner sitting next to me said, 'What do you think of Mickey's court case, Mr Bray?'

I said, 'I was full sure he'd be convicted. All the evidence was against him.'

'Do you think he bought the jury?'

I laughed. 'You can't buy a jury. Nobody can.'

He went on to tell me a story over the next half hour about just that.

Back in the early 1980s, the head of a large Dublin crime family had at last been caught red-handed and was on trial. He had tried every trick in the book to prevent the trial and he had succeeded in the past using some underhanded methods, but this time there was no escape.

He gathered as many of his gang and his associates as he could and had them sitting in a group. As his last throw of the dice, he was going to try to intimidate the jury by the massed presence of all these gangsters. This cut-throat crew stared at the jury all morning as the trial proceeded. When it broke for lunch, they repaired to the pub across the road and were chatting. One of the gang said, 'I know one member of the jury. I used to play football with him one time years ago.' That evening, the footballer received a visit, and a face he hadn't seen for years invited him out for a drink.

Over a pint, he was told what was expected of him. Under no circumstances was there to be a guilty verdict. He was scared shitless because he knew what would happen to his family if he didn't co-operate.

When the jury retired, eleven of them voted guilty, but one guy said innocent and nothing would make him change his mind. They fought for hours, but in the end he would only agree to guilty on the minor charge of possession of drugs for personal use. He said innocent on all the bigger charges.

The judge couldn't accept a split jury and the jury couldn't reach an agreement, so there was no option: the judge had to let the crime boss go, but he ordered a retrial. Two weeks after the first trial collapsed, a package was delivered in the post to the juror they had got at. He was very nervous, but when he opened it the package contained £2,500. The following day there was a second delivery – a second £2,500.

That was the first time I had heard of a juror being bought.

After he'd finished his story, the prisoner leaned back in his seat with a satisfied smirk. Everyone in the van, prisoners and officers, had been listening with rapt attention.

'That's a good story,' I said.

'It gets better,' he said. 'One of the gang members – we'll call him Mr Black – watched with care how the jurors were chosen.'

'Jury selection is completely random,' I objected. 'You just get a letter telling you to report for jury duty and you show up in court on the day.'

'True – but that's not where the flaw is. Have you ever watched jury selection carefully?'

I had to admit I hadn't. None of us had. The prisoner had our full attention again as he went on to explain what happened.

The Clerk of the court has small cards with the names of every potential juror. He calls out each name and if you answer when your name is called, the card gets put into a drum. The jury is selected from the names in the drum. If the name is not answered, that card gets put to one side. Once all the cards are read out, those who have not been answered get read out again in case anyone has arrived late or didn't hear their name the first time.

Then, the judge addresses the court and thanks them for coming and for doing their civic duty. He often refers to the fact that those who didn't attend could be prosecuted, but I've never heard of anyone being convicted of that. The draw then takes place for selection for the jury and, once again, names are read out. Both the prosecution and the defence lawyers can object to seven jurors taking their place on the jury without giving any reason. This is pretty common, but quite often the solicitor isn't even looking when the names are being called out, he just objects to seemingly random names.

So the big day came – the drug boss was up for the retrial and he packed the court with his goons, just like the first time. Now our Mr Black was bored, so to relieve the boredom of sitting down in a stuffy courtroom all day, he answered when a name was called out by the court clerk. No one else answered, so Mr Black just raised his hand and said, 'That's me.' With that, his name went into the drum. He was only a step away from getting on the jury.

'So he got on and his boss got off the hook?' asked a prisoner.

'What do you think this is, a fucking fairytale? The name wasn't called out and his boss got six years. But it set Mr Black thinking. You see, there was no ID check of any kind. When his name went into that drum, no one asked him to prove he was who he had said he was. He saw guys near him get selected, walk forward and step into the jury box and none were ever asked for ID. They didn't even have to bring the bloody letter summonsing them for jury duty.'

In those days, it wasn't unusual to empanel several panels of juries in one day and to be sent off to return at a later stage for trials.

'So a couple of months later, Mr Black got a bunch of people – men and women – and brought them to the court. Any time a name was called out and no one answered, one of his people would take a note and when the name was called for the second time they would answer, pretending they had been late for the first call. Once they were in the drum, they had a good chance of getting on a jury.'

The story goes that when he got somebody on the jury, he would then approach the criminal whose case was being heard and offer to sell them a jury. Around that time, £5,000 seemed to be the going rate.

The verdict had to be unanimous, so one person had the power to hang a jury. A return of 'not guilty' was the best result and the worst was a hung jury and a retrial. Later on, even when the jury system was changed to majority verdict, it was still of great value to have a friend or a spy on the jury, but the price then dropped to £2,500.

I don't know if I fully believed this story, but, at that stage, the whole van was silent, listening to this tale. Then another prisoner threw in his tuppence worth. He said that the name and address of every juror was on a notice board in the hall of the courthouse. 'It's easy to find out where they live if you want to,' he added ominously. I had heard enough.

Then, the discussion turned to those who weren't eligible for jury duty. The list included Guards, prison officers, vets, doctors, the clergy and barristers. As we were getting off the bus, it occurred to me that if someone didn't want to do jury duty, all they had to do was write in and say they were one of those exempted professions. I doubted very much if the circuit court had the manpower to verify each of these, so there was a good chance you'd be excused. I often wondered what happened to those who didn't answer at all and who didn't send in any excuses; I never heard of anyone being charged with non-attendance. Of course, nobody in Ireland is obliged to carry any photo ID on them. This must be one of the few countries in the world where you don't have to carry any proof of your identity on your person.

———

Unless you've attended the opening day of a circuit court session, you won't understand the utter chaos of jury selection. The courts are overcrowded to standing room only, with the queue going right out the door. All the potential jurors are in the court – many of them for the first time, and they're usually bewildered by the whole event – along with the Gardaí, barristers, solicitors, witnesses, crooks, the innocent, the prison officers, court officials, journalists and gawkers. For the potential jurors, they don't know where to sit or where to stand and they can't hear what's going on. There are a number of barristers who have to be at a number of places at the same time and are trying to get the business done as quickly as possible with the judge. I always got the impression that in the district courts, the judge's audience, as it were, was all the people in the entire room, but in the higher courts, it seemed as if only the legal eagles present were the focus of the judges. Most of the time, it's impossible to hear the barristers speak because they have their back to the court. The judges can also be hard to hear, as they direct their voices downwards. Amidst all this chaos, no one is ever asked for ID.

For years after hearing that prisoner's story, I watched the jury selections with care, and I think what he outlined could have very easily happened. Often while sitting in the body of the court, a person near me would answer the second call – how could he or she not have heard it the first time? Were they pulling the con job? How could anyone know?

———

I remember the first time I went to America in 1980 and showed my Irish driving licence to the car hire company, which was just a couple of sheets of paper covered in a red cardboard cover. The man behind the counter couldn't believe that it didn't have any photograph. He accepted my passport as a valid ID instead. In the 1980s, they sent a photographer around to all the prisons to photograph all the officers for new photo identification cards. When the cards were issued, we found that an official from the Department of Justice had stamped the cards with his name, B. O'Brien, across the photo, so it looked like we were all called B. O'Brien. But it didn't matter, because I was never asked to show it to anyone in all my years of service. I've been in and out of nearly every prison and courthouse in the country, including Mountjoy, in uniform and in civilian attire, and have never been asked to produce my ID card.

The only time my ID card was of any use was when I was holidaying abroad. Sometimes, they ask for your national identity card when in a shop or restaurant while using a credit card. I often had to suppress a giggle as the girl at the checkout carefully copied out the number at the back of the card, which she thought was my national identity number but was instead the phone number for the Department of Justice in Stephen's Green, Dublin.

Oh, and it did help me once when I was stopped for speeding in France, when I received a professional courtesy, for which I was very grateful.

Chapter 19
The Dope on Drugs

Everyone thinks they know all about our prisons. When people hear that I worked behind bars, they tell me all sorts of crazy versions of how our jails work. The big fallacy is that we turn a blind eye to drugs. I hear that a prison can't be run without a bit of hash inside, as it keeps the prisoners from going crazy. But no one ever told me that. None of my bosses or the governors or the Department of Justice ever told me to overlook a fellow who had a bit of dope.

If I caught someone with dope, I treated it the same as any other offence. It wasn't the fact that it was dope I had caught you with, it could have been anything. That was the point – if they could get dope in, what else could they get in?

If we found a prisoner with dope, it meant that something had slipped through our defences and that made us nervous. There would be no question of overlooking hash. Even some of the prisoners bought into the urban legend that a small bit was allowed, because if it wasn't they would go crazy and the prison couldn't function. But I think that was wishful thinking on their part.

Drugs weren't always a problem, though by the time I joined the service, they were beginning to appear in Ireland. From the beginning, we were watching the druggies, but we weren't ready for the influx and were playing catch up.

I wasn't in long when I saw a prisoner kissing his mother full on the mouth, and I thought I'd never seen anything like that before. It was weird. It took us a while to cop on to what was happening: she was passing him over something. Immediately, we decided to put an end to it. Any guy kissing his mother on the mouth, we'd strip search him afterwards. That worked for a long time. Then things changed.

Today, as soon as someone gets their hands on something they shouldn't have, they stick it up their backside. We don't go up after it. That's just not in the job description. We did it for the subversives, but we weren't going to do it to find a bit of smelly hash.

If someone had a drug conviction, was up on drug charges or had a history of drug use, we'd watch him like a hawk, but then they started getting other fellows to bring it in for them. I'd be watching the dodgy guy, but there would be a quiet fellow, a guy who was in for just a month, and he'd be the one who got the gear. Why would they risk everything if they were only in for a month? Some of them weren't even users themselves. The answer was simple: they were threatened and coerced into it, and their mothers were coerced into bringing it in for them.

My mother would clip me on the ear for cursing even at twenty-eight or twenty-nine years of age, yet there were mothers bringing in drugs for their sons. How do you square that up? You had to know the full story. How it worked was the prisoner – the guy we weren't watching – would ring his mother the day before her visit. He would be tearful and frightened.

'Ma, I've got into a spot of bother here and they're going to slash my face,' he'd say. 'They've said they'll let me off if you get €150 and go down to such an address and give it to the guy there. He'll stop me from getting slashed.'

'I haven't got €150,' she might say.

'Go down to the credit union or whatever. Just get it or I'm going to be destroyed.'

So his mother gets the money and goes down to the address and hands it over, thinking that that's the end of the matter. And then they tell her to come down again next week with another €150 and the door will be slammed in her face. When she doesn't have the money the following week, they visit her house. They knock on her door, in front of the neighbours, and demand their money. Then, they offer her the way out: they say deliver this small package to your son and we're square for this week.

So you have this young fellow in jail and his mother is bringing him in drugs. And we aren't even watching him. Scumbag is at one end of the table, hands down by his sides, nothing wrong, and we have all the cameras trained on him so that at any sign of an exchange, we would pounce on the prisoner straight away. But we're looking at the wrong guy. The quiet guy at the other end of the table is the guy we should be watching. And that's how a lot of the drugs get into the prison. It's got nothing to do with us turning a blind eye so that the prison will run smoothly.

The most common drug inside is hash. Occasionally, they try to sneak in a bit of coke or uppers and downers, but hash is the main drug of choice for a number of reasons: it's a drug you can enjoy on your own and many people think it's harmless. A prisoner knows their mother or father will smuggle in a bit of hash but won't bring in anything else because their mother or father might be smoking a little themselves. It's a bit like if you were in hospital and you weren't allowed to smoke. You'd plead with your mother to bring you up just one cigarette, and she'd probably bring it up. A mother might bring up a small bit of hash to the prison, but nothing else.

Many other methods have been tried to get hash into prison, and one method was the simplest of all: throwing stuff over the wall. I think this started in Cork, when ex-prisoners went to the waste ground outside the prison, filled tennis balls with hash and pucked them over the wall into the prison yard. The prisoners would pounce on them immediately before the officers could get to them, so nets were slung over the yard to prevent this from happening. Not giving in too easily, the prisoners came up with another idea: they cut the hash into pieces small enough to fit through the mesh of the net. They then put some hash into tomatoes and threw them over the wall to land on the net, hoping that birds would peck at them and the hash would fall down through the net into the yard. This method had varying degrees of success, but that type of smuggling was eventually abandoned because it was too unpredictable, since as much of the dope fell short of the target as got through.

Another way was to try to intimidate a trustee who would be able to walk around the prison unescorted. Visitors would try to hide drugs in the toilets and the trustee would go and collect them and bring them back into the prison. There was often serious intimidation involved in getting the trustees to co-operate. Recently, there was a rumour that people sentenced to, say, either pay a €200 fine or serve seven days in jail were reporting to the Garda stations volunteering to do the seven days. The suspicion is, of course, that their body cavities are packed with contraband. As usual with any law enforcement agency, there is an element of catch-up involved in detecting these plans.

It's a lot more difficult to smuggle the hard stuff inside.

Heroin is the dirty, stinking, rotten thing that we all despise and hate. Once you're hooked on that, you'll do anything to get more of it – anything. You need it all the time and you need it regularly. The minute you open your eyes in the morning, your whole aim is to get a fix. The reason that cars get broken into at traffic lights and grannies get kicked for their handbags is heroin, not hash. A fellow on the dole could probably afford a hash habit, but you'd want to be a millionaire to afford a heroin habit.

The problem with heroin is that when you take it first you feel high, but after that you're just taking it to feel normal. The best you can feel is the way you're feeling right now. You spend thousands on it and that's the best you can get – feeling normal. With the hash, there's a hit, with the coke there's a hit, with the ecstasy there's a fabulous hit, but with heroin you have to have it because it stops you feeling sick. And you are sick when you don't have it, not sick when you do have it. That's the kick.

You won't get much heroin inside in the prison, but there is a whole support system for addicts. If they're hooked on heroin, they get methadone. Methadone is the exact same thing as heroin except it has a different name. Prisoners get it for free, clean, from the doctor. They are better off inside than out.

E is probably what inmates would love the most, but everyone likes a bit of hash because you sit back and relax and everything on the telly is funny, and you're inside in a cell enjoying your PlayStation and forgetting that you're locked up. Or at least that's what they tell me. The only drug I have taken is alcohol, which has done more damage than any other drug. It's probably led to more people being locked up than any of the other drugs too.

There is zero alcohol in prison. Nothing gets through. You can't pass over a bottle of vodka by kissing, so prisoners go to great lengths to try to make it themselves. The best way is by fermentation, but for fermentation you need yeast, and that's almost impossible to come by.

How prisoners overcome this is by taking a pile of bread and soaking it in boiling water, then leaving it to stand. What they end up with is absolutely disgusting. Personally, I don't think there's any alcohol in the mix at the end of the process.

Most of the time, we find it, but sometimes we pretend we didn't. There's a good reason for this. Prisoners hide all sorts of things, including weapons. Often, for example, they'll make a knife for self-defence or a bit of security. They might get a shard of glass and wrap tape around one end to make a handle, or they might attach a razor blade to a bit of wood or a toothbrush. They rarely keep these weapons in their cells, or, if they do, they make sure they're hard to find.

When we find a fellow's hiding place, we don't always bust it, not for a bit of hooch. We'll wait until something serious is coming down. Then, we know the hiding place and we can pick up the weapon before he gets a chance to put it into use. Biding your time can be a lifesaver. Sometimes, we won't drain the hooch we find. Instead, we'll throw it out and replace it with some other liquid. The prisoner will just think his attempt at brewing failed. So we stopped him getting drink, but we also found out where his hiding place is without busting our cover.

Hooch comes in cycles. Christmas and St Patrick's Day are two peak times. Around Christmas, every inmate buys as much fruit as they can get to try to ferment it – apples, oranges, anything they can lay their hands on. They'd ferment their underwear if they thought it would work, but it won't because they haven't got the constant temperature that's needed.

It's comical at times. Gallon containers used by the cleaners go missing. We find them up on a height, propped up by a broom handle. We know it's hooch. We sometimes wait a few weeks, then put a hole in the container. It's a battle of wits. A prisoner is entitled to do anything he wants, and my job is to try to stop him. If he wins, score one nil, but if we are better than him, he loses. Obviously, the officers win a lot more often than the prisoners do. We need to.

I have seen prisoners go crazy with the hooch, but I think it's psychosomatic. They talk themselves into the state. I'm convinced it has no alcohol content, but I've never tried it. I don't know what sort of hygienic conditions it was made under, so I wouldn't drink it. And then there's the smell. Whenever we found a stash, the first thing I would do is smell it. Seeing me recoil, the fellow behind me would always know: hooch.

How anyone can drink it is beyond me. I like a drink, but I would go without it if that was the only alternative.

————

For all their efforts to smuggle drugs in or to brew their own alcohol, from the day I joined the service, the thing that cracks a prisoner most is the cigarettes.

I never saw a fellow shaking, begging me for a drink, though I saw plenty doing just that for a cigarette: 'Please, Officer, a cigarette. Please, Officer, please, a cigarette.'

Sometimes, prisoners had to be put in a padded cell for their own safety. We would get a fellow and throw him in a digger (a strip cell) take all his clothes off and leave him with just a mattress and nothing else. The first thing he cracks for is the cigarettes. Nothing else. It isn't hooch or hash he asks for. And, of course, we give it to him. I will give a cigarette to him out of the kindness of my heart and because it's a habit to give. And because it gives us control.

More than once, I have seen guys coming into prison in the back of a Garda car with three or four Gardaí sitting on top of them. The Gardaí would dump him inside the gate and drive off, and I would be inside on my own with this fellow. A few minutes later, the guy is sitting down smoking a fag with the assistant chief officer, calmed down. Score one nil. It's fabulous in that regard.

Prison is one of the few smoker-friendly places left. Minister Mícheál Martin banned smoking everywhere except prisons and psychiatric hospitals. He was afraid that there would be trouble if the ban applied to prisons. Maybe he should have tried it and left it to us to sort out the trouble. But smoking is ingrained in our culture and in the culture of the psychiatric service. Years ago, when we picked up a prisoner from the Central Mental Hospital in Dundrum, what always amazed me – apart from the weight he'd have put on from all the drugs – were the big bags full of cigarettes he'd had. The doctors and nurses gave them out in handfuls. When an inmate would arrive back at the prison, the other prisoners would be waiting for him and he would be everyone's friend for a few weeks, until the supply ran out.

Hundreds and hundreds of fags were given out free.

I know from my travels that cigarettes were so scarce in American prisons that they were worth $300 a pack. That never happened in Irish prisons. Cigarettes never became currency, but prisoners do use them for gambling and you can buy the odd favour with a handful of fags, so even guys who don't smoke carry some.

Unsurprisingly, with such a smoky environment, loads of guys inside have asthma. There are so many guys on inhalers, I formed the opinion that they were forcing down the hash smoke with the inhaler. It seemed to me that almost half of the prisoners are on inhalers – far too many for it to be chance. Personally, I think they're just too lazy to suck down the hash smoke.

Back in the good old days, everyone in prison smoked – officers, prisoners, the whole lot. Today, many of the officers have stopped smoking and a lot of the prisoners have stopped as well. I have great admiration for any prisoner who can quit inside. A couple of years ago, they couldn't find anyone with matches to light the candle for the Sunday mass in the prison chapel. That wouldn't have happened when I joined. Smoking is being phased out by officers and prisoners alike.

But for those who are still hooked on the weed, they can buy as many cigarettes as they like in the tuck shop. And they buy plenty. The prison tuck shop isn't like an ordinary shop; prisoners can't wander in and browse. It's a store with plenty of merchandise: biscuits, sweets, cigarettes, newspapers, basic foodstuffs, toothpaste, etc. Prisoners get paid a small amount by the state each week. It's called gratuity or 'the grat' and would just about keep a light smoker in roll-ups for the week. Many prisoners would have cash left in for them at the main gate by their visitors which is placed into their tuck-shop account. Sometimes, they could have substantial amounts lodged. Prisoners are brought in small groups to the shop and they order their supplies for the week, which they then bring back to their cells.

You would be flabbergasted if you could see what can be got in the tuck shop these days. It's as well stocked as your average corner shop. You can get all kinds of cereal, condiments, a variety of teas and coffees, soups, vitamins, a huge array of bars and sweets, several brands of biscuits, fresh fruit, biros, envelopes, newspapers, cigarettes, loose tobacco, cough tablets – just about anything, really. But when I started, you could fit the selection in your pocket: all they could get was one ounce of tobacco, two packets of papers and a box of matches per week, and if they didn't smoke they got a bag of Foxes Fruits. I'd come back from the tuck shop with fifteen ounces in one pocket, fifteen ounces in the other pocket and a couple of packs of sweets in the back pocket. Supplies were scarce and had to be rationed.

Before I joined, matches weren't allowed in the cells, so prisoners depended on officers for a light. Obviously, in the night-time, no one was going to come running down just to give a guy a light.

Later, matches were allowed, but they were precious and weren't to be squandered, so prisoners would slice each match in four with a razor, getting four lights from the one match. Others had more ingenious solutions.

Back in the 1970s, I saw the last of a thing that even then was extremely rare – a tinder box. It was a small Golden Virginia tin, which originally held loose tobacco, and it belonged to an elderly gent on D Class. I think he was a tramp. The prisoner had cut hundreds of tiny slivers off a sheet or a cord and had packed them into the box. He lit the wadding for a second, then closed the box, snuffing out the flame. Later, when he wanted to light a cigarette, he would open the box and blow gently on it, and it would light up enough to light the cigarette. Then, he would close it again. He could go for months like this without ever having to buy matches.

I spotted it in the cell one day and I asked him what it was. He was afraid I was going to take it off him.

'You can keep it, man,' I assured him. 'I just want to know what it is.'

'It's a tinder box. That's been lighting three months for me now,' he grudgingly admitted.

Three months – I couldn't believe it.

'I'll show you,' he said. 'Do you have a cigarette?'

I gave him a cigarette and watched as he opened the box and lit it. The tinder box was an extraordinary solution to the matches problem. It lasted for months, cost nothing, didn't burn his pocket and didn't get too hot. The tramp told me that soldiers used to use it in the Boer War and the Peninsular War, and that is where it came from. That was the last tinder box I saw. I found it fascinating. He got two cigarettes from me for that demonstration.

Back then all the cigarettes were roll your own. Poorer prisoners would pick up the butts in the recreational halls; they would never be short there. Often the smoke from the forty prisoners would be coming down from the ceiling so thick you could hardly see through it. Your clothes and your hair would stink and you'd be breathing it in. It was just disgusting.

It was the same with escorts, bringing six or seven prisoners up to court in a van, when the whole car would be filled with smoke. We smoked ourselves. If you didn't, it was just tough luck. There was no question of saying, 'Excuse me, I don't like smoke.' People would look at you like you had two heads and just keep puffing away. And when you'd get to the court, the smoke would be as thick there. You could still go up to the Four Courts and see all the solicitors and barristers in the rotunda in the middle, smoking away under the no smoking signs.

We felt Minister Martin didn't seem to care if the prisoners or the officers all died of cancer caused by passive smoking as long as the bar men didn't get it. But we cared. So we kind of brought in our own rules. Today, you can only smoke in your own cell, not out in the landings. We won't let the prisoners smoke next to us or in the recreation halls. At first, they'd try, but five or six of them were put on report and they stopped after that.

Someday, someone is going to bring a case against the state because he was put in a cell with a smoker. But, of course, he'll have to get cancer to win the case, so it won't be worth it to him in the end. Often these days a prisoner will complain that he is sharing with a smoker and ask to be moved.

'I don't want to be in with him,' I'd hear.

And he'd be told, 'It's optional – you didn't have to come into prison in the first place.'

It won't last forever. The smoking ban will eventually apply inside as well as out, but, until then, cigarettes remain a powerful tool. You'd get a couple of ounces of tobacco from the governor, or later a couple of cigarettes, and you could calm prisoners down or barter for information. The whole place operates on information. We need it to keep a lid on potential trouble.

Apart from not wanting to be in a cell with a smoker, the next big reason for wanting a change of cell was snoring. There can be nothing worse than not being able to get a night's sleep in prison. Cell mates will usually put up with most things in each other – body odour, spitting, farting, unusual eating habits, even going to the toilet in the cell – but not snoring. It was often the cause of fighting in the cells. Most felt the time spent in a good sleep was not really considered prison time and it was treasured. 'I had a great night's sleep last night, Officer, one up on the judge's arse, ha, ha.' There were a few single cells around but it was usually the lifers or other long-term prisoners that got them. If one was due to be released, the class officers would be flooded with requests for the cell. Each trying to out do the other with the most worthy reason for the move.

Chapter 20
Sex Offenders

It seemed to me that there were more teachers than any other profession inside the prison, and most of them were in for sex offences. It goes without saying that I know a huge number of teachers who are an example to all, but there's a bad apple in every barrel. Many of the teachers were priests or Christian Brothers, but the first sex offender I met wasn't a teacher, he was a manager with a big chemical company down in Munster.

It was April 1977 when I received him at the reception, fresh from his trial. I was surprised to see a big, handsome man in a three-piece suit, collar and tie and a hat. He was so out of place. Most of the other inmates were small and uneducated. This fellow was completely different. He reminded me of my father, a decent, respectable man, well presented and a few years older than myself.

We followed the normal admission procedure. He was taken downstairs and told to strip. He hesitated, but complied. We ordered him into the shower. He was slow doing this and he was trying not to wet his hair, so one of the officers went over and pushed him by the head. The officer jumped back with a scream as the prisoner's scalp came away in his hand. Your man had a wig on. It shocked me too for a minute. It was the first time I had seen a wig and he looked like a different man without it.

He said he was in for a barring order, though I found out later he had been convicted of incest. It was the first time I had come across it. His daughter had gone away on a retreat and a nun found out that her father was interfering with her.

While he was in prison, his daughter kept sending him letters saying how much she missed him and how much she wanted to be with him. She wrote that when he got out, they would go away together to England, where no one would know them. I thought it was the saddest thing I'd even seen. One of my mates disagreed; he said it was a victimless crime. She didn't mind, they were just having sex, so where was the harm? But her father was after taking her innocence off her. He had stolen her childhood and destroyed that unfortunate creature, putting a false love in place of real love.

The most extraordinary thing was that the wife knew. We learned this through the letters the daughter was sending. All letters, in and out, are censored. In a lot of the incest cases I came across, it seemed to me that the wife knew. In some cases, I felt she encouraged it to keep her husband away from her. That may not be pleasant to acknowledge, but that's my experience. I have come across at least three cases where the wife knew and made no complaint – cases where she backed the husband against the daughter or son in court.

None of the prisoners knew what this man was in for. We officers did. In some places, such as America, the wardens aren't told what the prisoners are charged with to ensure that everyone is treated the same. But Ireland is different; we had to inform ourselves. We knew, but we still managed to treat everyone the same.

Sex offenders usually got jobs in the laundry or the reception back then. Often two would be alone together on the reception. This kept them isolated and they were usually compliant and caused no problems. There was no way they were going to give hassle: in their own minds, they were fearful of the other prisoners. We had to protect them.

———

I was twenty-nine when I joined the service. I had a family and had seen the world, but Ireland was really innocent when it came to sex abuse then. So were my colleagues. Most of us didn't equate rape with sexual offenders. We thought of it as a hand shoved down the trousers, and that's the way we dealt with it at the time. It was only when I started going to court and hearing the horrendous testimony that I realised just what they were capable of.

Many sex offenders began to filter in. Some were picked on. I was

in the yard when the first of them got beaten up. It was 1980, and I was
on my own. The yard was full of prisoners and I had no backup, no
radio and no baton. The man was punched and knocked to the
ground and I didn't see it happen. The following day, I was called to
the office and asked about the assault.

'I was up near the gates dealing with someone else and it happened
behind my back,' I explained.

'But you're supposed to see everything,' came the smug reply.

'I haven't got eyes at the back of my head,' I snapped. They hated
that kind of answer. 'What I will do is I'll find out who did do it,' I
added and walked out. I didn't wait for an answer.

One of the prisoners told me who had done it: a small, baldy thief.
He had attacked the other man because he was in for a sex offence. I
went over and told him that he was going on report for assault.

'No one fucking saw me,' he said.

'Two fellows inside saw you, so you're going to be done,' I lied.

'Fuck it, just for a sex offender,' he said indignantly.

'The best thing you can do is go in and admit to the governor that
you hit a sex offender. The governor hates sex offenders more than
you, and you'll get off, guaranteed,' I urged.

The next morning, he went in to the governor and said he had hit
the man in the yard.

'Did you?' said the governor.

'I did. I clocked him. And you know why, Governor.'

'Do I?'

'He's a sex offending fucking bastard. You'd have done the same
yourself.'

'Would I? Lock him up for three days.'

Even sex offenders are entitled to be treated properly in prison.

Because some inmates were targeting sex offenders, we began
segregating prisoners around 1980. It coincided with the AIDS
epidemic and the opening of Arbour Hill Prison in Dublin, but it
came about by accident. Arbour Hill was initially for those with AIDS,
to separate them out from the general prison population. Prison
officers from all over the country did two-week tours of duty there,
and they were rough. We were dragging the prisoners off the walls.
They were going absolutely berserk – they all thought they were going
to die – so the Department decided to integrate them back into the
prison population.

The union wasn't too keen because that meant we would have a whole load of guys with AIDS and HIV and no way of knowing who had the disease and who didn't. We decided we had to treat every single body fluid as suspect – spit, blood or piss. Once we treated everyone as if they could have AIDS, it took a lot of pressure off us. And it worked. So the AIDS sufferers came out of Arbour Hill and now the prison was free for other inmates. It became a sex offenders' prison. Some other long-term prisoners, such as Malcolm McArthur, were also put in there. I worked in Arbour Hill for a short time while I was on a course. It was a pleasure to work there. There was no hassle of any kind.

After a while, some of the sex offenders were moved to the Curragh. They were mostly the paedophiles and Catholic priests. A mate of mine was working there. The Curragh Prison is odd – it's as if you took Limerick Prison and turned it into a doll-sized version. The doors were a third smaller, roofs were a third lower. Everything was shrunk. I couldn't even get into some of the doors. And the place was full of respectable-looking, middle-aged men just sitting around.

I asked one of the officers what it was like to work there, and he said he'd come down from Mountjoy, where he'd worked for twenty-two years, and he couldn't believe how easy-going it was to work here.

'Last Sunday, only one guy missed mass, and that was because he was sick,' he said.

'What happens here, Noel?' I asked my mate.

'Nothing. Absolutely nothing.'

'What do they do?'

'Nothing.'

'Do they give any hassle?'

'The only hassle is over who will get to feed the fish in the aquarium,' he said. 'And sometimes they argue over who is going to say mass.'

That's the paedophiles – very well behaved, often educated. No criminal history and no sense of guilt at all. A rumour went throughout the service that in the Curragh Prison, there were about thirty men walking around in full clerical attire, including roman collars. It's almost impossible to imagine such a scene and the Limerick branch of the POA even brought a motion to conference proposing that these people should not be allowed to wear clerical clothes while serving a sentence. I don't know if it was true or not, though, because I never saw them wearing those clothes any time I visited the Curragh.

It was odd to see my friend Noel in such a quiet place. The first time I met him was in D Class in Limerick. I had been told to take a prisoner down to have a shower. With only one shower in the prison at that time, prisoners didn't wash much and some were manky. This fellow was about six seven, and wide, like the Indian in *One Flew over the Cuckoo's Nest*, with long hair hanging down the back of his neck. He didn't even move when I came to him.

I said, 'Come on, man, you're going for a shower.'

He just slowly shook his head. *Shit*, I thought, *I'm going to have to dance with this guy, and I'm going to lose. He's huge.* My only backup was Noel, who was a lot shorter than me. He must have lied about his height to get into the job, but there are no height restrictions when it comes to bravery. Noel brushed past me and grabbed the big guy, then firmly led him down the stairs of D Class and to the shower.

'Get undressed now,' he said. He was always softly spoken. 'Go in and have a shower.'

And the giant, as meek as a child, did.

Although sex offenders are sent to Arbour Hill today, they can request a transfer to Limerick if that's where they come from, as it makes visits easier. We keep them on the top landing of B Class and they're the last down for food every day. If anyone wanted to have a go at them, they could, but it doesn't happen. Other prisoners don't care – and some of the hairies are tough enough to look out for themselves.

One of them, a big German – we'll call him Luke – was a boxer. Just a few months before I retired, he was working out in the gym on B Class. Three Limerick prisoners came across from A Class because their gym was closed and saw him punching the bag. The officer on duty told me that one of them said, 'He's a fucking sex offender, raping our fucking women' – as if it was their job to rape them.

So the three lads went over to Luke and began giving him some lip. He turned and dropped each of them with a single punch.

'What did you do?' I asked the officer.

'What do you think? I did nothing. I said, "Luke, do you want to go back to your cell?" He said fine, and I opened the door and let him off.'

Luke was later released and then done again for rape. But no one messed with him.

I did martial arts myself, but I didn't want the prisoners to know it. If I had a reputation as the prison Bruce Lee, it could push them into overkill – get Bray first because he's going to give us the most trouble. I'd try to keep it as quiet as possible, but occasionally there was a bit of trouble and some fellow would spot a move.

'Are you a ninja, Mr Bray?'

'Not at all, I saw it in the pictures.'

'You were in the French Foreign Legion too.' That rumour got out because I speak a bit of French. I always denied it, but it didn't make a difference. 'They always deny it when they were in it,' the prisoner would crow.

———

We had a large variety of sex offenders over the years, and some would shock you. A couple of guys were done for interfering with cattle – bestiality. You'd want to be very stupid to get caught for that. You'd think you'd be able to do that in private, wouldn't you?

Then, we had one guy from the North who was in for attempted rape. He tried to rape a girl but was so innocent he didn't know where to put it. But he was a big bloke and had done martial arts, so we had to be careful around him. And he was the only prisoner who ever beat me at chess. I could never best him, and it used to kill me. Yet he didn't even know the basics of the mating game. Extraordinary.

Some of the offences were quite horrendous. One of the early paedophiles I remember was a petty officer in the British Navy, a big, tall man who towered above me. He had raped a twelve-year-old girl. Normally, I didn't care what they were in for, just as long as they behaved themselves. I didn't judge people; it made it easier for me to do my thirty years. Most prison officers don't deal with it that way. They operate on the basis that if you don't mess with them, they won't mess with you.

But this day, as I was walking into court handcuffed to this guy, I said, 'Do you mind me asking? What the fuck do you see in children?'

He looked at me like he didn't quite understand. 'What do you mean?' he asked.

'Why did you pick on a twelve-year-old girl? You could have got any woman you wanted. You're a big handsome man. You could have got a woman for twenty pounds if you went to the right place. So why? She was only twelve.'

'She was a big twelve. She was big for her age,' he said.

He had no conception that he had done anything wrong, but he must have seen the look of horror on my face because he added, 'I think she liked it.'

People think that sex crimes are always committed by men, but women commit them as well. The difference is that if a thirty-five-year-old bored housewife brings a sixteen-year-old friend of her son into the house for a quickie, that's not considered being interfered with by an adult. He comes out and everyone thinks he's a lucky guy. Turn that the other way around and it's a crime. Having said that, we had a woman in once who was convicted for interfering with children. She was from the Waterford area, in her thirties, and you couldn't have said there was anything different about her.

———

Although in general the hairies didn't get picked on, it did happen occasionally. And it wasn't always by other prisoners. I was in the yard once with an officer who was down for a while from Dublin. There were two brothers walking the yard and they were Travellers. Every time these two passed him, he would mutter under his breath, 'Rapists, rapists.'

I told him to cop himself on and leave them alone.

'I'd prefer to be sitting up against the wall smoking a cigarette rather than rolling on the ground with those two,' I said.

'I hate rapists,' he hissed.

He kept muttering about the two brothers and, eventually, they cracked. As they were passing him, they suddenly went for him and I had to dive in. That's what I was paid to do. There was a tussle, but we subdued the two of them. After that, we had to put them on report. That's standard procedure. It's the equivalent of the Gardaí charging them.

The Dublin officer – we'll call him Bosco, because he was a fucking idiot – put the two Travellers on report and then went off on his holidays. Two days later, I was called up to the governor's office. The two prisoners were there and I was there, but there was no sign of

Bosco. The governor read out the report that Bosco had written: 'Governor, I respectfully wish to report the two prisoners for breach of the prison regulations...' and the usual old formal guff.

'First charge that the two prisoners assaulted me outside in the yard for no reason whatsoever. When I subdued them [on his own, no mention of me] they said they were going to rape the governor and his wife and his children, that they hated the governor and the chief, and they were going to burn the chief's house when they got out.'

Where the hell had that come from? This was a whole heap of lies, but I couldn't come out and say that. To make matters worse, the two prisoners were looking at me because I had the name of being fairly straight.

'Come on, Mr Bray. Tell him what happened,' said one.

'Is this true?' asked the governor.

'I didn't hear everything, but these two men did assault me out in the yard and I had to defend myself,' I said evasively.

'I know, but did they say they were going to rape my wife?' he persisted.

'I'll tell you now, Governor, and I am ashamed to say it, that in the heat of battle, I didn't hear that.'

The prisoners were getting annoyed. I was annoyed myself. Bosco's lies had landed me in it too. The two Travellers were both saying, 'He called me a reaper – reaper – reaper.' That's what it sounded like in their thick accents. The governor kept telling them to be quiet, but all he could hear was this mantra: 'He called me a reaper.'

Exasperated, he ordered them to be locked up for three days and I bustled them out of his office as quickly as possible.

When I returned, the governor said to me, 'Mr Bray, what is a reaper?'

'I think they were talking farming terms, Governor, because I really didn't understand it,' I lied.

So the two unfortunate prisoners got locked up for three days over nothing. I hated it when an officer did that, so I slipped them a few ounces during the week. But it was rare enough. Most of us got on well with the inmates. I can walk down the street and meet former inmates and there is never trouble. I've been approached by hundreds of prisoners. The day I retired, they were sticking their hands out the bars to shake mine. It took a lot of guts for them to do that in front of their mates. I built up a good rapport with them, and in some cases with their parents and even their grandparents.

In the last years of my career, there were guys coming in and I had locked up their grandparents. These prisoners would meet me when they came in and say, 'I was told to look for you – you'd look after me.'

One man approached me with a child who looked like he couldn't have been more than twelve. I suppose he was sixteen and should have been sent to St Patrick's Institution, but his solicitor had asked that he be allowed do his time with his father in Limerick. This man seemed to swell with pride as he approached me.

'Mr Bray, this is my son.'

He pushed the young lad forward and I shook his hand warmly.

'Now, if you have any trouble you are to look for Mr Bray – none of the other screws. He'll look after you.'

And as that boy smiled hesitatingly at me, I thought that I had locked up his father, his grandfather, his aunt, four of his uncles and at least six of his cousins. I had locked up every member of his family except his mother – and she was a well-known prostitute in the city. A story a Garda told me came to mind: they had raided this family's house once, a good dozen years earlier, and found the entire family – including children – sitting around naked watching blue movies. Rumour had it that the family was involved in the production of blue movies. What chance had this young teen had? But I did my best not to let his father down. I did look out for him.

————

The sex offenders were always known as the hairies, and for the life of me I couldn't explain why. They were no hairier than the rest of the prison population. Perhaps it's because it rhymes with Tipperary. Many seemed to come from that county. They didn't have the mark of the devil on their forehead or eyebrows that met in the middle. There was no way of telling what someone was in for just by looking at them. The most depraved-looking gargoyles could be in for quite innocent stuff, while the sweetest-looking individuals could be monsters. As a rule, we tried to integrate the hairies among the general prison population because it was safer for them. We always had a couple of hairies in the kitchen and they always worked hard and did a good job. If they didn't, I would have shipped them out. One of the best workers we ever had in the kitchen, who'd take over the place and could run the whole show, was in because couldn't keep his hands off his next-door neighbour's young son.

Everyone thinks that sex offenders get a rough time in prison, but that's a myth. If you are small and weak and vulnerable, you'll get a rough time. If you are big and strong and tough and have some connections, you'll have an easy ride, no matter what you're in for. I have seen a man who kicked a handicapped child to death walking around being backslapped and fêted because his fellow inmates were afraid of him. They knew he was a dangerous bastard. The hairies do sometimes get attacked, but it's usually by the lame and the inadequate. In other prisons, it was different, but in Limerick they integrated fairly well.

A big part of our job is to prevent bullying. Everyone hates a bully, but there is more to it than that – bullying is the cause of a lot of hassle. It drives people too close to the edge. If you bully a fellow enough, you back him into a corner. I've seen it loads of times. He's in a corner, fearing for his life, and he just loses it. One of my colleagues was down in C class serving tea when a young prisoner pulled out a home-made knife and started slashing wildly. He wasn't a tough guy or a nutter, but he had been driven crazy with fear. He had been threatened on a daily basis and couldn't take any more. He was striking out blindly; he didn't care if he cut an officer or a prisoner. That's one reason to prevent bullying.

Although sex offenders aren't given a hard time that doesn't mean they are liked. Other prisoners, especially the Dubs, tended to look down on them. It was ironic, really, as one of the biggest of the Dublin criminals was recently done for abusing his kids.

For a long time, we didn't realise what some of the prisoners themselves had suffered. Some prisoners would tell me they had been in the reformatory schools and had been abused. I'd say, 'Don't be telling lies about the priests and brothers, that's not necessary. I know they might not have treated you well, but there is no way that was going on.'

I was a bit ashamed later, and so were a lot of officers, that we didn't believe them. It was only years later that we found out that there was a gulag of schools and laundries run by the religious where children of both sexes were beaten and raped on a regular basis. From the reports, some Christian Brothers would pick out some boy from a dormitory, in front of everyone, take him out, abuse him, kick the shit out of him, and return him to the dormitory. The Nazis didn't even do that. Every one of those kids was inside in their bed, rigid with fear.

I had many vulnerable people under my care in the prison. I could have got them alone in a cell and they would have had no recourse to help, yet no prison officer has ever been convicted of a sexual offence. The clergy were supposedly our betters – they had a higher social status than us, more education and were better thought of than us. More was expected of them than of us. Our prisoners were the same vulnerable people the clergy were interfering with. When the prisoners told us their stories in the 1970s and 1980s, we didn't believe them. We should have. In many cases, the abuse they suffered turned them into the abusers they became – our hairies.

––––

There was a family of one father and two sons, and they interfered with everything in the house between the three of them: each other, the other children, the animals, everyone but the wife. The three were in Limerick Prison at the same time. We put them in the same cell. I suppose there was an innocence about us; we didn't realise what sort of people they were. But as it began to emerge from the court case just how dysfunctional their home life was, the decision was taken to split the three men up, so they were all put in separate cells, with other inmates.

We thought this was a good solution. Unfortunately, we hadn't thought about the poor unfortunates who had to share cells with them. I was on patrol one morning when a very angry prisoner accosted me.

'Mr Bray, that man has to leave my cell. He can't spend another night with me.'

'What happened?' I asked.

'I woke up in the middle of the night, and that prick was just after wanking off all over my chest. There was a pool of – '

'That's enough,' I said, putting my hands up. 'I'll move him.'

'See that you do.'

'What did you do?'

'I hit him, Mr Bray. I fucking smashed his face in. Then, I stayed awake all night.'

After that, we had to move the three back into a shared cell and keep an eye on them. We were afraid of what would happen if they were left in separate cells with other inmates. They seemed to have no conception at all of right or wrong.

———

Contrary to popular belief, homosexual rape almost never happens within the prison. It's another urban myth. There's a bit of consensual homosexual sex among people who aren't homosexuals, but in Ireland, I never saw any overt homosexual behaviour. I never saw a fellow mincing down the landing, dressing flamboyantly or pretending to be a woman. I have seen it in America and in other places, but never in Limerick or in any Irish prison, and I've been in them all. Obviously, the prison population has the same percentage of homosexuals as the general population, and we have caught fellows in bed together, but it was always consensual.

This thing about being raped in the showers is a load of shit. It never happens. I think it's an urban legend designed to keep middle-class people from going off the rails: you'll be put in a cell with Bubba if you don't behave yourself. It's the grown-up version of the Bogey Man.

Having said that, we had one case in the early 1990s where a fellow called Battery Head (he's dead now) concocted a very clever plan to abuse a fellow inmate. Battery Head was a Traveller, and the story was that he had been tied up with the dogs at a very early age under the caravans. He had a very sad and unfortunate life and was raped himself on a number of occasions.

Battery Head was in a cell with another prisoner on D Class. D Class is like a dungeon you walk up to. It was a shithole from the moment I walked into the prison until the day they knocked it and replaced it. Normally, it was kept for remand prisoners who were awaiting trial as it kept them away from the general prison population. What Battery Head was doing there, I don't know. D Class was originally the debtors' wing of the prison. Debtors could carry on their trades inside prison. They were provided with a room and a fireplace and they could pay to have food brought in for them and a bit to drink. It was one of these debtors' cells that Battery Head was sharing with the remand prisoner.

Battery Head told his cellmate that he was planning to escape. The cell had a chimney that was bricked up, but it was easy to take out the bricks. That would be his way out. Of course, if he escaped, the other prisoner would be in trouble, but Battery Head had a plan for that too: he had saved his medication over a number of days, and he would give that to his cellmate and then tie him up. That way, the authorities would have no suspicion of him having aided the escape.

The cellmate agreed to this arrangement. He took the medication and Battery Head tied him up. The next thing he remembered was waking up at three o'clock in the morning with Battery Head up on top of him, brutally raping him. Then Battery Head tried to kill him, wrapping a shoelace around his neck and pulling it until he passed out.

The next morning, we came up to open the cell. Upon opening the door, one of the officers found a black man inside lying on the bed – but there not supposed to be a black man inside in the cell. I was called to bring him to the hospital. I was stunned when I saw his face. It was completely black. It was the exact same as if you'd got a paintbrush and painted his face. It was black from a distinct line around his neck where the shoelace had been. From that spot down, he was pure white. At that stage, we didn't know he had been raped.

They made him undress in the hospital. During the course of undressing, I noticed he had blood on his underpants. I said to the nurse, 'You might have a check on that.' Slowly, the penny dropped that he had been raped a couple of times by Battery Head inside in the cell.

I was detailed to spend the night with him in hospital and I talked to him and pieced the whole story together. During the course of the evening, he said, 'Officer, I can't sleep. I just can't sleep.'

'Is there anything I can do for you? Can I get a nurse to give you some pills?'

'I'd be afraid to take them after what happened to me last time.'

He looked around and on the wall there was a crucifix. 'Is there any chance you'd give me the crucifix?'

Of course, I'm suspicious by nature when I'm on duty, but it wasn't much of a weapon, so I took a chance. His behaviour didn't give me cause to think that he might be dangerous. I got the crucifix down from the wall and I gave it to him. It was a large one, about two feet tall. He put it on his chest and crossed his arms over it. He lay down there on the hospital bed, and I sat there looking at this man with his arms crossed, clutching a crucifix to his chest, and his face extraordinarily black and the rest of him extraordinarily white.

That was the Battery Head for you. He was never charged with what he did to that prisoner and it didn't add a day to his sentence. The prisoner didn't complain. He said he was lucky to get out of it alive.

Battery Head was eventually released and he went to Dublin. We all knew he would rape again and, sure enough, he did. Within three days of his release, he dragged a girl down a laneway into a building site and raped her. He was back inside, this time in Arbour Hill. Sometime in the mid-1990s, he hung himself. Battery Head had suffered much misery in his life, but he inflicted much more misery on the lives of those who came in contact with him.

Chapter 21
Doing Time

Fortunately, prisoners like Battery Head were rare. Most were guys who were in for minor enough stuff who just wanted to do their time as easily as possible. There'd be a bit of craic with them. Occasionally, they played tricks on each other. When a new fellow would come in they would say, 'Are you doing anything in the morning?'

'Time,' he'd reply.

'Why don't you apply to walk the governor's dog? They're looking for someone. The last fellow is after getting out. You'd have to go up by the Fair Green, down by Garryowen, down the back of the Pike.'

'I wouldn't mind that at all.'

'All you have to do is ask.'

And the eejit would ask.

I was standing outside the parade one day when a tough guy walked out of D Class in a white singlet and white shorts. He had a pair of black socks and a pair of runners and the number 14 pinned on to him.

'Where are you going?' I asked.

'I'm going in to see the governor.' Every prisoner had that right.

'What for?' I asked.

'I'm going in for the bicycle race.'

I didn't want to tell this big bastard he was a fool, so to be gentle I said the race had been cancelled.

'I was told you'd say that, Mr Bray. I'm going for the race, and fuck you.'

'Fine, so. Get in the line.'

Everyone in the queue waiting to see the governor was giggling. Any time my friend got near the front of the line, I put him to the back.

'Bicycle men to the back,' I kept shouting. Every prisoner in the place saw him. Eventually, it was his turn to go in. He was the last man. The prisoners were all up on the landing waiting for this eejit to come out of the governor's office. If he had only listened to me, he'd have been all right.

'One more, Governor,' I announced.

'What is it?'

'I can't understand his accent. You better talk to him.' And with that, I ushered the man in the singlet into the office.

'I want to go in the bicycle race,' he began.

'Are you out of your shagging mind?'

'Governor, I tried to stop him coming in, but I don't think he's the full shilling,' I grinned.

The prisoner was livid. Suddenly, the penny started to drop. The last thing I wanted was for him to go down and kill someone, so I hustled him out and said, 'Didn't I tell you it was cancelled?'

And though he was no fool, he accepted that explanation and the penny never fully dropped.

I know he wasn't entering the race out of a love for sport – he wanted to do a runner. But, in general, the prisoners were trustworthy enough. For a while, I was bringing them up swimming in Roxboro. I was in charge of the gym at the time and I was up in Roxboro doing scuba diving practice, so they thought I'd be the ideal man for the job. Fifteen prisoners in a bus and me on my own – a recipe for a break-out.

The first day, we pulled up at the pool. Roxboro Swimming Pool is in the middle of Southill, and some of them could even see their houses from the bus. Before we opened the door, I said, 'Anyone who's planning on running, could you come up to the front of the bus and run now so I can bring the rest of them back. I'm not spending an hour counting you.'

But none of them ever ran on me. I'd be nervous, though. We would bring them in and they would be in the changing room and the public were there. We must have been out of our minds. But they never let me down.

Over the decades, I saw the prison transformed. When I joined first, all the laundry was sent out. The Good Shepherd Laundry, one of the gulag of sweatshops and Magdalene laundries run by the Church, received several large bags once a week. But you couldn't be showing a nun soiled underpants, so all the underwear was removed and washed in the prison laundry.

There were big ceramic Belfast sinks, and cold water. Socks, underpants and vests were washed by prisoners with carbolic soap, cold water and a washing board. Occasionally, someone would come out with a bucket of warm water. I don't know where they got it from, but you can imagine it only made a slight difference. Fingers were numbed in winter.

After washing, the undies were placed in a warming cupboard. This had a series of pipes that I never felt any warmth in; the floor was bare earth. The whole laundry was dank and unpleasant. It was next to the kitchen and very occasionally, perhaps once a month, some of the prisoners in the kitchen would wrap chips in silver paper and toss them into the laundry. The washers would fight like dogs for those chips. The food wasn't great back then. I once saw two prisoners fight over the skins of potatoes.

Today, the laundry is state of the art and handles all the prison washing. Nothing is sent out; we have top-of-the-range washers and tumble dryers.

Similarly, the prison kitchen has improved beyond measure and two wings were knocked and replaced with modern ones. Cells were brightened up and toilets and washbasins appeared in the renovated wings. We were particularly delighted when D Class was shut down and rebuilt. It now has proper sanitation and all the mod cons, including televisions.

It began to change in the 1990s as the Celtic Tiger dug its claws into the country and we began to admit people who had families and mortgages and central heating and gazebos and double glazing. They lost out badly when they were convicted. It was often drugs that brought those guys in.

These new convicts were used to better conditions, but, then, the conditions within the prison had got better. You're admitted in a custom-built reception and your cell has a television and kettle, and a small toilet and hand basin on c and d Class. Thirty years ago, you would have had just a bed, a chamber pot and no water.

The televisions were introduced in 2003, initially as a means of reducing suicides, by the late Governor Pat Laffin and had a great effect on the prisoners. The Black Panthers in America were furious when they brought in televisions there. Up till then, they had been discussing political philosophy on the landings. Then, they were discussing soaps. And that is what happened in Limerick.

A beautiful silence descends on the prison when *Emmerdale* and *Coronation Street* come on. From seven to eight, there's peace. Most of the prisoners don't even come out for recreation any more; there are two officers sitting above in the recreation hall on their own. The prisoners have about a dozen channels. I remember a month before I retired, they found one channel that was showing Traveller sulky races on the main road. Thinking back, someone must have managed to get a video and hook it up so the whole landing could see it.

I don't care what anyone says about the prison having become too luxurious – the televisions really worked. It calmed prisoners down, made them more manageable and reduced suicides. They also had GameBoys and PlayStations, though we didn't provide those. A lot of times, I saw prisoners repeat the same pattern they had at home, which was to play computer games until four or five in the morning, skip breakfast, then get up for the dinner and go back to bed again.

———

While most of the prisoners behaved well enough, there could be flashpoints. I was over on a Class when two Cork lads came back from a visit. Visits were a pain. Inevitably, it would happen that one fellow would come back and say, 'My bird says she saw your bird out drinking.' This was the biggest fear they had – that their girlfriends or wives were out socialising and meeting God knows who. And often it wasn't true at all.

These two young bucks came back, and on the way they had some kind of an argument. They were growling at each other. When they came into a Class, they went for each other. I saw them coming up the stairs, then start fighting on the very narrow landing. Though they were both bigger than me, I got between them to break it up. In fairness, prisoners don't often hit you. I have walked into the middle of loads of vicious rows and came away with no mark at all. This time was no different as I pushed them back.

'Lads, for fuck's sake, knock it off,' I roared.

Then, down at the end of the landing, I saw this fellow who looked like a troll – a very short, stocky man who only came up to my hip; Big Dwarf was his nickname – come charging down the landing, bellowing, 'Get the screw! Get the screw!'

Stunned, I shoved the lads aside and side-stepped this guy. As he careened past me, I kicked him in the backside and he went running down the stairs. I went back to the prisoners and they shook hands, but to cover myself I had to put the troll on report the next morning. I didn't bother putting the Cork lads on report; they had shaken hands and promised no more trouble, and I trusted them.

The governor knew I didn't start trouble. I was a straight guy and he trusted me. He was horrified.

'Who attacked you? Bring him in.'

Next thing, Big Dwarf walked in. The governor looked up at me, looked down at Big Dwarf, and said, 'You better tell me what happened.'

I was giving him a brief outline when Big Dwarf interrupted.

'Governor, I wouldn't hit this big man. He was above fighting with two prisoners and I came running down and I shouted, "Everyone come and help the screw! Help the screw!"'

This caught me off-guard and I hurried the prisoner out of the office.

'I think we should let him off this time,' I muttered.

'I think we should,' agreed the governor.

So Big Dwarf went off up the stairs and I gave him twenty fags afterwards. He was happy enough. To this day, I still don't know if he was telling the truth or not.

————

Most of the Limerick prisoners were like Big Dwarf: they came in, did their time, then went away. But some of the Dublin lads wanted you to do the time for them.

'Oh, Mr Bray, it's an awful bleedin' shithole,' they'd complain.

Or you'd hear from a southerner: 'I want to be down in Cork, like. What am I doing up here?'

But the Limerick prisoners just got on with it. And the other prisoners in Ireland were afraid of them. Even the weakest and most innocent of Limerick men commanded respect in other prisons. We've had some tough Dubs, and they were very nervous at first when told they were coming down to Limerick.

'Mr Bray, what's it like down there?' they'd ask, as I was escorting them down.

'It's grand, man. It's lovely.'

'Fuck off – what's it really like?'

Tough men lose a lot of their hardness inside. It's not just fear. If you are outside with three or four fellows and you've had ten pints and a bit of hash, you're afraid of no one. But it's a different story if you're on your own with no place to run. If they tried it on, we could press a button and a load of blokes would come, and they were going to lose. But still, they did it, and I often wondered why – why start a row they knew they were going to lose?

They'd say, 'I'm not going into the cell.'

'Man, for crying out loud, you're going into the cell. I'm going to turn my back and count to ten, and you better be in when I turn back.'

But no. So I'd have to press the button, and the next thing he's in a world of pain and fear and noise and I'm standing there restraining him and saying, 'What the hell did you want this for?'

I realise now he was playing out the only scenario in his life that he'd ever had control over, which was getting the shit kicked out of him by everyone he knew, everyone he loved, everyone he went to school with, everyone he met on the way home and everyone he met at home. This was what he could control. I wasn't in control at all. From a psychological point of view, it holds up. He was doing a repeatable thing with a predictable result. It was better than the mind-numbing boredom of looking at a wall. And he could always say, 'It took six fucking screws to bring me down. Six of the fuckers.'

The truth is, it doesn't take too many men to bring one fellow down. But if they take their clothes off, it becomes a lot more difficult. It's almost impossible – you can't get a grip on them. Thankfully, that didn't happen too often.

One fellow we had from Carlow had killed a man who lived in a caravan on waste ground in the town. This was almost thirty years ago. I knew the man from when I was a child, as I had relatives down there. The killer was caught because he left his wallet behind, but he got off on a technicality. He left Carlow and went to England. He killed someone there too, but this time he didn't get off. He got a life sentence and was transferred to Ireland to serve it under the repatriation scheme. He wound up with us.

He was big and tough and full of anger. I had him in the kitchen and, a couple of times he got very angry. There was a big stirring ladle that I kept close by, and the prisoners would say to me, 'Are you nervous, Mr Bray?'

'Not a bit of it.'

'So why have you got the spoon with you?'

The ladle was four feet long with a wooden handle, and I held on to it. If he got out of control, he was going nowhere. It was just common sense and self-defence on my part.

This man went on hunger strike and I was asked to speak to him. It was nothing to do with me, but I went down to his cell anyway.

'Can I come in?' I asked at the door.

'Are you on your own?'

'Yes.'

'Come in, so.'

He told me he was on hunger strike and he gave me a long list of reasons.

'How long have you served?' I asked.

'Fifteen years.'

'Do you know when you should have started this hunger strike? Fifteen fucking years ago. What's the use of dying now when you're almost through the whole thing?'

He looked at me for a moment, then nodded.

'You're right. Tell them I'm off it,' he said. Problem sorted.

About four months later, the prisoner fell down inside in the cell. Officers found him on the floor. The medical officer went in to check that he was all right. He caught the medical officer with one large hand and dragged him down.

'Hold me, Officer. Don't leave me on my own,' he whispered, then died in the officer's arms.

The governor had decided that when a prisoner died in prison or committed suicide, the parents would be allowed in to see the place. This man's mother came in and I was asked to bring her around. She was a lovely woman. At the end of the tour, she turned to me and said, 'How long more do you have to do?'

I was about to reply that I had ten years till retirement when I realised she thought I was an inmate. I got a lot of slagging over that.

Chapter 22
Piss Pots and Punches

Prison has taught me that violence works. That is a sad reflection on us as a species, but it's undeniable. The IRA fought their way into the Dáil and Stormont. The Israelis fought their way to their own country. Yugoslavia is split into three parts now because of violence. And violence works in prison. If an inmate has the name of a hard man, he'll be left alone. And that applies to us too. If a prisoner challenges our authority, we must meet that challenge on the landing, not by putting him on report the following morning.

Although I wasn't a brave man, it was better to have never shirked from those challenges. I was hoping I could look after myself. The attitude of a violent man was a different matter. There are very few naturally violent men, and I'm lucky enough not to be one of them. They are the monsters, the psychopaths who can't switch it off. The rest of us have to work at the violence.

What I found was that after the first few fights, the fear became less and less. In reality, it's difficult for one unarmed man to do much real damage to another unarmed man. All you suffer are cuts and bruises, and they heal, so I wasn't too afraid to get stuck in. My attitude was that if you attacked us, we would respond at once. Today, as the years have taken their toll, my attitude is that if you take me on and I lose, I'll get a few bob as compensation. An element of doubt has crept in with advancing years, though. Perhaps it's as well I'm retired.

We make rules to survive inside. The first is that if you don't interfere with me, I won't interfere with you. Another rule is that the prisoners' living conditions are my working conditions, so it's in my interest to make those conditions as good as possible. By my rules, I get the same money for standing around doing nothing as I get from rolling on the ground with a prisoner, so I will avoid unnecessary confrontation. There has to be discipline, so that's where the confrontation comes from. But it's never personal.

Limerick had a more laid-back approach than the rest of Ireland's prisons. I have walked down the town with my wife and not get hassled. A chief can come in and find us reading the paper and ask how things are going. When we say all quiet, he knows that we know what's going on, and it's all quiet. One chief transferred from Cork to Limerick and on his first day saw three officers standing around drinking coffee. He later told me he almost put them on report, but he let it go. Now he joins them with the coffee because he sees the prison works like a Swiss watch. But you shouldn't confuse easy-going with weak.

Many prisoners made that mistake, but they usually weren't from Limerick, and it wasn't a mistake they made twice. When the Dubs came down first, they had to learn the hard way. They thought we were pushovers, so they pushed – but we didn't go over. What prisoners hated – and what myself and other officers hated – was the kicker. He was the sneak that stuck in a boot when no one was looking. If I was tussling with a prisoner, he would get behind us and kick the prisoner on the back or bring down a baton on his head. No one would know who did it. The problem was that I was the last face the prisoner saw and he'd go away rubbing a sore head and saying, 'I didn't think Mr Bray would do that.'

Mr Bray wouldn't – and he didn't.

But the kicker was my colleague and we stood together. I couldn't run after the prisoner and say, 'It wasn't me who kicked you.' What could I do? Kickers were sneaky, cowardly bastards, but they were rare. Why didn't they understand that when a guy is down, what the hell do you want to hit him for? The game was over.

Unfortunately, violence is getting more and more common in prison, and it's generally between prisoners. When the alarm sounded, I assumed it was two prisoners fighting, and nine times out of ten I was right. However, prisoners do attack officers. It has happened and there are horror stories. Today, there is a compensation scheme in place for officers injured by prisoners. When I joined first, there wasn't – and we wouldn't have wanted it. You would be ashamed to admit that a prisoner had blackened your eye.

Prisoners are entitled to look for compensation too if they get injured inside for any reason. We have an obligation to provide them with safe custody. Quite a lot of the cases are thrown out of court, as judges realise it's impossible to swaddle the inmates in cotton wool.

If one prisoner wants to get another prisoner, there are ways. One is to get boiling water from a kettle and put sugar in it. The prisoner waits until his target is in bed, then rushes in, pulls back the covers and tries to cover as much skin as possible with the scalding mix. Adding sugar means the boiling water sticks to the skin and the damage is far worse. A couple of those cases came to court, with the prisoners claiming we hadn't provided safe custody, but the judge said that the man in charge of the landing did all that could be expected of him if he was in charge of thirty people. An attack takes place over a couple of seconds, and it's unreasonable to expect one officer to be able to prevent every incident. After that judgment, compo claims went down.

But in recent years, a whole new set of claims have started going through the courts: hundreds of prisoners are claiming compensation for having to slop out – which is having to use a pot in the cell at night and having to empty it into the toilet in the morning. This happens because the older cells don't have their own toilets. The cells on c and d Class, which have been completely refurbished and modernised, have toilets, but a and b Class are still relics of Victorian rule and are furnished accordingly.

In 1980, I brought my father to New York to visit his brother, Bill. Bill had been on the losing side of the civil war in Ireland and refused to recognise the Irish state. He wouldn't open letters from Ireland or answer phone calls or even take the IRA pension he was entitled to. My father hadn't seen him for forty years. I knew my uncle had been locked up in Limerick Prison as a young member of the IRA, so I wasn't sure of the reception I would get from him. But Bill turned out to be a wonderful and welcoming man.

We spent hours talking into the night and when I described Limerick Prison to him as it was that day, he was amazed – it was exactly the same as it was when he had been there as a young boy of sixteen. Nothing at all had changed, it seemed. They were put fifteen in a cell and the cell doors were left open. A water-cooled Lewis machine gun was mounted at the end of each landing. He said you had to put your hand out if you wanted to go the toilet and say, 'Going to the toilet, Boss,' and an English voice would call out, 'All roight, mate, one at a time, make it smart.'

Slopping out still happens on A and B Class, the same as when I joined. All prisoners in those cells get a piss pot, but they don't have to use it – there are toilet unlocks. If a person bangs on the door after eight and says he needs to do his business, we let him out, but we are slow to do it after a certain time. By then, they have had loads of opportunities.

So in the morning, you have forty-six prisoners trooping down a landing four and a half feet wide, their pots brimming over with piss and shit. At the end is an officer guarding the toilet. They troop past him and pour their pots down the toilet, clean them out at the tap there, then go back to the cells. The toilet on A Class is beside the kitchen. There is a big slop hopper (or sink) with two taps. Prisoners have no taps in their cells, so they fill empty Coke bottles and bring them back as their drinking water – not the most hygienic of systems. Every morning ,they come in with the piss pot in one hand and the Coke bottle in the other. Seven years into the new millennium, on the day I left the job, I looked out of the kitchen and into the toilet and that is what I saw: a guy emptying his piss pot at the hopper and putting his Coke bottle in underneath to get water.

Prisoners have a problem with slopping out. As you can imagine, it must be demeaning to be walking around with the contents of your bowel and bladder in a tin container first thing in the morning. I also think it's a serious hygiene problem. In fact, three days before I retired, some gouger blocked the toilet in A Class and flushed it so that the place was covered in piss. Word went out that if any prisoner cleaned it up, they would be slashed, so an officer had to do it. I was in charge of the kitchen on the day, so that officer was me. It was either get on with it and mop it or let that slop get into my spotless kitchen, so I got a squeegee and pushed the mess back into the toilet.

Another problem with slopping out is that a lot of prisoners have HIV, TB and other infectious diseases. Some have hepatitis and their body fluids were slopped all over the place. We were very aware of the possibility of contamination by contact with these fluids. Occasionally, it got on you, and that was disgusting. The only plus side was that you would get a new uniform, and if the old uniform wasn't too badly damaged, you would have a spare. But being sloshed with piss was right up there with spitting – we treated it as a deliberate affront. If someone spat at you, you reacted straight away, no debate about it. Any physical contact was the same; to maintain discipline, it had to be treated as a challenge. One time, a fellow came up behind me and stuck a finger in my back and said, 'Hands up.' I spun around ready to defend myself. I didn't wait for a jury to decide whether he was joking or not. He was joking and he was horrified by my reaction, but he never did it again, which is what I wanted.

Fortunately, it's rare enough that a prisoner will lose the head and throw a full piss pot, but an empty one is often used as a weapon – they are made of brushed steel. If you got a belt of a piss pot on the back of the head, you would know all about it. The first question you'd ask was: was it full? The contents are more dangerous than the pot itself.

I have been very lucky – I only had a pot upended on me twice in thirty years. One fellow claimed it was an accident, but I didn't accept that. The second one was deliberate, but it wasn't aimed at me. It was aimed at another officer, and I only got some of the contents.

The first chamber pot landed on me in 1980. The prisoner was on remand and I never knew what he was in for. He could have been charged with rape, murder, anything – even simple pickpocketing. A fellow bumped off me and spilled his piss down my leg. Using my skill and judgement, I decided it was deliberate. I could walk down a narrow landing with a pile of prisoners coming against me and I don't have to turn or move. None of them bumped off me. Not by accident.

The prisoner denied it was deliberate, but he was smirking at me. When I spoke to him about it, he attacked me. It was very confined – fighting surrounded by a room full of guys all holding on to their pots – but we went for each other. Instant reaction. There were a couple of punches thrown and then he was down and the fight was over. There wasn't a mark or a scar on either of us and he never threw a pot at me again. The spectators went about their business. Funny how they managed not to spill a drop while a wild fracas broke around them.

The following morning, I put my man on report for attacking me – a precaution in case he or I were injured. In his defence, he said he didn't mean to do it, but he never did it again in the seven months he was there.

In the mid-1990s, a second rain of piss hit me, though that one was aimed at a different officer. We were on the ground floor of B Class. A whole lot of fellows were getting stuff in the tuck shop. Suddenly, dirty liquid came spraying down on top of me and my colleague, and above us we could hear laughing. But stupid me, I thought someone was after throwing lemonade at us. Why would someone throw a piss pot?

Apparently, they wanted to get the officer next to me. He had stopped a visit for one of the prisoners a week earlier and the guy had said he would get him. We went up to find out who did it. They all denied it, but we found the guy. We had a few quiet words with him, he went away and he never threw a pot at us again.

Slopping out is something that the governor would love to be rid of. He would love to run a modern jail with toilets and washing facilities in each cell and we would love to patrol that prison. But it's a question of money and priorities. You can't always get what you want.

In Mountjoy, they have a policy that the doors will be opened any time a prisoner needs to use the toilet, so for the past ten years, they have eliminated slopping out. Most Limerick prisoners would prefer to use the chamber pot rather than bang on the door and wait ten minutes for an officer to bellow, 'What do you want?'

With slopping out becoming a legal and human rights issue, I believe an officer should put in a claim. I have had gallons of piss and tons of shit pass my nose in thirty years, and maybe I should get some compensation.

There were other dangers, too. Just two nights before the first chamber pot hit me, I had an encounter with a man from Kerry, on remand for murder. He was huge, and strong with it. I was in the cage on A Class giving out the breakfasts when he took offence to something I said.

'You wouldn't say that if the gate was open,' he said.

Like a fool, I opened the gate, and he caught me under the chin with a peach of a punch. I was knocked back. But you learn from that.

The Kerry man had hit me with his left hand. He had a teapot full of boiling water in his right. I picked myself up and said, 'Put down that tea and we'll have a fair fight.'

Of course, as soon as he turned to put down the tea I clocked him. I caught him on the chin with my knee – sorry, no Queensbury rules here – and this time it was his turn to hit the floor.

I met him about four months later. He was doing life. I was on my own with about twenty prisoners in the yard, next thing I know, the

Kerry giant struggled out. I thought we were going to dance again, so I got into a defensive mode, getting my feet in the right position. He walked up to me and put his hand out.

'Jesus, you have a great right hook,' he said. He didn't realise I had kneed him on the chin. We got on great after that.

You learn to be ready – and I got a lesson that time. Paradoxically, you also have to learn to switch off. I would always switch off if a prisoner was mouthing off. He could be on a rant, working himself up into a fury about some perceived slight or wrong, but I knew it had nothing to do with me. I was the target of the anger sometimes, but never the cause, so I learned not to listen. Instead, I would watch his body language. I couldn't care less what he said; it went right over my head. I was just looking, waiting, judging, and wondering if he was going to go for me. I had switched down the volume. There was no sound, just the fury, but if he made a move towards me, I had to be ready.

We had to give them a free shot, and I hated that. We had to let them take the first punch, even if we could see it coming. That way, we were defending ourselves. But though I hated it, it gave us a certain righteousness.

Normally in a violent situation, the alarm will be sounded to bring in reinforcements. Often, the alarm was set off before the fight because you could see it coming. It was easy to be brave if you knew the cavalry were on the way. But, in fairness, that was hardly ever abused. In my experience, it was rare for an officer to attack a prisoner. We would take or dodge the first hit before we responded. Most of us are not violent people, even though we are capable of violence. We use violence in our jobs. Real violent people are a different breed.

It's a strange thing – I wouldn't be brave enough to start a fight, but I am cowardly enough to finish it. As a prison officer, I can't afford not to have the last word. Discipline would break down.

We hear a lot of threats, but very few are carried out. I have had guys look me in the eye and say, 'I am going to rape your wife, I am going to rape your daughter and then I'm going to come back and do you.'

I would just smile and say, 'Would you ever cop yourself on? You couldn't even organise a piss-up in a brewery. And be careful the next time you give me lip. I mightn't be in such good humour then.'

It's not a big thing; it's disgusting, that's all. It's like a prisoner throwing a punch at you. But a lot of these prisoners are cowardly. In the middle of the night, surrounded by their mates, or on a street with their friends, they're very brave. But they're not so brave when they're on their own facing a man who is six feet tall and able to take care of himself, who can press a button and bring a whole world of pain and misery down on them.

———

There are very few genuinely tough guys, either officers or prisoners, when it comes down to it. And I wouldn't count myself among them. A truly tough man is as rare as a truly violent, evil man. Some of the toughest guys we had inside had played a lot of sports and had probably instigated a lot of violence on the pitch. You would see indications of that in other aspects of their lives too. Often what a prisoner is in for will give you an indication of his capacity for inflicting violence. If they have done it before, there is a possibility they will do it again. There are people who often attacked officers, but we would have them marked down. There would be no hesitation about getting stuck into those guys if they started something.

Over the years, our initial lack of training was more than made up for by our experience on the job. We had dealt with the IRA, the Dublin Mafia, the feuding Limerick gangs and the Prisoners' Revenge Group. Then, management decided we needed to be trained to tackle the big stuff. In the early 1990s, a number of us were chosen for riot training.

This was fantastic. I was still fit enough to really enjoy the most physical workout I had had in years. Training consisted of hand-to-hand combat, followed by the most realistic of simulations.

We were trained in how to tackle a single troublesome prisoner. Prior to this, we tended to rush in, all getting in each other's way. Now we had a procedure. We tackled violent offenders in teams of four. The first man came charging forward behind a large Perspex shield and pinned the troublemaker to the wall. Men two and three grabbed an arm each while the fourth man went for the legs. Then, the man with the shield could back away; the situation was under control, with no one, including the prisoner, injured.

That procedure could be adapted for everyday use without the riot gear. If a prisoner needed to be restrained, one of us would go for each arm and a third would take the legs; situation sorted.

After the hand-to-hand training, we moved on to riot simulations. We were being trained in an army facility which could be made up to look like a prison landing. I remember our first simulation. We were issued with full body armour. It was like getting dressed up as a medieval knight – we could have been hit with axes and we wouldn't have felt it.

Over the body armour, we wore flame-retardant black overalls and we topped off the ensemble with a crash helmet and shatterproof visor. In place of a sword, we used a police nightstick, a long baton with a side handle which could be used both offensively and defensively.

As I was standing there waiting for the exercise to begin, one of the training officers shouted, 'Fab, look out!' Then he swung a broom handle viciously at me.

Reacting instinctively, I raised my arm to block the blow. The wooden handle caught me square on the forearm – and shattered. I didn't feel a thing. He grabbed another stick and swung it at my chest. He hit me with all his force and the second stick broke. I felt I was invincible.

Two guys were selected to be the rioting prisoners and were sent upstairs. Our job was to storm the stairs, but to storm it like a disciplined force of Roman soldiers. We were trained to act like the Roman tortoise, marching behind our shields. Those at the front of the attack held their shields forward. Those behind them held their shields over their heads, making a moving phalanx of men who couldn't be stoned, poked or assaulted. That was the theory. We were about to put it to the test.

The whistle blew and we charged. I was in the second row and my shield was over my head. A hail of missiles rained down on us – bits of furniture, shoes and old tin cans. Then, there was an almighty clatter and my shield shook but didn't give way. Through the thick, transparent Perspex, I saw a flash of yellow and realised that one of the men upstairs had lobbed down a big gas cylinder. But it had bounced off harmlessly. Moving inexorably forward in tight formation, we were like a tank.

I felt great, but after the gas cylinder, I braced myself, ready for anything. Up we went. We swarmed the landing and the riot was over.

We had been trained to use grappling hooks to remove barricades, and this had proved to be very effective.

Over and over, we practised this simulation until we were perfect – and our arms were hanging off us with exhaustion.

After the day's training, we retired to the pub for the post-mortem.

'You're a mad bastard, Fab,' said one of my colleagues, who had been an upstairs rioter.

'Why's that?'

'When I jumped on you and landed on your shield, you just kept coming. I rode up those stairs standing on your shield like a surfer!'

We found out afterwards that our simulation had breached all regulations. It was phase two of our training, and we should have only been pelted with shoes and slippers. Later phases involved handling fire and smoke, but they were cancelled after a couple of trials. I was too old for the later training. Looking at how phase two went, perhaps they had a point.

When they returned to the prison, they were ready for anything. They were the Men in Black, ninja warriors ready for anyone.

Chapter 23
The Charming Conman

Of course, not all the prisoners were violent – some were surprisingly gentle souls. One day, Barry, a colleague, told me that there was a French prisoner on B Class whom I might be able to persuade to work in the kitchen. It wasn't that his French heritage would guarantee a good chef; it was just that I was trying to bone up on the language. A Belgian prisoner had been transferred to Mountjoy, leaving me with no one to practise on.

'What's his name?'

'Jack Deverioux – he's a conman,' Barry grinned. 'He's doing six months, if he behaves himself.'

I went up to B Class to check him out. Six months was just what I needed to polish my French.

'Jack Deverioux,' I bellowed, putting a Gallic spin on the pronunciation.

'Yeah – who's asking?' came a reply with rather less of the Gallic than I expected.

'*Jack, vous aiment travailler dans la cuisine?*' I asked in my best French.

'What?' came the startled reply.

Bugger, I thought. *I must not have said that right. I'll try again.*

'*Voulez-vous un travail fonctionnant dans la cuisine?*' I shouted, adding a bit of volume to make up for the shaky pronunciation.

'What?'

'Come down here, I want a word with you.' I was getting tired of roaring at this surprised man. A skinny, grey-haired man in his fifties came down to me, looking a bit wary.

'What do you want, Officer?' he asked cautiously. I began to wonder if the guys were having a joke at my expense.

'You're not French, are you, Jack?'

'No – what would make you think that, Sir?'

'I'm sorry. I was told you spoke French.'

'I do, a bit,' he said.

'Great,' I said, adding under my breath, 'A bit is better than nothing.'

'*Combien de français avez-vous?*' I said, hoping for any kind of a response.

'I don't understand what you're saying, Sir,' he replied.

'How much French do you know?' I snapped.

'Crème de Menthe.'

'Is that it?'

'*Oui*, Monsieur Bray. But I'm a quick learner,' he grinned.

'Come on then, Jack, you're a kitchen worker now,' I said, warming to the cheeky fellow.

I always had a soft spot for conmen, and of all the conmen I've met, I consider Jack to be the best. Conmen are usually non-violent, very intelligent and very personable. Jack was all these and more. Born in a small town in County Galway in the late 1950s, he got a young girl pregnant and did a runner. He ended up in London and tried his hand at the building trade, the old stand-by for Irishmen in the big smoke. But Jack wasn't cut out for hard labour and soon started on the scams.

He began by stealing a pick-up truck from a huge building site. He changed two numbers on the registration plate and had transport that was so innocent it was unnoticeable – perfect for the scam merchant. He drove around the city looking for road works outside shops or restaurants or offices, small jobs such as gas and electricity maintenance. When he found the right spot, he would get out of the pick-up with an accomplice and begin walking the site, pointing to poles and wires and cables. Once he was sure that he had been spotted, he would enter a shop or restaurant and ask for the proprietor.

'We're doing some work outside and we need to cut off your electricity for a short while,' he'd begin. He would have chosen his time carefully: just before lunch at a busy restaurant, for example. The proprietor would be horrified.

'I can put it off an hour, but I need to see your fuse board,' he'd continue.

Owners were always willing to comply and the fuse boards were usually in the office, or near enough. Jack would look at the fuse board, then say, 'Give me ten or fifteen minutes, and I mightn't have to cut the power at all.'

The delighted owner would go away and leave him in peace. Of course, Jack didn't bother with the fuse board; he searched for valuables. Often cash was lying around, and more often than you would imagine, the safe was lying open. This was because the safes back then had very heavy, secure doors with stiff locks. Once they were opened in the morning, they tended to be left open. Jack would take his time and clean out the office before slipping away before anyone copped that he wasn't part of the road works team outside the premises.

He told us about one scam that we were never really sure was true, but it went something like this. When they were bringing the natural gas line from Cork up through Ireland, Jack and some of his friends would approach farmers whose field the gas line was going through. They would offer to connect him to the gas line, therefore guaranteeing him free gas for life, for £3,000. A narrow trench would be dug up across the farmer's fields to his house and a gas pipe would be fitted to his cooker or his central heating system. The appliance was turned on and it worked perfectly. The farmer was delighted. A couple months later, the cooker would stop working and the farmer would trace back along the line to see if there was a leakage or a blockage. What he found at the bottom of his field near the main pipe was three big cylinders of bottled gas that were empty. He wasn't connected to the pipeline at all and, of course, he had no one to complain to. Jack always said you can't con an honest man – it's only someone who wants something for nothing, or less than nothing, who you can catch.

Another favourite scam of his was selling knock-down cigarettes to publicans. This didn't work too well in England because all the pubs were run by managers who answered to the breweries, but, in Ireland, he felt some unscrupulous publicans could be easy game, always willing to bend the rules if it meant a few extra quid in their back pocket.

Jack would find a house in some nondescript Dublin housing estate with a good shed in the back. He'd make sure the house was unoccupied, then phone around a few pubs until one of the landlords bit. He'd offer him a consignment of cigarettes which had 'fallen off the back of a lorry' at a price the publican couldn't refuse. But it had to be cash upfront, Jack explained, because he had been stung by a few bouncy cheques.

He would lead the unsuspecting publican to the house he had cased and show him the shed. He was always very friendly – it threw them off the scent.

'Back your van up to the shed there – I'll go in and open the gate for you,' he'd say as the publican handed over the money. As often as not, Jack didn't bother to count it.

'I trust you're being straight with me,' he'd smile, then he'd nip around the back to go and open the gate. Only he didn't open the gate – he kept going through the house and got into his car. He would be well away before the publican realised he had been had.

'They never reported me to the cops. They had too much to lose by admitting they were trying to buy cheap cigarettes,' he told me. 'Never' is an exaggeration, though – a few publicans did report him, and he did do time for that particular scam.

Like most conmen, Jack had a talent for passing dud cheques. About once or twice a month, he'd get hold of a stolen chequebook. He'd pick a Sunday and travel around the country, visiting petrol stations along the way. The owners were rarely in on Sundays – they would be off at a football match or playing golf or just relaxing with their family. The stations were manned by young relatives or inexperienced employees. Jack would boldly walk in and strike up a conversation, making out he was a good friend of the owner. After a few minutes, he'd ask them to cash a cheque for him. Nothing too big – perhaps £50 or £100 – and quite often they would cash it in the mistaken belief he was a friend of their boss.

'On a good run I could clear £1,000,' Jack boasted. 'But I was always careful not to revisit the same garages. I didn't want to be known for passing bad cheques.'

I looked at him with incredulity. 'I can't get cheques cashed in garages where they know me, and you're telling me they'll cash cheques for you, a complete stranger?'

'Ah, but Mr Bray, you look like a conman,' he grinned.

Jack finished his time with us and went on his merry way. But it wasn't the last I saw of him. He was a habitual offender and he reappeared on B Class regularly down the years. I always enjoyed his company. Unfortunately, though, he was an alcoholic and had a chronic inability to hold on to what he had. He often found himself without a place to stay, and rather than sleep rough he would go to a Garda station and ask them to put him in a cell for the night. Normally they'd run him, so he would break a couple of windows on one of the squad cars. That would get their attention and he would be arrested. 'It would have been cheaper if you had taken me in at the beginning,' he'd say.

Jack told me that he was known at a number of police stations both in Ireland and the UK, and many of them would put him up for the night when he asked rather than have to face all the broken glass in the morning.

Over the years, Jack began to lose his charm as the booze took its toll. It became more and more difficult for him to con anyone, and as he couldn't do any physical work, he had to rely on the charity of the state. It was soul-destroying for him to have to live in hostels and bed-sits without any family or support. The burden of the wasted years began to eat away at him.

During his last sentence in Limerick, we got a phone call to go to a local hostel and pick up his belongings. An officer went down to the B&B and collected two black plastic bags, one large and one small, which held all of Jack's life's possessions. When the bags were brought into the prison reception and checked, it was found that the smaller one held nothing but some women's underwear. Jack said that he'd picked them up by mistake and that they were meant to go to the laundry, but some wag put it out that there were clothes pegs in the bag and that he'd nicked the undies off a line. He got a terrible slagging over that.

During that final sentence, I saw a huge change in Jack. He wasn't eating and stayed in his cell for days on end. We became very concerned about him, but couldn't cajole him out of the dumps. The old sparkle in his eye was gone and the bounce in his step was no more. The worst thing for a conman is to lose his confidence.

It was with great sadness that I heard last year that Jack stole a couple of Valium and a bicycle and cycled into the River Lee in Cork. In the end, the ones who mourned his passing the most were the ones charged with keeping him under lock and key.

And I will always regret that I didn't manage to teach him a single word of French.

Chapter 24
Up on the Roof

In the 1990s, a new trend hit that certainly broke the monotony of a working week, but that didn't mean we welcomed it. A rooftop protest is no fun for anyone. It's dangerous and messy, and if you handle it wrong and a prisoner falls, then you're in real trouble. Fortunately, they are rare; I was only involved in two in my thirty years of service.

The first happened on 24 April 1990. I suppose that one was inevitable. At the time, there was a huge rooftop protest going on in Strangeways Prison in Manchester, with a whole pile of prisoners camped out under the stars for over a month. It was on the radio every day and the pictures were filling up acres of newspaper space.

The Strangeways protest was in its thirty-fifth day when we had our equivalent. Four Limerick prisoners broke out onto the roof of D Class. They managed to break open a trap door into the attic and they clambered up. I have no idea why. I asked one of the four afterwards and he just shrugged and said, 'I followed the other two up. I don't know why.'

After they got into the attic, it was a simple job to break through the slates and get onto the roof. It was a fine afternoon and it must have seemed like a lark – until they looked down at a forty-foot drop onto concrete. That was a bit hairy.

Of course, it wasn't long before they were spotted. We were immediately on high alert and we all swung into action. I was in charge of B Class that afternoon and I locked up all my charges. That left me free to come and help. I took charge of the D Class prisoners who were not involved in the protest and brought them over to the B yard, which got them out of the way for a while. I later brought them back for their tea, then locked them up and went to assist in ending the protest.

Of the four prisoners who went on the roof, two came down almost immediately. I couldn't blame them – forty feet up and looking down on cold concrete was not a place I would have wanted to spend too much time. The governor and the chief appealed to the other two to come down, but they refused. They said they were going to stay up until conditions improved on D Class. They had brought up a bag of food and water, so we had to take them seriously.

We were all a bit edgy because we knew how long the Strangeways situation had been dragging on. Some officers decided we needed to do more than shout up at them to come down, so around five of us got through the trap door and went into the attic ourselves.

Our aim was to make life uncomfortable for the prisoners, to make them think it would be better to come down, so we began to poke batons through the slates. The prisoners had made a large hole in the centre of the roof and, by poking our heads through, we could see them clearly. But, obviously, they could see us and throw things down on us. How could we sneak up on them?

The governor unwittingly provided our distraction. While he was talking up at them and they were shouting down at him, one daring officer made a snatch and grabbed their bag of provisions. We were making a rooftop sleepover a lot less attractive – they were without food, drink, jackets or coats and we weren't going to give them anything, so the longest the protest could last was however long they could survive cold and hungry.

While this was going on, I managed to make a hole in the roof near one gable end while some other officers managed to do the same at the other end. This was done to restrict their movements and to impress upon them the futility of their protest: we weren't going to just watch them.

The negotiations went on throughout the afternoon, but we couldn't find out what they wanted. They kept changing their minds and we quickly realised that this was an aimless protest. They had spotted an opportunity for devilment and had taken it, with no plan in mind. The stalemate dragged on into the afternoon.

At one point, the governor and the chief withdrew for a few minutes. An officer took that opportunity to act. Without warning, he ran out onto the roof, closely followed by two others. The prisoners were caught unawares, but reacted with typical bravado. As the first officer approached them, one prisoner shouted, 'I'll drag you down into the fucking yard with me!'

'No you won't, Sonny,' the officer replied as he laid hold of him and shoved him towards us at the hole in the roof. Holding him firmly by the shoulder, he pushed him down towards us waiting officers. We grabbed him and dragged him into the attic.

The second prisoner began to throw slates at the three officers on the roof. The first officer went at him with a shield, then pushed him down towards us. We leaned up and began to pull him inside.

The second prisoner seemed to be resisting. Tempers were running high and he got a few clips as we tried to drag him inside. Then I noticed that his leg had got caught in one of the rafters. I released his leg and he went down without further protest. The situation was over.

What none of us realised at the time was that the governor and the chief were in a state. They had been walking away from the yard and heading for the governor's office when they heard a commotion. They looked up and saw three officers running across the roof, then the two prisoners dropped from view. They thought the worst – that the prisoners were sprawled on the concrete, a mangled mess in the D yard. They didn't realise that they had been dragged in through the hole in the roof. They came running back to D class in a hurry, but the situation was resolved. It was shortly before five and we were knocking off for a break.

We returned to duty and nothing was mentioned officially, but as we were going over the events months later, I asked the first officer who ran across the roof what had possessed him to do such a foolhardy thing.

He said, 'I was on eight to five, and I wasn't going to stay late that day. I had two days off and was heading away with the wife and kids. If that bloody protest had gone past five, my time off was at risk. So it wasn't going beyond five.'

'Are you seriously telling me you risked life and limb to get off at five?'

'We don't get many days when we get off at five,' he said.

That's how precious those free days were to us. What was even more extraordinary was the reaction of the prison management to our successful intervention. Nothing was ever said. No one in authority spoke to the officers involved. There was no praise, no condemnation. It was never mentioned again. At least not to my knowledge.

The only official reaction I received was a call from the assistant secretary general of the Prison Officers' Association, demanding to know if all officers had to risk their own lives from now on. Did I not know the risks? We had set a dangerous precedent for other riots. What were we up to in Limerick?

It amused me to read the papers the following day: all the pictures of us prison officers risking our lives on the roof were mislabelled Gardaí. We got no credit. And the Minister for Justice, Ray Bourke, who ended up getting to know the prison service rather more intimately that he might have wished, was quoted as praising the governor for his 'quick resolution' of the situation.

In the yard that following afternoon, I chatted with the two prisoners we had dragged down as they played handball. Neither could tell me why they had done it, but they had no hard feelings about the way we ended it. Even now, years later, if I meet one of them I'll shout, 'Are you doing any climbing today?'

'Not today,' they laugh.

But the POA general secretary was right: our spontaneous action in Limerick did set a precedent. A few weeks later, some prisoners got onto the roof of Mountjoy and the prison officers were instructed by the Minister to go out onto the roof and bring them in. So the officers in Mountjoy climbed onto the roof and began removing slates one at a time, passing them back along to other officers who stacked them neatly in the attic. Within a short time, nothing remained of the roof and the prisoners had no place left to go. They had no option but to come down. Then the trades officers quickly replaced the tiles and rebuilt the roof.

Months passed and I spotted an unusual memento in the governor's office – a slate with an engraving from Strangeways Prison. They had obviously been in contact with him, presumably praising him for his speedy resolution of our rooftop protest. But, as far as I know, he never passed the praise on to the men who had ended the protest.

———

Eighteen months later, another group of prisoners managed to get onto the roof, but this time the situation was a lot more serious. These were hardened criminals from Dublin and they couldn't be intimidated, bullied or pushed back inside. They were some of the toughest prisoners we ever dealt with. They were prepared to take us on physically at any time and most of them had spent hours training in the gym.

Around that time, I was in charge of the gym, and as part of my duties we set out circuits for the prisoners to do. Occasionally, the prisoners would challenge me or one of the other officers to complete the circuits with them. I was fit enough, and once I started the circuits there was no way I was going to admit to not being able to keep up with the inmates. Likewise, none of them were going to give up and admit a screw was their better. This led to some savage training sessions, and we gym officers became quite fit.

Unfortunately, the prisoners became quite fit too. It was some of these men who managed to break a hole near the ceiling of a cell on the top floor of A Class. It was quite a small hole, just above the window, but it was enough for these daring gymnasts.

One by one, they squirmed out on their backs, facing the sky. Their companions held on to their legs as they got out of the cell, with a forty-foot drop below them if that grip loosened. Once they were halfway out, they had to reach up to the gutter, then pull themselves completely out. That left them hanging by their fingertips and they had to clamber up over the gutter and on to the roof. It was a far more daring feat than that of the Limerick guys who had come through the attic.

There were eight of them on the roof, and they were all serious men. Needless to say, none of us were planning on running out after them. It was 4:30 P.M. on a warm Tuesday when they broke out. We could see that this was no whim; they had brought food and water with them. Luckily, they hadn't been able to stockpile too much, but they were prepared to sit it out for more than a token few hours.

The eight were in great humour, laughing, cheering, shouting and jeering at the lads underneath who had missed the chance to get out. As word began to filter through the prison of their daring action, the prisoners in the A and D yard began throwing them up food, so we cleared both yards fast and kept them clear until the situation was resolved.

That took a full three days. They slept out on the exposed roof for three nights with nothing but their prison clothes to keep out the cold. During that time, we were on full alert. The army boxes on the walls of the prison were in the process of being refurbished and were derelict, but the army men were still on the walls among the rubble of their sentry posts. The gable end of A Class was only about fifteen feet away from the soldiers and the prisoners were goading them constantly. The soldiers never rose to the bait and ignored them completely.

As is usual in these situations, the first thing the rooftop prisoners ran out of was cigarettes. They would occasionally shout across to the soldiers for a cigarette, but that didn't produce results.

The roof they were on adjoined the circle. In the roof of the circle was a window which had a hinged panel of bars. We secured this with handcuffs to prevent the prisoners from entering the tower. From the circle, they could have gone anywhere, and then we would have had a real problem. We also occupied that room, along with an armed soldier.

A number of officers were detailed to get blankets and a supply of water and to station themselves in the attic to prevent the protesters from removing slates and getting back inside that way. The first night of the protest, I was one of those officers on attic duty. I spent a miserable night in that hot, airless space, not knowing if the Dubs were going to break down into the attic or not. The second night, I was on duty in the tower, which was more comfortable. I could look out the window and see the eight men and there was an armed soldier with me. A couple of times during the evening, the prisoners slid along the top of the roof and came to the window of the tower. While staying a safe distance away, in case I grabbed one of them, they asked for cigarettes. Occasionally, I tossed one over and they would sit and chat for a while. It was a good-humoured affair, even though we treated it as a serious situation. We certainly felt no anger towards the protesters. I think they had a good supply of hash, which kept their spirits up. During the course of a long night, the soldier fell asleep and was snoring contentedly on the floor. I let him be.

The soldier was armed with a Sauer rifle, which was new to the Irish Army at the time. It was of a bullpup design, made from a plastic compound, and had a fixed sight which magnified 1.5 times. I have always been interested in guns, so I was curious about this new weapon. I picked it up and studied it.

One of the prisoners chose that moment to come scuttling across the slates towards me, bored out of his mind. He was looking for a chat and a fag. I saw his dark shape moving in my direction. Quick as a flash, I raised the rifle and pointed it straight at him.

'Get back or I'll blow your fucking head off,' I growled.

His jaw dropped and he backed away from me, shouting, 'The screw has gone mad! He's going to blow us all away!' With a laugh, I returned the weapon to the sleeping soldier and returned to my guard duty.

Many years later, when I was on a training course in Mountjoy, a group of prisoners under escort passed by me. One of them shouted to me, 'How are you doing, Mr Bray?'

'How do you know him?' asked an ACO who was accompanying him.

'He nearly shot the whole lot of us one night below in Limerick, the mad bastard,' laughed the prisoner.

The protest eventually ended after three days and three nights. The eight men began coming down in dribs and drabs. The last one came inside at 9:30 P.M. on Friday evening, but there's no doubt that the few days of protest generated huge overtime – I didn't spend a night in an attic and a second night in a tower for the good of my health. I was going on my holidays three weeks later. We were off to Australia, which meant that the cheque for that week arrived in my account while I was away. It amounted to a couple of grand, which I spent on a holiday within a holiday – we flew out to a coral reef island for a few days of scuba diving. So the rooftop protest worked out, for me at least.

———

A few months later, the army were gone. They were no longer on the walls and the machine-gun post over the main gate had been removed. The Gardaí had been phased out a bit prior to that. The prison was returned to the officers and the inmates. We were no longer a high-security unit.

Chapter 25

Suicide

Our high-security status might have ended, but we still had to be alert. If you were on nights, particularly inside nights, you had to watch for two things: suicides and escapes. Escapes were a rarity; anyone wanting out waited for a hospital visit or a court appearance or some other suitable opportunity. Thankfully, suicide wasn't common either, but whenever you encountered it, the experience was traumatic.

Peering into a cell through a small spyhole at three in the morning trying to see if someone was alive or dead was nigh on impossible. If a man was asleep in the bed and not moving, how could you tell whether it was slumber or something more sinister? If you flicked the light on and off he might turn over and moan or curse you. This worked early in a man's sentence, but if he had been in for a while, he just slept through that disturbance, leaving you none the wiser.

The spyholes were covered in glass, and, over the years, that got scratched, reducing visibility. Some prisoners smeared the inside with butter or hung a sock over the hole to give them privacy. So what were we to do?

As a rule of thumb, if the spyhole had been obscured, it was for a reason, so we opened the door and found out why. Otherwise, we just flicked on the light and looked in. Over the years, the glass on several of the spyholes became broken and wasn't replaced. This gave us a clearer view, but presented its own problem: a prisoner could be waiting to poke us in the eye when the light came on. It wasn't so bad when the cells were lit by regular bulbs – the light came on too fast, and we could get our look in and remove our eye from the hole – but the cells that had fluorescent bulbs were a problem. The bulb would flicker for several seconds before coming to life, giving a prisoner ample time to get into position.

You had two choices: put your eye to the spyhole as you turned on the switch and wait, looking into the darkness, for it to fire up, or stand back for a few seconds until the cell was illuminated, then look in. This flickering delay annoyed some prisoners and you didn't want a landing full of inmates cursing you. In fact, at one time, management ordered us to wear slippers on the landings at night so as not to wake the prisoners! The Prison Officers' Association went to the governor about this, pointing out that regulations forced us to wear the shoes we were issued with, so he offered us the runners the prisoners got. Needless to say, that scheme didn't fly.

As I patrolled the cells in the small hours, I often felt guilty that the main reason I didn't want someone to kill himself that night was that I would get into trouble and would end up with a pile of unwelcome paperwork. *If he's going to do it, please let it not be on my watch,* was the prayer of more than one officer.

Of course, if it happened, we would react with thorough professionalism and to hell with the trouble and the paperwork. And we laughed at the urban legend about prison officers finding a dead prisoner and putting him up against the radiator to keep the body warm so that the authorities wouldn't know he died on their watch. The reality was that we prevented a lot of suicides over the years.

There are so many things that drive a person to the ultimate act of despair, and no one really knows what's going on in another's mind. I still remember with sadness one case where a prisoner hanged himself the night before his release. He had served his four years and none of us could figure it out. He was a model prisoner who had produced some beautiful wooden works of art in the craft shop. He was on his own in the cell, so there was no question of foul play. In another case, a prisoner killed himself just hours after his committal. Who knows why?

One of my colleagues, Harry, wasn't long in the service when he came back from patrolling D1, the ground floor of D Class. As well as remand prisoners, D Class housed prisoners who had asked for protection for one reason or another. Often it was because they were depressed – bad news from home could trigger an attack. Getting news from home and knowing you were inside and that there was nothing you could do to help was the worst. The cells in C Class contained a fireproof mattress, a pillow and some blankets, and nothing else. It was thought that you couldn't do much harm with those tools.

But Harry was agitated when he returned from his patrol and told the class officer that he thought he had seen blood on the floor inside one of the cells. The class officer knew that the floor was painted red, so the chance of seeing blood was a bit of a long shot, but he went to investigate. Sure enough, there was a sticky patch seeping under the blanket, glinting in the low-wattage landing light. Harry and the class officer opened the door and found the prisoner lying covered by a blanket.

'Are you all right?' asked Harry.

'I'm fine, Officer,' the prisoner replied.

Harry pulled back the blanked and recoiled in horror. The prisoner had cut the skin in the hollow of his elbow with a crude plastic knife and had tried to extract and sever a vein. They had stopped him in the nick of time.

The man was immediately brought to the hospital. Harry was sent as escort and he asked him why he had done it.

'It eases the tension in me when I draw blood,' was the reply.

It was not uncommon to look into a cell and find a prisoner standing in the middle of it with his arms covered in blood, waiting for you to deal with it. Some people call these incidents of self-harm a cry for help. In most of the cases, you found that they had made numerous small cuts rather than one deep and effective one, and often the cuts were on the front of the arms rather than the back. There was no fear of them bleeding to death, and they knew it as well as you did.

Sometimes, there were old scars from earlier incidents. A doctor told me that patients presenting with multiple scars like that were generally victims of sexual abuse. The act of cutting themselves was thought to help them take their minds off the horrors they had suffered when they were younger.

More bizarre was the sight of a prisoner who had tried to cut his own throat. That was no cry for help, that was a genuine suicide attempt, though it didn't succeed. More than once, a prisoner managed to draw blood, but it must be harder than you think to dig deep enough with a plastic knife for it to be fatal.

The weirdest suicide attempt I ever saw was very well thought out – and completely unworkable. A prisoner filled his chamber pot with water and stood barefoot in it. He unscrewed the light bulb in his cell, stuck his finger in the socket and waited for the night guard to come around. When the officer flicked on the light to check the cell, there was a small flash and the prison was plunged into darkness. The prisoner had shorted the circuit, and all he got for his trouble was a slight scorch on his finger.

Unfortunately, one method does work: hanging. There are two ways to hang yourself. If the rope is long enough and the drop big enough, your neck snaps and you die instantly. If the rope is shorter or the drop not sufficient, then you choke to death painfully. The confined space of a prison cell does not allow for a long drop.

Even though I'm retired, I'm not completely out of the loop. Recently, an officer called out to see me and he was very upset. When he told me his story, I could understand.

He had been on patrol one night, checking the cells as we all did. He looked into one cell and the bed was empty; the prisoner was on his knees praying. That was a bit unusual, but where's the harm in praying? He moved on, but something wasn't right, and after checking the next cell he came back to the first and looked again. There was something about the posture of the man on his knees...

The officer hurried off and got the key, then came running back in a panic. He pushed open the door and ran forward, but it was too late. The man on his knees was dead, with a noose drawn tight around his neck. That is one of the most horrible sights. More than once I have looked at a neck and checked for any scratch marks. Did the prisoner change his mind and claw at the noose, trying to buy some more precious time on earth? I have never found those scratch marks.

In this case, what had happened was that the prisoner put the noose around his neck and attached the other end to the bedpost. Then, he had put his hands behind his back, knelt down and leaned forward. The weight of his body on the noose was enough to slowly squeeze the life out of him. What was so upsetting was that he had left his arms behind his back and never made an attempt to save himself. No last-minute change of heart.

Months later, the officer who found him still isn't right. But how could you be right after seeing that?

Sometimes, prisoners aren't suicidal, but they have other problems which reveal themselves in self-harm. We had one fellow who always lost it after a few days inside. He would bang his heads off the walls repeatedly. We had to handcuff him and shackle his feet. I remember once handcuffing him to a radiator, shackling his legs and putting a crash helmet on him because he was going crazy and would have killed himself. We had straitjackets as well when I joined, but they were rarely used and have now been phased out.

Another form of self-harm was slashing the arms. Sometimes, a prisoner would be admitted with dozens of scars on his arm. If he was right-handed, the scars were on the left arm, and vice versa. Prisoners used to have razors, and the blades could be used on themselves or on others, so we switched to electric razors. For a long time, there was glass in the cells, but that also provided potential weapons.

But a resourceful prisoner can use all sorts of things. I saw fellows make weapons out of the most unlikely stuff. If you melted a toothbrush, you could draw that to a point and use it as a knife. You could break a bulb or a window or a bit of a spring from the mattress was a potential weapon. If you saw a saggy bed or if someone asked for a board to make his bed firmer, you knew there was trouble coming. You had to search for the weapon and keep an eye on the prisoner.

The worst case of non-fatal self-harm I encountered came from the women's prison. At the centre of it was a girl barely out of her teens, from a small town. She was a tiny, petite nineteen-year-old and I can't remember why she was inside. I do remember getting the call to go to the women's prison and help bring a prisoner to the main gate for transportation to hospital.

When I got there, I met two female officers leading this poor girl out. She had tried to gouge out her eyes. I don't mean there were scratches around her eyes – I mean she tried to get her thumbs into the backs of her eye sockets and tried to force out her eyes. I'll never forget her face. As she passed me, I could see what looked like two red, raw, golf-ball sized swellings where her eyes should have been.

The girl was crying and begging to be allowed to finish the job on her eyes. It was heartbreaking. One of the female officers had tears streaming down her face. I never saw that prisoner again, but I often wondered what could possibly drive a poor soul to commit such an act on herself.

One self-abuser called Radar would eat anything he could get his hands on. He ate batteries, cutlery, coins and razor blades. It wasn't unusual to check his cell at night and find the light wasn't working because he had eaten the bulb.

Radar was in and out like a yo-yo. He was the biggest problem for the Gardaí in his hometown. Once, he stole their radio and tormented them with false alarms and abuse. He told me it was the most fun he ever had, until the battery ran out. Instead of eating it, he tried to recharge it, but that didn't work. The radio exploded, ending his fun.

There wasn't much fun in Radar's life, but his episodes of unusual gluttony weren't considered suicide attempts. We thought they were an extreme way of getting attention.

He was always in foul form but, then, his life had been no bed of roses. And we could see no improvement in his immediate prospects. He was constantly getting in trouble for what we called anti-social crimes: being drunk and disorderly, causing an affray, staggering around town roaring and shouting and making a nuisance of himself. He had never worked a day in his life and had no intention of ever doing so. This man could be quite abusive if you crossed him. We gave him a lot of breaks because of his tough life and because he was small and weak and vulnerable. There was no way he could have carried out any of the threats he made against us.

But a transformation came over him when we brought him to hospital. His humour would improve and he became friendly and chatty. The nurses and doctors loved him. Before he was x-rayed, he would say, 'Guess what it is this time. Bets on a knife? A spoon? A razor blade? A battery?'

His stomach was crossed with scars from all the operations. The medical staff only saw the jovial side to him. They had great sympathy for him and showered him with little treats. But the sad thing was that no one ever visited him during his numerous stays in hospital. He had nobody.

He would transform back to his moody, aggressive self when he was home and shades of the prison house began to form about him once more.

If anyone was truly at home in prison, it was Radar. He was the first prisoner I met who had been born in the female prison. Radar was put into care when he was still a baby, and, as a result, had spent more of his life in one form of institution or another than any man I ever met.

He was actually quite proud of his place of birth and would say to officers, 'I was in this fucking prison before you were even born.'

And, in most cases, he was right.

Chapter 26
Diversity in Prison

Over the years, I've seen many different ethnic groups pass through the prison. We got about ten Chinese fellows in a few years ago. They were rounded up because they were in the country illegally. Only one spoke any English, and from him I learned that they were mostly slaves. They were on the run from their jobs in England, where, they said, they got no money, just accommodation and food. They weren't allowed to leave the accommodation or the restaurant they were working in under any circumstances. They said they were riddled with every disease going – STDs, TB, the whole lot. We had great sympathy for them and were concerned that they wouldn't be able to eat our food, so we got two or three of them and brought them down to the kitchen to cook. That didn't last long.

The Chinese didn't work out because a lot of people confuse kindness with weakness. It's in the nature of an Irish person to be friendly towards you, but the Chinese started abusing this and making big demands. Then they started coming down and claiming two dinners. They weren't in long and they all looked alike to some of the officers, so it was difficult to detect this scam at first. We got fed up with them and their time in the kitchen came to an abrupt end. So we gave them ordinary food and they loved it. They were the first down every day, eating anything we gave them.

We had two Filipinos who did five years with us during the 1990s. Their fingerprints were all over about €10 million worth of drugs shipped into Foynes. They no more owned the drugs, no more had a beneficial interest in them or were no more in charge of them than you and me. I thought they were just two mules who probably got an extra few pounds for carrying their deadly cargo. In our eyes, these guys weren't major drugs dealers.

But they had magic hands. They could get an old can and turn it into a rose or transform a bottle of Coke into the most beautiful shapes. They started building Spanish galleons out of matches without the heads. Selling those ships made them a fortune. They made more money in Limerick Prison than they got working on the drugboats.

They were the best. We had them down in the kitchen and they couldn't stop working. They had beautiful manners, a beautiful attitude and were always in good humour. They were very popular prisoners. Everyone knew they weren't drug dealers. The St Vincent de Paul Society visit the prison regularly, and these two were among their clients. The Filipinos carefully kept everything they were given. When they were released, they went home with a couple of hundred euros each, which was big money for them. They had suitcases full of the tiny bars of soap, toothpaste and toilet paper. We didn't begrudge them.

Then we had two guys from Thailand. They could cook. Everyone in the kitchen had some privileges – they were allowed to take some of the food and prepare a sandwich or whatnot to bring back to their cell. These guys didn't bother with sandwiches – they used the bones of chickens for a broth with eggs.

The Jamaicans were rays of sunshine, real happy-go-lucky fellows. One guy we had was dying of AIDS and was let out early because of that, but, again, he was a pleasure to detain, if that can be said.

Among the strangest ethnic groups we have had were the white South Africans. They were often sacrificed by big drugs lords. A major dealer in Nigeria would recruit four people to bring drugs through to Ireland and then he would tip off the customs about one of the four. That guy would be caught, which provided a distraction to allow the other three to get through. But the fellow who was caught wasn't off the hook when he was released; he was still responsible for the drugs and he had to pay the dealer when he got out.

Those guys had nothing. One had been a policeman until the collapse of the apartheid regime, and now he had nothing. He said, 'We were princes in our country until the blacks took over. Now we are paupers.' He hated the blacks. He did two or three trips to Ireland before he got caught.

Another guy told me that the gangsters came into his house one night with AK47s and threatened to blow his wife and kids up unless he smuggled the drugs. He felt he had no choice.

The white South Africans may have been full of anger, but they conformed and they gave no trouble.

We didn't get too many black Africans in prison. I have heard judges say that black convicts get a hard time in a white prison, and they use this as an excuse to reduce their sentences. It's complete rubbish. I have seen black guys walking down A Class and shaking hands with all the inmates there. They don't do the time any harder. I never saw anyone ever get abused because of their colour.

Perhaps the two most unlikely inmates were a pair from Algeria. They were brought by a Russian ship into Foynes. They had paid the Russians to bring them to America. The Russians took their money and passports and set them ashore, telling them they had arrived in the US. You can imagine two black fellows in Foynes weren't hard to spot. They were arrested and landed up with us.

Neither spoke English, but one had French, so I was called in to translate. I felt so sorry for them that I tried to negotiate a deal with the governor to give them €10 to start them off in the tuck shop. In the end, he gave them €60 each. They were absolutely delighted. They had been in Limerick Prison for three days, and until I translated for them, they thought they were in a refugee hostel. After a few days, they were transferred to accommodation in Ennis.

There are always English prisoners in Limerick, and they get on fine. They don't get a hard time for being English. I think it's the same across the water. You often hear of Irish prisoners saying they were discriminated against in English prisons, but a lot of that is talk – they can't come out and admit they were treated well, can they?

We've also had our share of diversity in terms of religion. We've had a few Muslims, both refugees awaiting processing and real prisoners. No one cared what they were. In some prisons, they're given a compass and a prayer mat, but not in Limerick. But we would be mindful of their food – they don't eat bacon, for instance.

Neither do Jews, but we rarely had any of them. Under regulations, all Jews served their time in Dublin because there was a rabbi there. But like any other prisoner, they could apply for a transfer. We had one fellow in the 1970s from Garryowen, a suburb of Limerick, who claimed he was Jewish, but I think that was to avoid being called for mass. Back then, Sunday mass was compulsory – you could be put on report for missing it. There were two chaplains attached to the prison, a Catholic one and a Church of Ireland one. Obviously, the Catholic chaplain was the busier of the two. The priests had a very hard line to walk between the officers and the prisoners. Naturally, an over-familiarisation with one side or the other could cause friction. They had to do a balancing act between serving the prisoners and not antagonising the officers – an almost impossible task, but it was carried out brilliantly by all the chaplains.

One particular chaplain was having a television documentary made about him, and a large part of the documentary was filmed in the prison. I was in charge of B Class that day when the priest, Fr Pat, came in with a television crew to do some filming. I asked one of the camera crew if he was nervous about being inside in a prison. He said that he wasn't, that he'd been in Mountjoy a couple of times and it was all the same to him. We chatted for a couple of minutes and then he turned to me and said, 'Jaysus, where's my camera?'

There was his camera, gone. Now, this wasn't a small hand-held camera, this was a shoulder-held camera, a big camera. He said, 'That's worth a fortune! We have to get that back.'

The prisoners on the landings were looking down roaring laughing. To the tune of 'Where's Your Momma Gone?' they started singing 'Where's your camera gone?' and the officers sang back in response, 'Far, far away.'

As we now had to start a general search on B Class, the poor camera crew weren't as relaxed on their way out as they had been on their way in. Of course, we found the camera undamaged – the prisoner had only taken it as a joke – and filming continued uninterrupted. I often slag Fr Pat about it to this day.

Another priest who came in regularly had spent some time working as a chaplain on a Native American reservation in the US. His name was Fr Joe, so of course he got the nickname Indian Joe. The prisoners flooded to mass to hear his sermons, as they always included wonderful stories about his time with the Native Americans. But this was the cause of a small problem for us, because the longer the mass went on, the less time we had for our breakfast. The union went to the governor to see if they could ask Indian Joe to cut back on the sermons a bit, and of course he did.

He was a lovely, friendly man with a big, open, smiling face and a wonderful personality. He got on well with everybody, both prisoners and officers. He was almost what you could call the perfect priest. Then Indian Joe went home one night and shot himself in the head with a shotgun. Jesus, we were sad. What a loss.

Thirty years ago, men and women shared a mass, separated by a barrier, but that changed when we began to get the female IRA prisoners in the late 1970s. Then, there was a separate mass for the men and the women, as we couldn't risk mixing them. Back then, every officer had to go to mass. If thirty of us were on duty, twenty-nine went. You can guess the odd man out. Every prisoner was also expected to go and most did.

Today, there are over 100 officers on duty every Sunday for a prison population of 300. And I'm told you might get maybe three prisoners and twelve officers at mass. Mass is almost a non-event. All it means for the prisoners is that they get an hour extra in bed.

Protestant prisoners can get a weekly service inside if they want it; the chaplain can be called up every week, though, in practice, that didn't happen. There was a small Church of Ireland chapel just inside the entrance that was rarely used and, when it was, it wasn't used appropriately. Some of us would break in during the night and sleep there – it was quite comfortable. It was very close to the furnace room and so was a lot warmer than the draughty landings. Back then, there was no heating provided for the officers.

The chapel is gone now, but if a service is called for, a discrete room can be provided.

And of course, we still observe Christmas.

The officers celebrate by knocking off as early as possible to be able to go home to their families. The prisoners celebrate by spending a month trying (generally unsuccessfully) to make hooch.

Christmas Day dawns with a fry-up for breakfast. This gets everyone into the festive spirit. In the middle of the afternoon, they get a full Christmas dinner – an absolutely gorgeous Christmas dinner. There is soup and rolls with turkey, ham and all the trimmings, all followed by Christmas pudding with custard. It used to be produced inside but for the past three or four years, it comes prepacked, with beautifully presented portions. In the evening, a turkey and ham salad is served, but a lot of prisoners don't bother coming down; they're stuffed.

We always made an effort. A couple of times, we put on a Santa hat to serve the dinners and the prison is dolled up for Christmas, but when men do that sort of thing, they make a horse's backside of it. There might be a Christmas tree in four or five locations without decorations and lights wouldn't be plugged in. There was a crib for a number of years, but an officer, who left the job, put a condom over the Virgin Mary's head. The management rightly freaked and there was no crib after that.

The prisoners tried to get some drugs or to make some booze to have something in for the season. We'd try to crack down on that, particularly the booze because it was horrible stuff that would make them sick. Plus, if they got their hands on it, our job was always more difficult.

There used to be a bit of drinking in the prison among the officers in the olden days, a drop of whiskey, but none got to the other side of the bars. But that doesn't happen any more.

Some prisoners used to get temporary release at Christmas. Most came back, but a lot didn't. Then there were a couple of joyriding incidents in Southill. In one incident, a Garda was badly injured. Then, two fellows on temporary release killed two children, pinned to a wall with a stolen car in Cork. After that, the Justice Minister issued an order that there was no temporary release for joyriders.

After some more trouble, that order was extended to drug dealers. The Minister thought he was doing a great job, but now a prisoner knows that no matter how well behaved he is, he isn't getting home for Christmas or getting out early. We have fewer carrots to control his behaviour.

———

Luckily, not everyone is a common criminal. A lot of today's drug dealers are committed working men with families and mortgages. The days of only the hoodies coming in for drugs offences are gone. These days, we often get businessmen, guys who ran their own trucking companies, say, and had a number of men working for them. These are hard-working, future-committed men who saw a way to make a few quick quid. Outside, they have a family and a huge mortgage. Inside, they have nothing, not even the prospect of temporary release for Christmas.

A lot of them end up in the kitchen because they want to be working, not idling in the yard. We like those guys. This new breed never took drugs themselves, but I think that's worse. I'd admire them more if they were selling drugs to their own children as well as mine – at least then they wouldn't be hypocrites. But though I had no admiration for what they did, I found I had more in common with those lads than with a fellow who rolled out of bed at three in the afternoon because he was out robbing until four that morning.

Seeing working men inside is a lot sadder to me than seeing someone who never worked, will never work and whose children will be brought up not to work. Many of them don't even finish school. From the day they are born, the state wipes their backside, yet they moan that they hate the state – the state that gives them free money, free legal aid and free drugs counselling. They say fuck the system, and the system is what is keeping them alive. At the end of their days, they will find a nice bed in a nursing home beside some poor sucker who worked all his life and had to sell his house to get his bed. Go figure that one.

Enough of the rant. Back to the prisoners, and one group I always liked: the Travellers.

It's not true that Travellers don't take to prison well. Most of the Travellers have no problem doing time. They don't suffer discrimination from either prisoners or officers. We have employed Travellers in the kitchen and got great work out of them. It throws all the stereotypes out the window: they were intelligent, kept their mouths shut, no fights, no problems. Everyone thinks that Travellers are free spirits who can't take being locked up, but Travellers actually have very little freedom. They oppress themselves far more than we oppress them. The freedoms they have are not real freedoms – the freedom to beg on O'Connell Street or live on the side of the road are not freedoms I would fight for.

Often, the only structure they get in their lives is when they're in prison. And when we give them responsibility, a lot of them step up to the mark. They can work seven days a week, they can be polite and tidy and can make a contribution. Their cells are spotlessly clean.

From my experience, the Travellers cause fewer problems than any other group in the prison. They come in and do their time and go away. They don't want anything to do with 'the buffers', as they refer to authority. They keep their heads down and their mouths shut.

If someone said there were four Travellers who wanted to work in the kitchen, I would say send down five. If someone said there are four Dubs who want to work in the kitchen, I would say send down the Travellers. They rarely let us down.

Chapter 27

Inside Out

Violence has always been a part of prison life, but by the turn of the millennium, the nature of the violence had changed. In the mid-1980s, the Dublin Mafia had set up the Prisoners' Revenge Group (PRG) with the intention of targeting Gardaí and prison officers. They were particularly strong in Dublin. In late 1984, a list of names came to the attention of management. There were six Limerick officers on the list, but thankfully I wasn't one of them. None of the six came to any harm, but the union wrote to the Minister for Justice asking for burglar and smoke alarms, stab-proof vests and a guard in the prison car park.

We were instructed to change our routes home regularly, break our routines and check under our cars for bombs.

Rather ludicrously, we were also told to organise codes with our wives. If I came home and found the bathroom light on but the upstairs landing light off and the curtain half-drawn in the front bedroom, it meant she was being held hostage. Needless to say, we ignored these directives and we had no trouble.

But by 2000, we had a different class of prisoner behind bars and the threats against us had to be taken more seriously. A particularly sinister note was struck during a general search of the prison near the end of 1999.

General searches were called for various reasons. Often we would get a tip-off that there were weapons or drugs hidden within the prison. In later years, it was mobile phones we were searching for. General searches were always very disruptive. Prisoners were strip searched in the cell and then every item was taken out and searched –

lockers, clothes, letters, books, mattresses, pillows, the lot. There was quite often a bit of trouble during this and, sometimes, a prisoner's personal property got broken.

In a nutshell, prisoners didn't like general searches. I sometimes felt they were called just to show who was in charge and at other times to disguise the fact we had specific information relating to one cell.

When I first started, you could search a prisoner's cell in three minutes because he had absolutely nothing except what he stood up in and what he slept in. He never had pyjamas, sleeping mostly in his underwear. But as the years went on, the amount of stuff in cells increased. For example, the cells were decorated with posters. Samantha Fox and Farrah Fawcett were very popular. Some men would get a silk scarf and lay it over the light to give atmosphere. We encouraged all that, as it made the place more homey, but it made for a lot more work in a general search.

During searches the landings would be full of noise and banging and clashing. They were always done first thing in the morning. Our breakfast would be delayed, and so would the prisoners'. I was always careful to try and pair up with an officer who wasn't a nutter to reduce the possibility of a flare-up. All the officers were involved and the process took two or three hours. As we went through one wing, the prisoners in the other wings would be banging on their doors demanding their breakfast. We couldn't tell them that a general search was going on because that would give them the opportunity to hide stuff, but inevitably they found out, so we put a guy in the yard to spot anything coming out a window.

Often we found nothing. Sometimes, we got makeshift weapons, hooch or hash. Phones turned up more and more regularly. But that search in 1999 chilled us. We had gone through the entire prison and found nothing. Everyone was locked back in their cells with their breakfasts and peace reigned. We went off to the canteen.

Thirty minutes later, an officer was returning from his breakfast when he spotted two 9 mm bullets on the floor of one of the landings. The message was clear: we were being threatened and defied. The prisoners were saying, 'You searched the whole prison and we were able to keep these from you.'

What was frightening was the possibility that there was a gun in the prison. We didn't know who the potential target was – a prisoner or one of the officers? No one was happy.

——

A few months later, the reality of the new situation struck home forcibly. If you work long enough at a job, some people become particular friends. One of my closest buddies in the service was Alan Kavanagh, an officer with a young family and an impeccable record. Like me, he was heavily involved in the Prison Officers' Association.

On 5 January 2000, Alan was the class officer on D3. He was coming to the end of a long day. At seven thirty, he went around the landing and unlocked all the cell doors. This was to allow any prisoner who had stayed back during recreation to come out for his supper and to allow the other prisoners to return to their cells. He could hear the prisoners coming up the stairs from the recreation halls. It was a normal evening, and in less than an hour, he would be home with his family.

As the prisoners began pouring in the gate to the landing, Alan saw a look flicker across one man's face. That look saved his life. He began to turn just as three men jumped on him from behind. But he was too late to avoid the attack. Two men pinned his arms and wrestled him to the floor. The third caught him by the hair and looked him in the eye, shouting, 'Die, you bastard, die! I'm going to fucking kill you!'

He then slashed Alan across the throat with a razor.

Back then, prisoners were allowed to have razors and the one they favoured was the Gillette G2 because it had a double blade. But they didn't want the double blade for a closer shave; their interest was more sinister. If you slashed someone with a double blade, it tore out a strip of skin and the scar would never heal. They would slash from the middle of the cheek to the corner of the mouth and the resulting permanent scar was called the Garryowen Smile.

I remember once having a prisoner in the kitchen with this mark. It looked vicious. Some time later, I was shocked to see a young child of about two visiting this man. The child had the same scar.

'What happened to your son?' I asked.

'When they called to do this to me,' he said, indicating the scar, 'I was out, so they slashed my son instead. As you can see, they got me in the end too.'

'And do you have any idea who did it?'

'My brother.'

Those were the sort of people we were up against and those are the sort of people who went for Alan Kavanagh that evening. But they weren't trying to give him the Garryowen Smile – this was an out and out attempt to kill him. They had removed the blades from the razor and melted them into a toothbrush handle. His attacker slashed viciously, and if Alan hadn't been struggling, the blade would have severed the artery. Alan told me he saw the blood spurting everywhere. The ground became slippery with it, which hindered his attackers as they tried to drag him into one of the cells to finish him off.

They had him halfway in and he knew if they got him fully inside he was a goner. He could feel the blood flowing from him, and with a desperate effort, he managed to free one hand as his attacker came in for the second, deeper slash. He lashed out wildly, still holding the key for the cells. The key caught one guy in the hand and he loosened his grip. This gave Alan the room to get up and he staggered towards the gate at the end of the landing. He could feel himself getting weaker by the step. His three attackers were thundering down the landing behind him and all the other prisoners had miraculously disappeared. Alan barely managed to reach the gate and pull it shut behind him in time. It saved his life. He collapsed against a wall, blood pouring from his wound.

A prisoner who wasn't involved puked in the landing. Every officer was ashen faced. More and more officers were pouring onto the landing. Prisoners were hustled into cells and one officer ran into the first cell he saw, emerging with a towel. Holding it firmly against Alan's throat, he led him to the prison surgery. An assistant chief officer came down and looked at the damage. He knew immediately how serious it was and Alan was bundled into a car and rushed across town to the hospital. I was off duty at the time, but I got the message and I arrived at the hospital as he was coming in.

My first reaction was a massive sense of relief that Alan was still alive and would pull through. Then, the second reaction hit me: it could just as easily have been me. I didn't want to make big deal of that thought, but it was at the back of my mind. I stood in the casualty ward with his wife and children and saw every one of the seventy-four stitches going into my friend's throat. I went home that night worried, angry, frightened and relieved.

Alan was lucky. He made a fabulous recovery. He showed great mental strength and can joke about it now, even though he still bears the scar. But he never returned to work.

While I was in the hospital, an assistant chief officer took complete charge of the situation on D Class. One of our men had nearly been killed and the situation could easily have got very ugly. But this officer made sure that nothing stupid was done. He ensured that none of the prisoners were touched and that the scene was preserved properly for the Gardaí. As a result of his diligence, there would be no cock-ups when it came to prosecuting the three attackers.

He got a hand-picked team together and took the attackers' clothes for forensic examination. He put guards on the doors of the three attackers' cells and made sure everything was done by the book.

'No one is to be allowed into those cells. I don't care if it's the fucking governor – no one in,' he said. 'We want this done right, so not a hair on their heads is to be touched.'

It was done right and his precautions worked: the prisoners were convicted and were given a total of twenty-one years for what they had done. But, to this day, we have no idea why they attacked Alan.

———

In the immediate aftermath of the attack, there was an agreement that twelve extra officers would be put on duty at the prison. But that was only for a month, pending a review of security and staffing levels. We wanted that cover extended to six months.

Two weeks after the attack, the Prison Officers' Association called a ballot of all officers. We passed a motion of no confidence in the governor and considered industrial action. At the end of it all, the only real change we got was that razors were removed from the prison; from then on, all inmates were issued with electric razors.

Meanwhile, Alan was compensated for his injuries and returned to civilian life.

As Alan was recovering in hospital, my wife revealed to me that there hadn't been a day that she didn't go out of her way to make sure she told me she loved me and to ask me to take care of myself. At the back of her mind, there had always been the possibility that the same could happen to me.

We didn't talk about it, but she was affected any time she heard of a soldier, a fireman or a policeman being killed in the line of duty. The same thought crosses all of our minds: we're doing this job for a few bob to support our families. We shouldn't have to die for the money.

But you put the fear in your pocket, and if you leave it there long enough, it will stay there.

Six months after Alan's attack, another of my closest friends was targeted. This time, it happened to a man who was off duty and at home. Joe went outside in the evening for a smoke. He was standing at the side of his house when he heard a noise. He turned to investigate and saw someone writing 'screw' on the wall of his house. As he went to confront the man, someone snuck up behind Joe and struck him a blow on the back of the head. He dropped like a sack of coal. Disorientated and semi-conscious, he picked himself up and ran back into his house. He was completely out of it. When he got to the hospital, they discovered he had many knife wounds. His steely determination saved his life.

I got a call within minutes and was straight over. When I got there, he was hyper. The shock of someone being vicious enough to attack him like that angered Joe. He was one of the good guys and no one had a right to have a grudge against him. He saw it as a personal assault with no regard to his wife or his health. It was the thoughtless savagery that got to him.

Joe, like Alan, never returned to the prison. Many people suffer injuries in sport or in traffic accidents. We get over those knocks, but the scars from an assault like those run a lot deeper.

Soon one of the city's most notorious criminal gangs began targeting prison officers in earnest. One was eventually convicted of assaults on three officers. He had also threatened to kill one.

Shots had been fired at another officer's house and hoax bombs were planted outside three houses. An officer's car was set on fire. Even the prison wasn't safe from attacks. One evening, two pipe bombs were lobbed over the wall of the prison from the jail boreen. Seemingly, the plan was that the two bombs would land on the net over A yard. The first was supposed to go off, showering the yard with shrapnel. The second one was supposed to fall through the net, explode and finish the job.

That day an officer said to me, 'Come out. I think there's a bomb here.'

I went out and saw what looked like a pipe bomb about a foot long and six inches in diameter against the wall of the kitchen. I pushed a big wheelie bin over it in a vain effort to reduce its power.

The prisoners on A yard reported another bomb which had fallen short of the wire that lay on the ground on the other side of the kitchen. So there was now a bomb on either side of the kitchen. The gas was turned off and everybody was evacuated from the kitchen, officers and prisoners alike. Now, the next problem was how to feed the prisoners, so we went where generations of Limerick families have gone for their meals for many years: the local chipper. We rang them up and asked if we could have 300 fish and chips please. The joke around the prison was that the response we got back was, 'Do you want salt and vinegar on them?'

We collected the food in relays in the prison van and gave them out. The prisoners had no complaints about the dinners that day.

With all this going on, and after serious assaults on two friends of mine, I had to question things. Most of us began to wonder if the job was worth it. In the end, most of us concluded that it was. I had only seven years to go before retirement on full pension, and I stayed with the prison service. I was caught in the velvet trap.

Chapter 28

The Last Lap

I was nearing retirement. The end was in sight and, for the first time, I began to think about the money. I was about to escape the velvet trap, but I needed to make sure my pension was all it could be, so I put myself forward for some extra overtime to pump up my contributions (I found out later it made no difference).

Be that as it may, I was in the prison one day when I was called upon to bring a prisoner to the regional hospital for a physiotherapy appointment. I had seen the same prisoner walk around the prison on numerous occasions with no difficulty, so I was a bit surprised to see him hobble up to me on crutches. I suppose he had to put on the show to get the day out – and perhaps to get some sympathy from a pretty nurse.

The office gave me the documentation for the prisoner, then I handcuffed him to an officer friend of mine who was coming as my assistant on the escort and we headed off for the regional hospital. On the way, the prisoner was extraordinarily friendly and cordial, which caused me to be suspicious. I was on high alert by the time we got to the hospital. There is a fully equipped gym there for rehabilitation. As we walked into the gym, the nurse smiled at us.

'If you take off the handcuffs, we'll get him up on this treadmill,' she said.

But the prison is a civil service outpost, and everyone covers his or her backside. The management, rightly, always covered themselves by issuing instructions that handcuffs were not to be removed. That way, if a man escaped, the officer who had removed the cuffs was in trouble, not his superior. I wasn't about to screw up a perfect record with just weeks to go before my retirement.

'The cuffs have to stay on,' I said.

The nurse looked at me with surprise. The prisoner objected, saying, 'I'll refuse treatment if you don't take off the cuffs.'

'That's fine by me, I'll be home an hour earlier,' I responded. 'Nurse, you can cancel the appointment. I'm taking this man back straight away.'

Suddenly, the prisoner's attitude changed completely and he was willing to do anything to stay in the hospital. This increased my level of suspicion.

At that, the prisoner got on the treadmill and proceeded to jog. It was a comical sight to see him trotting along with an officer handcuffed to him, standing immobile beside the treadmill. Then, the officer began to enter into the spirit of the thing, jogging on the spot in time to the running prisoner. The two nurses were over in the corner giggling at the spectacle, which nearly brought me to my knees with laughter.

After a few minutes, the prisoner slowed down.

'I need to go to the toilet.'

'Again?'

'I get nervous in hospitals.'

We went into the toilet and released the handcuffs, allowing him to go into the cubicle while we waited outside. There was no outside window, so I wasn't worried, but something about the frequent toilet breaks was making me suspicious.

I had checked the toilet before the prisoner went in, which is the norm. I was fairly confident he had something on him when he came out, so I wrote on a bit of paper: 'The prisoner has drugs on him. We will search him when we get back. Say nothing.'

I passed this note over to my colleague, who was re-handcuffed to the prisoner. Jogging over, he was now leaning up against the wall smoking.

'Can you check the spelling on this form?' I asked him, passing him over the piece of paper and making sure he could see my scribbled note. He got the hint, and read what I wrote.

'Not quite right,' he said, taking out a pencil and adding to my note: He has something on him. I can guarantee it.'

The bullshit detector inside my head was beeping furiously.

When we got back to the prison, I brought the prisoner straight up to the reception and performed a strip search. Strip searches were never pleasant, but we worked out a way to minimise the embarrassment. The prisoner first took off his top clothing – jacket, shirt and vest. These were examined and handed back to him. He put these back on, then the bottom clothing was removed – trousers, underpants, socks and shoes. These were then examined and handed back.

We searched this man, but we found nothing. He had looked slightly worried at the start, but now he was positively gloating. He started slagging me, saying, 'You thought you had something on me.'

He was jumping up and down in glee. I was annoyed, but you do lose some. Then I spotted something odd about this jumping jackass – his underpants looked a bit flabby. I realised that he had a second pair of underpants on. When he had removed his bottom clothes, his hanging shirt had prevented me seeing the second underpants. I saw one coming off and assumed he had stripped right down – as I mentioned earlier, we weren't in the habit of looking up backsides unless it was absolutely necessary.

We found almost two pounds of hash on him that day. He was going to get into big trouble with whoever he was bringing it in for. Score one nil for the good guys.

It was the biggest haul of drugs I had in thirty years of service, and I had found it just weeks from my retirement. You can't beat experience.

Chapter 29
Final Day

I was glad to be near the end because the prisoners I was dealing with were getting rougher and more ruthless. What had happened? I had no idea.

I remember a few months before my retirement talking with some prisoners about a story in the newspaper. A man had been blown through a window by a shotgun blast.

'That's complete rubbish,' said the prisoner. 'When you shoot a man, he drops down, he doesn't go flying backwards. It doesn't matter if it's a shotgun or a nine mill, that stuff you see in the pictures is pure crap. I never saw anyone move more than a few inches in my life.'

Looking at him, I didn't doubt it.

'I'll tell you another thing,' he went on. 'If you shoot a man in the back of the head, a funny thing happens. His two eyeballs will pop out of the front of his head and just hang there on stalks. Ha, ha.'

How he came by that information, I can only guess, but again, I don't doubt him.

The sooner A and B Classes are knocked, the better for everyone in Limerick Prison. No amount of patching up the place, built in 1821, will work. There is no water in the cells and the prisoners have to fill two-litre bottles to have water overnight. There is only one place to fill the bottles, and that's at the tap over the slop hopper, where the chamber pots are emptied. The day I left, there was a queue of prisoners for the hopper, two with chamber pots to empty and one at the end waiting to fill his bottle after them.

At the end of the shift, I went to stores and got a spanking new uniform. For my last day on the job, I was going to doll myself up.

The following morning, I polished my shoes until I could see myself in them and appeared at the main gate as dapper as can be imagined. I looked good – or at least as good as I possibly could look for my age.

It's a tradition that the last day is a sort of lap of honour around the prison. You don't work until five then go home. You have no duties. So I didn't get up at six and rush in for seven. I took a leisurely breakfast and presented myself at the gate at ten. Unlike my first day, I wasn't searched this time, but this wasn't because thirty years of service had made me trustworthy: it was because searching of all staff had been stopped about six years earlier.

In common with many of my colleagues, I was sorry to see the searches end. No matter what pressure was put on a prison officer, he couldn't smuggle anything into the prison because of those searches, which gave us some security. Now there are two sniffer dogs on duty. The prisoners are against the dogs. One prisoner asked for a meeting with the governor a few days after the dogs were introduced and put the most ludicrous suggestion to him: 'Will you remove the dogs if we promise to smuggle in only hash?' he had asked.

The dogs aren't there twenty-four hours a day, and if a visitor shows up and sees no dogs, a call will be made and suddenly a horde of visitors will come flocking in. Draw your own conclusions.

When I got into the prison, I walked every landing and every section. Thirty years of memories came flooding back as I walked through the Victorian wings, the new wings, the circle, reception, yards, workshops, gym and the women's prison. I shook hands with everyone I met. What touched me as much as anything else was the number of prisoners who shook my hand.

One particular memory stands out. I was passing through the gym attached to c Class and prisoners were stretching their hands out through the bars to shake mine. I treasure that. Some of those guys had had hard words with me and some had even fought me, but it was never personal, and we left it behind afterwards. None of them begrudged me my retirement and my health and sanity.

All of the staff shook my hand too, but I could read it in their eyes: they were just waiting for the day they, too, could leave prison.

It was a bittersweet experience in that I had invested thirty years and many long hours into the prison, and I knew from speaking to other officers that when you're gone, you're gone. The place wouldn't fall down without me, and in two or three months' time, if my name was mentioned at all, they would be saying, 'Officer who?'

I felt I had contributed in some way to the prison. I had been involved in all aspects of life inside: the Prison Officers' Association and the social club and I was a founder member of the golf club. I had also seen and contributed to the genuine rehabilitation of prisoners who worked in the kitchen. I met a group of men that enriched my life and made firm friends. Some thrived while others just hung in there. However we felt about it, we all knew that being a prison officer wasn't like another job. Certainly, there was nothing in the civil service that could match it. The rewards were there, but we ran the constant risk of violence – we were involved in fights and quelled riots. But I'm retired now, and I have no scars, either emotionally or physically. It can't have been all bad, this life behind bars.

That was something to feel good about. But it's all over now.

This is only a small part of the story; thirty years' experience behind bars would take a lot longer to tell. As I walked out the gates for the last time to go for a farewell drink with my former colleagues, an era in my life was drawing to a close. My life behind bars was over.

The score, I felt, was at least one all.